Table of Contents	Page
Preface	2
Legal and Civil Claims Investigations	3-6
Risk Mitigation & the Insurance Claims Investigator	7-14
Licensing Rules and Regulations	15-22
Getting a Foot in the Door	23-29
Professional Ethics	30-40
Legal Issues	41-49
The Private Investigator	50-60
Database and Record Searches	61-67
Locate Investigations	68-74
Surveillance Investigations	80-102
Equipment of the Professional Investigator	103-110
Safe Guarding and Restriction of Information	111-115
Report Writing	116-134
Common Investigations & Reports	135-158
Being a Witness	159-163
Terrorism Today	164-171
Statement Taking	172-186
Statement Case Studies	187-220
Being Ready for a PI Position	221-225
About the Author	226

Preface

In order to Investigate Civil and or Criminal matters on behalf of the public, the Investigator in most states must have a Private Investigator's License.

The full-time profession and part-time profession of a Private Investigator can be very different. The entry level career of a Private Investigator and the second career choice of a Private Investigator can also be very different. Many second career professionals bring with them experience from another area or profession and incorporate it into a private marketable service.

Our industry is a cross section of several types of professionals. The career PI has the analytical nature of an Investigator merged with the legal training of a Paralegal and the aggressiveness of an Attorney.

Entry Level Career Investigators are most suitable for large firms that have the infrastructure to teach and mold the investigator for the work he/she will be doing. Large PI Firms that offer such as entry level position will specialize in Business Risk and Claims Investigations (BRCL). You will be taught that your job is not to just gather the facts and the facts only. Your job will be to look for contradicting points in a person's claim or allegation to provide counter claims in the defense or mediation of a claim. Your job will be to identify causes, safety violations or solutions to prevent a similar incident.

Our world has become very litigious and if you read a complaint of most any type if will be filled with an array of claims or accusations. Career Professional Investigators working in the Business Risk and Claims Investigations Industry are called Claims Investigators. Their job is to investigate incidents and accidents and provide information helpful in the defense of these accusations. It is not to sit on the fence or produce a report with no useful information. We MUST look for information and evidence that will create counter claims, completely reject the accusation or provide insight as to how exactly the incident or accident occurred. If more technical assistance is needed in a forensic exploration, it is our job to either make the recommendation or offer to include the forensic evaluation as part of our investigation such as sending a specimen to a lab or a piece of evidence to a forensic engineering firm. Another possibility, and there are many, is to have a forensic accountant review a company or professional's books.

As a Claims Investigator you must have imagination and be willing to be resourceful. We aren't knowledgeable in all areas, but we will get cases in all areas so we are constantly learning. Looking up information and educating yourself along the way is a requirement of this career path. An Attorney friend once said that he practices law, because he is always "practicing". The same holds true for the professional investigator, we never stop "investigating".

Chapter One
Legal and Civil Claims Investigations

I. Introduction
   a. Define a Legal or Claims Investigator
   b. The Career Modern-Day Private Investigator
   c. Qualifications and Characteristics
      i. Problems solver
      ii. Mechanical or Analytical
      iii. Aggressive but even keel
      iv. Adventurous
      v. Confident
II. Defining Claims
III. Types of Legal and Civil Claims Investigators

1. Introduction

The US Bureau of Labor and Statistics reports that the investigations field particularly, Private Investigations is one of the fastest growing industries. The term Private Investigator simply means the investigator is not a Law Enforcement Officer. Also most large Private Investigative Firms don't work Criminal Cases or if they do, it is usually a small part of their practice. Today's Modern-Day PI or Staff Investigator mostly works civil matters that may constitute a tort or law suit and for firms that specialize in Business Risk Mitigation and Claims Investigations. This particular area of business has been the fastest growing industry for the professional Private Investigator over the last 30 years.

The term Private Investigator may conjure up many images in your mind but probably your image is far different than the current professional in the industry. The real image of a private investigator is very much just like the image of any professional office co-worker you have worked with that is reliable, interested in getting the job completed and somewhat inquisitive. They are usually well educated and hold bachelor degrees in various areas of study.

The Investigations industry is on the rise due to the litigious nature that exits today. It is also on the rise due to the affordability and access people have to legal representation. In order to build a career in an industry, one must choose a field that will provide ongoing work.

The earnings of almost every civil lawyer in the United States are funded by the insurance industry. Insurance can best be described as the mother's milk of the law profession. The civil defense lawyer is paid by an insurer for each hour he or she works. The civil plaintiffs' lawyer is usually paid by taking a percentage of any judgment entered in favor of the plaintiff, which judgment is usually paid by the defendant's insurer. In almost every situation in which a civil lawyer practices the funds for that work comes, either directly or indirectly, from insurance. Consequently, lawyers must use their wits and energies to avoid or to pursue litigation to the benefit of the client. Both sides understand that an insurer will eventually pay one or both sides in the dispute. Insurance is important to every civil dispute and even some that fall within the criminal courts.

Every lawyer retained to represent or defend a civil suit will begin the representation with a serious effort to find insurance coverage for the benefit of the client or the defendant the client is suing.

Auto Accidents

With the increasing number of cars on the roads of the US each year, car accidents have unfortunately become a very common sight. The majority of car accident victims are the drivers, then the passengers of the car, followed by pedestrians, and lastly cyclists.

Every 12 minutes, one person dies because of a car accident. Every 14 seconds, a car accident results in an injured victim.

According to the car accident statistics 2002, released by the United States Department of Transportation's (USDOT's) National Highway Traffic Safety Administration (NHTSA), there were around 6,316,000 car accidents in the US, with these causing about 2.9 million injuries. In 2003, the total number of car accidents was 6,328,000 and the resulting injuries stood at almost 3 million.

In a slip and fall claim, both the property owner and the slip and fall victim can be held to varying degrees of responsibility. A slip and fall lawyer can explain to both parties slip and fall law and what evidence and documentation is required to file a slip and fall lawsuit.

Slips and Falls

Slips, trips and falls make up the majority of general industry accidents. According to the U.S. Department of Labor's Occupational Safety & Health Administration (OSHA), slips, trips and falls account for 15 percent of all accidental deaths, and are second only to motor vehicles as a cause of fatalities. Slips, trips and falls kill over 16,000 Americans each year. Slip and fall accidents are among the most common injuries in the workplace and can lead to fractured bones, brain injuries, and even death.

There are approximately 540,000 Slip-Fall injuries requiring hospital care occur ring yearly in North America. Of these over half a million cases, 300,000 result in disabling injuries.

Sexual Harassment

According to the US Equal Employment Opportunity Commission there were 7256 cases filed for Sexual Harassment in which 44.6 million was paid out in settlements. Of course these are just the cases that found their way to the EEOC, however tens of thousands of such claims are made by employees each year that never rise to the stature of making it to the Nation's top equal rights office.

Work Place Accidents – Workers' Compensation Claims

The most common injuries in the work place are sprains and strains. In a recent study, they accounted for 41 percent of all workplace injuries requiring days out of work. In fact, more than 4 out of 10 of injuries and illnesses were sprains or strains, most involving overexertion or falls. A major cause of sprains and strains is the use of improper lifting techniques. Musculoskeletal disorders (MSD) accounted for 30 percent of the injuries and illnesses requiring days out of work. According to the U.S. Department of Labor, an MSD is "an injury or disorder of the muscles, nerves, tendons, joints, cartilage, or spinal disks." They do not include disorders caused by slips, falls, trips, or motor vehicle accidents.

A new study released by the National Academy of Social Insurance (NASI) indicates worker's compensation benefits rose by 1.3% to $61.9 billion in 2012 with employer costs rising by 6.9% to $83.2 billion.

Medical Malpractice Claims

According to the National Practitioner Data Bank 2006 Annual Report, the number of medical malpractice lawsuits per year varies from about 15,000 and 19,000. In 2006, for instance, 15,843 malpractice payment reports were received. The most current malpractice reasons are: diagnosis, surgery and treatment, respectively. The mean payment for malpractice lawsuits in 2006 was $234,635.

A new study published in the New England Journal of Medicine reports that one in 14 doctors faces a malpractice suit every year.

This results in almost every physician having to deal with a malpractice lawsuit — or more than one — during his or her career.

The physicians with the highest risk of being sued were the neurosurgeons, with an annual risk of 19.1 percent, followed by the thoracic-cardiovascular surgeons, with an annual risk only slightly less at 18.9 percent, followed by the general surgeons, with an annual risk of just less than 15.3 percent. The physicians with the lowest risk of being sued were the pediatricians, with an annual risk of 3.1 percent, followed, lastly, by the psychiatrists, with an annual risk of 2.6 percent.

Overall, the study authors said, 75 percent of physicians practicing in a low-risk specialty will have been sued by the time they are age of 65 years, 19 percent will have made an indemnity payment. For those in the high risk specialties, 99 percent will have been sued by age 65, and 71 percent will have lost.

Obstetricians often pay the highest premiums for malpractice insurance of any specialty. According to figures from the federal government, from 2003, the average rate paid by an obstetrician/gynecologist was $64,000 a year, or more. That compared with $28,000 to $50,000 for a general surgeon and $6,000 to $11,000 for an internist. In Florida, where malpractice premium rates tend to be the highest, an obstetrician/gynecologist can pay over $100,000 a year — sometimes well over.

Claims

Keep in mind that the word or term *Claims* is very general. If I say you ran over my dog then I am making a claim that something occurred. A claim is a statement or assertion that something is the case, typically without providing evidence or proof.

In legal ease, it is a 1) v. demand for money, for property, or for enforcement of a right provided by law. 2) n. the making of a demand (assert a claim) for money due, for property, for damages or for enforcement of a right. If such a demand is not honored, it may result in a lawsuit. In order to enforce a right a claim must be filed first. If rejected or ignored then the demanding party has the right to file a lawsuit.

Many claims are made and investigated and never actually go to trial or are argued in a courtroom. Many claims are settled in meetings before a trial is set. These meetings are called mediation or arbitration where both sides present their positions. In a workers compensation case, both sides present their case before a Labor Department Judge. There is no jury just one Judge who makes the determination of benefits.

Modern-Day professional Private Investigator

So the modern-day career oriented legal claims investigator will find him or herself working in the Claims Investigations field. It has a steady flow of work, to substantiate a solid career path and ongoing training in as many different subjects as you can imagine from dog bites to work related accidents.

Chapter Two
Risk Mitigation and the Insurance Claims Investigator

I. Risk
   a. Transfer of Risk through Insurance
   b. Costs/Loss
   c. Insured
   d. Insurer

II. Understanding Insurance Coverage and Terms
   a. Commercial General Liability
   b. Auto Insurance
   c. Homeowners Insurance

III. Human Resource Actions
   a. Job related lawsuits and Claims

IV. Managing Risk or the Threat of a Lawsuit

2 Business Risk Mitigation and The Insurance Claims Investigator

Risk mitigation is defined as taking steps to reduce adverse effects. One way to reduce risk is to transfer it and most businesses do this by buying insurance. By buying insurance businesses and people transfer much of the risk of a loss to the company that issued the policy. The policy holder or Insured will pay a relatively small amount in premium rather than run the risk of not protecting themselves against the possibility of a much larger financial loss. The costs of righting, investigating and or settling the claim is called the loss.

In business insurance, as in personal insurance, we can decide which exposures we want to insure against. Some decisions, however, are already made for us in laws stating that businesses must carry Workers' Compensation.

There are also other coverage's that may be required and not necessarily chosen by the business owner or private individual. A business may not be able to lease a building, space, acquire financed inventory, finance property acquisitions or construction unless it is adequately insured.

In personal insurance, we cannot register or finance a vehicle without insurance. Since many losses are transferred from people or businesses to insurance companies, claims investigators are utilized to investigate and verify an assortment of claims many times clarifying and verifying coverage.

Understanding Insurance Coverage and Terms

It is through insurance policy that risks are transferred from people and businesses to the Insurance Companies, called the Insurer. Those who are covered are called the Insured. As a Claims Investigator you should have the basic understanding of the different types of common business and personal policy coverage, what they are called and how they protect people and business.

Commercial General Liability Insurance

In the course of doing business, businesses interact with employees, contractors, clients, vendors, and others. Any one of them could claim that your business caused them injury or loss and take legal action against you. Whether you need to defend yourself against claims of property damage, bodily injury, libel, slander, or something else, your General Liability Insurance policy would cover you.

What Is General Liability Insurance?

Commercial General Liability Insurance protects small-business owners from claims of injury, property damage, and negligence related to their business activities. The indemnity provided by a liability insurance policy helps your business owner cover the costs associated with mounting a legal defense.

In addition, many small-business owners find that their clients require them to have General Liability Insurance (sometimes referred to Commercial General Liability, or CGL, insurance) before they'll sign a contract. This means that having the right coverage in place can make a significant difference in a business owner's ability to land clients and bring in revenue.

How Commercial General Liability Insurance Protects people and Businesses
In simple terms, a Commercial General Liability Insurance policy protects businesses by providing the financial resources necessary to defend a lawsuit or claim (such as a client injury that leads to a lawsuit)

Costs Covered by Commercial General Liability Insurance

A general liability insurance policy provides financial protection from the risks that any business owner, no matter how careful, might incur. A typical policy covers the following expenses:

The costs of defending or investigating a suit or claim against the business, including court costs, witness fees, attorney's fees, and police report costs
Judgments or settlements resulting from covered suits, including interest required on the judgment and the injured party's medical expenses, if the businesses defense is unsuccessful

People Protected by General Liability Insurance

A general liability policy insurance policy covers the business, of course, but it also covers many of the other people involved in the business: If you the business owner has a joint venture or partnership, all of your partners, members, and their spouses are protected if they are sued for something they do in an official capacity related to the insured business.

If the business is a corporation, the policy covers all of your business's executive officers, stockholders and directors while they are acting in their official capacities.

If the business has subsidiaries, the policy's liability coverage extends to any subsidiary where the business owner owns at least 50 percent of the stock
The policy protects employees from claims that result from actions they take in their capacity as employees.

If there is a written agreement to indemnify a person or organization, such as a vendor, that person or organization would be protected against liability claims for property damage or bodily injury as a result of selling or distributing your products.

People legally associated with the business, including volunteers working under the insured owners direction, are covered for liabilities that result from the work they do for the company, and for the use or maintenance of the property that is in their care.

Specific Coverage Offered by General Liability Insurance

- Bodily Injury

It may be difficult to imagine how a business could cause another person serious harm or even death, but it literally happens tens of thousands of times a day.

- Property Damage

Even if you're careful and take precautions, it's still possible that something your business does – or something it doesn't do – could damage another person's property. It's also possible that your actions might prevent the property's owner from being able to use it. In such cases, business liability insurance coverage compensates for:

- Physical damage to the property, or Loss of use of the property

It is important to note that property damage liability coverage often does not cover damage caused to client property you are working on or have in your possession.

- Products-Completed Operations

Commercial general liability insurance policies generally include liability protection for services or products completed by a company. So if something an insured company manufactures or a service a company provides causes an injury, the policy would pay for any resulting legal expenses, as well as damages up to the policy's limit.

- Contractual Liability

The commercial liability insurance coverage would cover liability that a business might take on when entering into various contracts.

- Liquor Liability

If the insured business does not manufacture, distribute, sell, serve, or furnish alcoholic beverages as a business, the GL policy will cover the business and owner if held liable for a liquor-related accident. This coverage would be pertinent if alcoholic beverages were occasionally used or served at a company picnic or office holiday party. The business would be covered - as long as they didn't charge money for the alcohol.

- Employee Injuries

It's important to know that if an employee should sue a business over an injury on the job, the commercial general liability insurance policy **would not cover** the damages. This type of coverage would be provided by the company's **Workers' Compensation Policy.**

- Fire, Explosion, or Lightning Damage

The property insurance portion of general liability insurance covers damage that may be caused to other people's property as a result of fire, lightning, or explosion; whether the property is owned by the business or rented. This coverage even applies to other areas in a building that may be damaged as a result of negligence on the insured's part. Let's say a fire breaks out in the insured office space on the building's second floor and causes damage to another company's offices below. The insured's policy will pay for the damage to the downstairs office space.

- Hired Auto and Non-owned Auto

Most businesses add an option to their general liability policy called "hired auto and non-owned auto" insurance. If you don't have any vehicles in your company's name, this option meets the requirements of any contract that requires you to have commercial auto coverage.

Additionally, if you or an employee is driving a personally owned vehicle on company business, and you have an auto accident, non-owned auto coverage protects you should the company be sued. However, the policy will not cover a suit against you or your employee personally – that would be covered by a personal auto policy.

- Legal Defense Expenses

Even if your company is not found liable for a claim, the process of mounting a defense is expensive without insurance. A business liability insurance policy will generally pay for the cost to defend or investigate a suit or claim against you, including court costs, witness fees and attorney's fees.

- Medical Payments

If a person should be injured, either directly by you or at your place of business, your commercial liability insurance coverage would pay for medical expenses incurred within a year of the accident. For example, if one of your clients slips and falls at your office and requires medical treatment, your policy would cover the cost of that treatment.

- Personal Injury

Personal injury is the part of the commercial general liability policy that protects you should someone claim that your business caused damage that isn't physical. In the following examples, most liability policies would protect you against any lawsuits related to:

- Publishing, in writing or verbally, false information that libels or slanders an organization or person
- Publishing material that violates someone's privacy rights
- Falsely detaining, arresting or imprisoning someone
- Maliciously prosecuting someone
- Evicting someone wrongfully
- Advertising Injury
- Should you ever be sued over something that happens while advertising your company's products or services, your business liability insurance protection will cover the claim.

> Advertising injuries can arise from:

- Publishing, verbally or in writing, false information that libels or slanders a person or organization
- Publishing material that violates an individual's privacy rights
- Copying another company's style of doing business, or advertising concepts

❖ Infringing on another business's title, copyright or slogan

Auto Insurance Coverage and Terms

The value of an auto insurance policy goes beyond replacing or repairing a vehicle if it's damaged. It's about limiting risk and exposure.

Car insurance coverage provides all the coverage needed to protect people and businesses from losses should you be held legally responsible for an automobile accident that causes death or injury to another person. This coverage also includes the legal expenses for your defense in a covered suit.

- Property Damage Liability

Protects you from financial losses should you be found liable for damage caused by your automobile to other people's property, such as fences, light poles or another vehicle.

- Uninsured Motorist Bodily Injury

Pays death or bodily injury costs for you and any passengers in your vehicle if you should be hit by an uninsured driver, or if you're struck by a "hit-and-run" driver you can't identify.

- Uninsured Motorist Property Damage

Pays for damage to your vehicle should it be hit by a hit-and-run driver, a driver with no insurance, or a driver whose property damage liability limit is not enough to cover the damages incurred.

- Underinsured Motorists

Pays benefits for the death or bodily injury of you and any passengers in your car, should you be in an accident caused by a driver who has some insurance, but that insurance is inadequate to cover the losses resulting from the accident.

- Personal Injury Protection (No-Fault)

Covers the cost of personal injuries that result from an auto accident, regardless of who was at fault. This coverage applies to injuries only, and does not include damage to a car or any other property.

- Medical Payments

Pays necessary and reasonable medical expenses that directly result from an auto accident, up to selected limits. Covered expenses might include medical care, rehabilitation, recovery and remedial care, as specified in the policy.

- Collision

Pays for damage to a covered vehicle, less the deductible amount and up to actual cash value, for losses caused by a collision. "Collision" is defined as contact with a physical object, such as another vehicle or a structure. If you choose to buy collision coverage, choosing a higher deductible typically reduces the cost of your policy. Collision coverage is available only for those who also carry comprehensive coverage, and is often required when your car is financed or leased.

- Comprehensive

Pays for damage to your covered vehicle, less the deductible amount and up to actual cash value, caused by events such as theft, fire, riot, glass breakage, hail and windstorms. If you choose to buy collision coverage, choosing a higher deductible typically reduces the cost of your policy. Comprehensive is often mandated if your car is leased or financed.

- Full Glass

Pays for a covered glass loss, without deductible.

- Towing and Labor

Pays up to the chosen limit for towing your inoperable vehicle, regardless of whether there has been an accident. To get this coverage, you must also secure comprehensive coverage.

- Rental Reimbursement

If your car should become inoperable as the result of a covered loss, and you need to rent a car to get around, this coverage will pay for the rental car, up to your policy limits. To get this coverage, you must also carry comprehensive and collision coverage.

<ins>Homeowners Insurance Coverage</ins>

Standard home insurance coverage policies provide the following types of coverage, up to the limits outlined in the policies:

- Dwelling — Pays for damage or destruction to your house and any unattached structures and buildings, such as fences, detached garages, and storage sheds.

- Personal Property — Covers the contents of your house, including furniture, clothing and appliances, if they are stolen, damaged, or destroyed.

- Liability — Protects you against financial loss if you are sued and found legally responsible for someone else's injury or property damage.

- Medical Payments — Covers medical bills for people hurt on your property. Medical Payments coverage also pays for some injuries that may happen away from your home, such as if your dog bites someone.

- Loss of Use — Pays for additional living expenses if your home is too damaged to live in during repairs. Most standard home insurance coverage pays 10 to 20 percent of the amount of your dwelling coverage.

Human Resource Actions

Legislation such as the Family Medical Leave Act and the Americans with Disabilities Act, plus a growing number of job-related lawsuits and claims, have created the need for Human Resource and Risk Managers to recognized potential risks to their business.

When accusations are made Managers will immediately jump into actions to determine the facts of the allegations. When they escalate the business manager may seek legal representation and hire an investigator. Situations where an investigator may get involved are in the following areas:

Gender, age and other types of discrimination, sexual harassment, wrongful termination or discipline, negligent compensation, promotion or hiring decisions, breach of contract for employment, invasion of privacy, libel or slander and employee benefits mismanagement. These are just a few of the common claims and one the most frequent claims is sexual harassment.

Managing Risk and the Threat of a Law Suit

Insurance is the transfer of the risk of a loss, from one entity to another in exchange for payment. It is a form of risk management used to hedge against uncertain loss. An insurer, or insurance carrier, is selling the insurance; the insured, or policyholder, is the person or entity buying the insurance policy. The amount of money to be charged for a certain amount of insurance coverage is called the premium. People and businesses protect themselves from lawsuits through Insurance. Before a lawsuit is actually filed, "a claim" is made, an accusation or accusatory statement usually asserting who is at fault; you hit my vehicle or I slipped on that grease please get your manager! Claims Investigators, investigate these accusations on behalf of the insured party. In other words, if you have auto insurance with Allstate auto insurance and you are in an accident, an Allstate hired investigator, will investigate the incident to make certain you were not wrongly blamed.

Chapter Three
Licensing Rules and Regulations

I. Licensing and Training
    a. In-House Investigator
II. Private Investigators
III. Private Investigative Firms
IV. Laws
V. Regulated Activity
VI. Types of Licenses
VII. Advertising
VIII. Equipment
IX. Costs
X. Future
XI. Firearms
XII. Use of Force
XIII. Other Prohibited or Discouraged Acts
    a. Use of State Seals
    b. Use of Badge
XIV. Unlawful Symbols of Authority
XV. Confidentiality
XVI. Divulging Investigative Information

3. Licensing Rules and Regulations

Most states in the US regulate the activities of private investigators working as legal or claims investigators. These subjects if working for an investigative firm are called Private Investigators. The term Private Investigator is very general and reflects the business of conducting investigations for the public or private businesses.

If the investigator is working in-house for the insurance company or law firm then he/she may be excluded from licensure depending on the states licensing guidelines. However since most law firms, insurance companies and business do not have an adequate staff of investigators, most use Investigative Agencies to assist in the claim verification process.

To secure a Private Investigator's license each state has specific laws and regulations to assist applicants for licensure in understanding the basic requirements and restrictions of the industry. Please note that this section reflects on the general rules and regulations found in many state licensing statutes. Individuals seeking a more comprehensive understanding of the laws for their state are directed to carefully read and study the specific laws regulating Private Investigators in the state you intend to reside and work in. First of all contact or query your local licensing body that issues your states Private Investigators licenses. Secondly, printout any state statutes or administrative codes pertaining to Private Investigative licensing requirements, training and regulated activity.

Regulated Activity – Private Investigation

Definition — the investigation by a person or persons for the purpose of obtaining information with reference to any of the following matters:

a. The identity, habits, conduct, movements, whereabouts, affiliations, associations, transactions, reputation, or character of any society, person, or group of persons.

b. The credibility of witnesses or other persons.

c. The causes and origin of, or responsibility for, fires, libels, slanders, losses, accidents, damage, or injuries to real or personal property.

As a Claims Investigator working for a Private Investigative Firm, you will be required to be licensed and sponsored or work under the direction of an Agency. The Agency is the brick and mortar business that employees and trains investigators and links the trainee or newest agents with a more seasoned Investigator as a mentor. Many agencies will also have managers who supervise a larger group of investigators usually partitioned by regions or states.

Types of Licenses

Many states allow lessor trained individuals without any experience to be licensed or registered under another experienced Investigator as an intern or apprentice. A couple of states that immediately comes to mind that have this type of programs are Georgia, California, Tennessee and Florida. Each state usually has a program to allow newcomers to the profession who lack any field experience. Searching out the programs will be as easy as determining the types of Private Investigator Licenses and applications available in your state.

Any individual who performs investigative services as an intern or apprentice under the direction and control of a sponsoring investigator may not subcontract; they must work for the person or company the sponsoring person works for.

In-House Investigators – No license required

Definition — An *unarmed investigator who is solely, exclusively, and regularly employed as an investigator in connection with the business of his/her employer when such employer does not provide, or advertise as providing, investigative services for a fee. An unlicensed investigator may not provide investigative services to any person or business other than his/her employer.

*The carrying of a firearm for employment requires a separate firearms license.

Example: An individual may be employed to investigate matters specifically related to his/her employer's business such as an Insurance Investigator employed by an insurance carrier in the Special Investigative Unit or SIU. Or an investigator hired to work within a Law firm.

While the Private Claims Investigator needs to be licensed and the SIU and Legal Law Office Investigators do not, their roles are almost identical in that they all investigate claims. The SIU typically handles investigations within his/her region and subcontracts out any over-flow or excess work he/she cannot handle to an Investigative Agency who employees a full staff of investigators. The typical law firm will use paralegals that perform research and while they may also have a limited investigative staff, most large firms also outsource the greater volume of investigative work to Private Investigative Firms.

PI Firms

Like law firms a PI Firm practicing statewide would consist of perhaps 25 – 50 investigators, management and supporting staff. An Investigative Agency that is Nationwide would have hundreds of staff investigators. These investigators are specifically trained to handle complex civil claim investigations.

Training and Test Requirements

Many states require applicants for a Private Investigator's license to pass a qualification exam. This exam will determine your knowledge of the state's statutes and regulations governing the Private Investigations Industry. The test may also cover regular and customary practices, legal issues and professional ethics. While the specific statutes and regulations will come from your state, this book will address all other areas of information needed.

College course work related to criminal justice, criminology, or law enforcement administration, or successful completion of any law enforcement-related training received from any federal, state, county, or municipal agency, can usually be applied towards your training requirement so be prepared to describe any such training you have had on your application. If it is work experience you are using to qualify for licensure, make sure you can adequately relate how your experience conveys to experience needed as a Private Investigator.

For Example: If your job required you to interview people and sometimes you needed to do some digging to find information about the subject that could be used to track them down in order to conduct the interview then you have been conducting investigative work. How you write that experience down on your application will be important.

Firearms

Smaller usually independent Private Investigators with former Law Enforcement backgrounds may choose to carry a firearm. However, firearms, are not required nor is firearm training a mandatory part of the job. In fact, most large Private Investigative Firms will have a policy **prohibiting the carrying of a firearm** during the course of any business activity.

If a firearm is going to be carried, most states require a separate license to carry a firearm during the course of employment. In many states this is different from a concealed weapons permit which permits an individual to carry a personal firearm. Firearms carried **on the job**, usually require separate and specialized training and licensure. Never assume your concealed weapons permit allows you to carry a firearm at work.

Use of Force

a. Private investigators are not law enforcement officers and are not granted any police powers regarding arrest or use of force.

b. Deadly force may never be used by a private investigator except in self-defense or defense of another from imminent death or great bodily harm. The use of deadly force to protect property or to prevent property loss is prohibited by law.

c. Non-deadly force may be used by private investigators to the extent necessary for self-defense or defense of another against the use of unlawful force or to prevent or terminate trespass or "interference" with persons he/she has a legal duty to protect.

d. Firing a warning shot for any reason, including an attempt to stop a person suspected of the commission of a crime, is prohibited.

Company Identification Cards

Most states require a licensed investigative agency to furnish to its partners, principal corporate officers, and all licensed employees an identification card with the name and license number of the holder of the card and name and license number of the agency. The identification card should be signed by the individual licensee and a representative of the agency. The identification card should be in the possession of the licensee at all times while engaged in regulated activity.

Agency identification cards are issued solely for the purpose of identifying the licensee and his/her employer. The use of any state seal is forbidden in many states. Whenever possible it is always a good policy to avoid any terms or images on a license that may be misinterpreted or imply the bearer has some official government status. Always remember that inferring or representing ones self as a law enforcement officer is a felony.

Agency Advertisements Require License Number

A licensed agency should always include its agency license number in any advertisement in any print medium or directory, and should include its agency license number in any written bid or offer to provide services.

Example: An agency's license number should be included on bids, Yellow Page listings, trade journals, etc.; however, employment advertising does not require the agency license number.

Other Prohibited Acts

a. Impersonating, or permitting or aiding and abetting an employee to impersonate, a law enforcement officer or an employee of the state, the United States, or any political subdivision thereof by identifying himself/herself as a federal, state, county, or municipal law enforcement officer or official representative, by wearing a uniform or presenting or displaying a badge or credentials that would cause a reasonable person to believe that he/she is a law enforcement officer or that he/she has official authority, by displaying any flashing or warning vehicular lights other than amber-colored, or by committing any act that is intended to falsely convey official status.

b. Fraud or willful misrepresentation in applying for or obtaining a license.

c. Use of any fictitious or assumed name by an agency unless the agency has Division of Licensing approval and has registered that name with Department of State, Division of Corporations.

d. Being found guilty of or entering a plea of guilty or *nolo contendere* to, regardless of adjudication, or being convicted of a crime which directly relates to the business for which the license is held or sought. A plea of *nolo contendere* shall create a rebuttable presumption of guilt to the underlying criminal charges, and the department shall allow the individual being disciplined or denied an application for a license to present any mitigating evidence relevant to the reason for, and the circumstances surrounding, his/her plea.

e. A false statement by the licensee that any individual is or has been in his/her employ.

f. A finding that the licensee or any employee is guilty of willful betrayal of a professional secret or any unauthorized release of information acquired as a result of activities regulated under his /her license.

g. Conducting activities regulated by law without a license or with a revoked or suspended license.

h. Proof that the applicant or licensee is guilty of fraud or deceit, or of negligence, incompetence, or misconduct in the practice of the activities regulated under the Private Investigations Licensing Statutes.

Example: It is misconduct to refuse to provide a copy of an investigative report to a client upon demand when such report resulted from investigative activity paid for by the client.

Example: It is deceit in the practice of regulated activities to refuse to provide a client a bill itemizing all charges upon demand by the client.

i. Commission of an act of violence or the use of force on any person except in the lawful protection of one's self or another from physical harm.

j. Knowingly violating, advising, encouraging, or assisting the violation of any statute, court order, capias, warrant, injunction, or cease and desist order, in the course of business regulated under the Private Investigations Licensing Statutes.

k. Soliciting business for an attorney in return for compensation.

l. Transferring or attempting to transfer a license issued pursuant to the Private Investigations Licensing Statutes. Employing or contracting with any unlicensed or improperly licensed person or agency to conduct activities regulated under the Private Investigations Licensing Statutes when such licensure status was known or could have been ascertained by reasonable inquiry.

n. Failure or refusal to cooperate with or refusal of access to an authorized representative of the licensing department engaged in an official investigation pursuant to the Private Investigations Licensing Statutes.

o. Failure of any partner, principal corporate officer, or licensee to have his/her agency identification card in his/her possession while on duty.

p. Failure of any licensee to have his/her license in his/her possession while on duty.

q. Failure or refusal by a sponsor to certify completion or termination of an internship, apprentice or acknowledge experience of a trainee or new investigator.

r. Failure to report to the department any person whom the licensee knows to be in violation of the Private Investigations Licensing Statutes.

s. Violating any provision of the Private Investigations Licensing Statutes.

Use of the State Seals Prohibited

No agency or licensee should use the Great Seal of any state on any badge, patch, credential, identification card, correspondence, advertisement, business card, or any other means of identification used in connection with investigative services.

Badges

a. Some states have established that the five-pointed star badges are reserved for sheriffs and deputy sheriffs in their state. Any badge or insignia of such similarity to the official sheriff's badge which is indistinguishable at a distance of twenty (20) feet should be prohibited for use by individuals licensed under the Private Investigations Licensing Statutes.

b. Licensed private investigators and private investigator interns should be especially aware that the use of any badge in the course of investigative activity could create the suggestion that you are affiliated with law enforcement. The act of impersonating a police officer would constitute misconduct in the course of any regulated activities. It is strongly suggested that ONLY the agency identification card and state issued identification are needed for identification purposes while on the job.

Unlawful Symbols of Authority

The unauthorized exhibition, wear or display of any indicia of authority including any badge, insignia, emblem, identification card, uniform or any colorable imitation thereof which could deceive a reasonable person into believing that such item is authorized by a law enforcement agency or the bearer is a law enforcement officer is prohibited. All non-official persons and agencies are prohibited from the use of the words "police", "patrolman", "agent", "sheriff", "deputy", "trooper", "highway patrol", "Wildlife Officer", "Marine Patrol Officer", "state attorney", "public defender", "marshal", "constable", or "bailiff" when the use of such words or combinations thereof could deceive a reasonable person into believing that such person or agency is a law enforcement officer or agency.

Divulging Investigative Information

It is a common practice and most Private Investigations licensing statutes will specifically prohibit a licensee or any employee of a licensee or licensed agency to divulge or release to anyone other than his/her client or employer the contents of an investigative file acquired in the course of licensed investigative activity.

This however does not apply when the request is being made by the state agency that licenses Private investigators and Private Investigative Firms. If a formal request is made to review business, operational records or an investigative file, by an authorized representative of the department engaged in an official investigation, inspection, or inquiry pursuant to any regulatory duty the authority has as a result of their licensing authority, full compliance should be granted. If the state request is to review a private file concerning an investigation made, the person who requested the investigation should be notified and asked if they want their investigation report released. If they do not grant access, the government agency should seek a court order to acquire the investigative report.

Chapter Four
Getting a Foot in the Door

      I.   Interns and Apprenticeship
      II.   Entry Level Investigative Work
      III.   How are Investigators Hired
      IV.   Insurance Company Structure
      V.   Standard Business Procedures and Market Industry
      VI.   Private Investigations as a "Stepping Stone" to Law Degree or Federal Investigator Job.

4. Getting a Foot in the Door

I. Interns and Apprenticeship

Many states offer intern or apprentice licenses or investigator employee registrations. This enables the recent college graduate or new recruit the opportunity to enter the field in an entry level position to learn the profession. This again throws out the concept or idea that only a seasoned investigator or Law Enforcement Officer can work as a Private Investigator. Like any profession, the Private Investigations industry needs fresh young people willing to learn the business and build a successful career within a particular company and perhaps stay there their whole career.

In Clams Investigations, we use one tactic very often and routinely. This tactic or activity is called "surveillance" which many in the industry have been known to say is a "young person game". Fortunately for many, while it is true young people can quickly pick up the concept and play an important role in the business, this same newcomer can also spend a career doing surveillance work. Surveillance is both scientific and artistic. Like any art, you get better over time with practice. So those in the industry doing a lot of surveillance learn how to make surveillance more productive but at the same time less arduous. So while a younger person just entering the field can do the job, they will get better and better at the art while at the same time developing other more challenging investigative skills such as interviewing, taking statements and conducting more complex investigations through research and creative thinking.

In some states interns are given licenses while other states, interns are registered. In both scenarios, the intern or apprentice as I like to say, must work under the guidance and direction of a seasoned investigator with usually a minimum of two-year's experience.

II. Entry Level Investigative Work

Most large professional investigative firms will specialize in claims and business risk mitigation investigations. Most insurance companies will have Special Investigative Units called the "SIU". Most law firms will use legal investigators to meet, interview, collect pertinent information and even sign up or contract the person for representation. So the market is quite large if your job search is organized and your research thorough.

Let's first start with Private Investigative Firms because they have the least exposure and are the hardest to find. This also means that they don't get the bulk of the resumes for this industry. First of all most CJ majors or those interested in doing investigative work, send their resumes to Police Departments and Federal Agencies. It's probably rarer for an applicant to send a resume to an insurance company applying for a position in the SIU. And when it comes to Private Investigative Firms, they don't advertise who they are and usually want to maintain a low profile. For many people they are even surprised to hear there is such a profession and when they hear they have unfilled positions this too comes as a surprise.

To target a potential job as Private Claims Investigator you need to investigate the market. The claims and business risk industries are primarily made up of businesses, municipalities and insurance companies. Most large businesses and municipalities will have a Human Resource Department. They may even have a Risk Management Department. Within one of these two departments, the company will have a focus on their own employee's health, welfare and safety. They will also deal with accidents by patrons, visitors and possibly criminals looking to target their company with fraud schemes. The role of HR or Risk Manager may even be played by the owner of a small company who finds him or herself facing a serious claim or lawsuit. In any of these scenarios, the private investigator would be working in a defense strategy mode, as a defense investigator. Working to minimize the risk or exposure of the claim, accident or incident caused.

III. How Investigators are Hired

As investigators we may work directly for the insurance companies as a staff investigator referred to as a special investigator working in the special investigations unit (SIU). We may be a staff investigator working for a Law Firm or we may be independent investigators licensed as Private Investigators working for a Private investigations Firm who contracts with Law firms and Insurance companies.

Private Investigations Firm – An entry level full-time staff investigator's hourly rate with an Investigation Firm would be between $18.00- $20.00 / hr., plus expenses or on a salary of between $500.00 –$700.00 per week. As experience and billable capability take hold, the investigator will see their income increase over time to $40.00 -$50.00 per hour.

Employee vs. Independent Contractor

There are hundreds of small Investigative Agencies with less than 15 investigators. While this may not be the best career route or offer the best benefits, it may still be a way to gain experience. Many of these smaller agencies lack sufficient business experience or are faced with operating in a business known for high operational costs and thin margins. Running an investigation company means having people in the field with cars and equipment. It's an expensive business and many look to short cuts to save money and increase profits. One of the ways to save money as an Agency may be to use or classify workers as subcontractors or Independent Contractors.

A subcontractor or independent contractor is a person or a company hired by another entity to perform part of the work of a job. For example, an Agency might have an abundance of work and their staff investigators are unable to meet the demand of the extra work. Subcontractors may be hired to handle the "over flow of work". This generally happens in certain busy seasons or with an agency experiencing rapid growth. It could also be the result of a seasonal anomaly or events such as a hurricane that causes an enormous amount of property damage that needs to be inspected and or investigated. Or the ending of a growing season when the migrant workers are no longer needed in the area or when a large plant is closing down and there is a rash of layoffs followed by claims of personal injuries from the workers uncertain about their futures.

It may not be an option for you to argue how you are classified and if it comes down to being an independent contractor or no job, I choose the job and experience. There are some simple steps you can take to protect yourself, by forming your own company, LLC or corporation. Having an agreement in writing which allows you to work for other firms will also enable you to get more experience and exposure.

Many seasoned investigators who choose not to work for one agency freelance working on a regular basis but for many different agencies. The Agency does not employ the investigator as a regular employee in most cases because he/she is not needed on a permanent basis. The investigator gets a higher hourly rate and is expected to be self-sufficient, with little supervision or questions asked about insurance. But having formed a separate company like an LLC you can insure yourself with Professional liability (with E & O) and Workers Compensation Insurance.

Once an Investigator is familiar with the industry or if they are adventurous enough to go out on their own, they may offer their services to other agencies as a subcontractor. While this practice is very common, it is frowned upon if the Investigator has not formed his/her own business. An area of concern for this practice is what happens if the subcontractor is hurt on the job or worse yet, hurts someone else. If they are working your case, and they are not insured, the liability will fall on the firm. If the firm did not properly identify that it was using a subcontractor on the job, then the insurance company make not insure the incident leaving the business owner and investigator responsible for the damages.

If you use subcontractors, your insurance company should be fully aware of the practice and their names so that your insurance can be extended to any subcontractors you use. As a subcontractor, you provide instant assistance to the Firm when work picks up yet the Firm is not responsible to keep you busy, withhold taxes or provide insurance or benefits. The benefit to the investigator can be a higher hourly rate of between $25.00 –$50.00 depending on the investigators experience. This hourly rate may also include expenses.

IV. Insurance Companies

Insurance companies use investigators to investigator claims and potential risks bought to their attention by their business clients. The business clients of the Insurance Companies are called the "Insured". Insurance companies rely on their own staff of investigators as well as other Investigative Firms to assist them. The insurance Companies own investigative staff, work within a group called the Special Investigative Unit, or "SIU". Many Insurance Companies don't have the staff to investigate all matters so they contract outside investigators for over-flow work. This is how work comes from the insurance industry to a Private Investigator or Claims Investigator. Some insurance companies rely on their Defense Counsel's suggestions when hiring an over-flow investigator and some set out to find their own list of qualified investigators. Insurance companies usually appoint one member of the SIU team that is called the "Vendor Manager" who specifically looks for qualified and reliable investigative firms to partner with to handle their overflow work. The approved Investigative Firms will go on an approved "vendor list" which is maintained and often reviewed yearly by the SIU.

In order to make the Vendor List as an Investigative Firm, rates, area of coverage and investigative staff will be vetted and approved before any work is given. Rates are set by competitive industry pricing so knowing the industry standards is important. Flat Rate Pricing for Surveillance, Activity Checks and Background Investigations is often the norm. Special complex investigations are usually billed our hourly plus mileage (75.00 Hr. and .55 per mile). Charges for travel time to and from a job as well as many other incidental expenses are frown upon as they represent unknown factors.

V. Standard Business Procedures and Market Industry

Insurance Companies have become use to industry standards when it comes to investigative forms reporting and formats. We refer to the people we investigate as Subjects or Claimants and routinely put pictures in our report of the subjects we interview, p[;laces we visit or the equipment involved in the incident. We summarize interviews to make the matter as easily to understand as possible: using pictures, drawings and well written reports. We secure Written or Recorded Statements of subjects or witnesses to memorialize what is fresh in their heads following an incident or accident. From the time a case is received, we attempt to work the case within 5 days and provide a client with a full written report within 10 days. The turnaround time is very important to the client. Large companies provide clients with daily updates as soon as a case is worked.

IV. Show Case Examples of Actual Investigations

1. Dispel the assumption that it takes a super sleuth to be a PI

2. We spend most of our time straightening out simple miscommunications.
3. We investigate routine accidents and incidents such as:
A. Property and Casualty Claims
i. Property
a. Automobile Accidents Damaged Cars
b. Stolen Cars
c. Cars set on Fire
d. Determining Permissive Use
e. Determining Premium Fraud in Garaging Issues
f. Burglary
ii. Casualty
a. Injuries associated to an automobile accident
b. Work Place or Business Liability
B. General Liability Claims
i. Slip and Fall in a business location
ii. Assault in a business location
C. Workers' Compensation Claims
i. Slip and Fall / back / injury at work
ii. Assault at work / robbery / shooting / fight
D. Human Resource Concerns
i. Sexual Harassment
ii. Harassment
iii. Assault
4. We utilize different investigative techniques for different type of claims
A. In defending a personal injury cases, Surveillance is used routinely
B. In Theft cases we take a lot of statements, pictures and conduct canvasses of the area for witnesses.

C. In Assault cases, we look for other similar crimes and their frequency to determine if more security measure should have been in place.
i. We request Crime Grids from the local policing agency
ii. We check the time the incident occurred for lighting
D. Virtually every type of case you can think of has been worked before and a routine outline of how to proceed is available.

This is the specific market a large professional private investigations firm targets. So joining or finding the investigative agencies that services this market is your objective when considering pursuing a position as a defense investigator.

Every year the insurance claim industry has conferences that focus on fighting and defending claims. In fact, there are many different types of conferences for as many different types of insurance offered. Each type of Insurance will represent its own type of potential claims and need for services. At a Workers Compensation Insurance Conference they will discuss issues regarding work place injuries and accidents. At a Liability Insurance Conference they will discuss issues regarding liability and minimizing risk and exposure and defending claims. Law Firms specializing in Insurance defense work also hold conferences. Conference are held and attended by the association members of Risk Managers, Human Resource Managers and Self-Insureds.

Some common purpose of these trade shows or conferences is to:

- Educate Members
- Offer Continuing Education for Professional Designations
- Discuss Issues Facing the Industry
- Exchange Information
- Initiate Policy Changes
- Share Ideas and Knowledge
- Review The Latest Products and Services
- Discuss Best Practices

The professional private investigative firm offers services to all of these groups of attendees and will be present to discuss their company's services and find customers.

A yearly Workers Compensation Conference may have two hundred vendor exhibitors made up of chiropractors, transportation companies, prosthetic companies, rehabilitation

companies, nurses and of course, INVESTIGATIVE AGENCIES.

Scour the internet for any conference or trade shows involving insurance claims, Liability, Property and Casualty Claims, Homeowners, Automobile, Workers Compensation or Medical Malpractice Insurance. Do the same for Human Resource and Risk Managers Conferences.

If you go on-line and query, workers compensation conference you will find state and national events. The same holds true for Property and Casualty Conferences and Risk Mangers Conferences. The Internet will be very helpful in determining if there is an event you can attend or visit. Try to contact the conference organizer to ask about investigative agency participants or a list of investigative agency participants from last year's event. Typically, a statewide event will have mostly local or agencies servicing that state with perhaps a third of the participants with operations in other states and nationwide. After determining the conference with the most participants make sure you attend the event with plenty of resumes and time to talk to the men and woman present at the company's exhibit booth. Most of the time there will be local investigators in the booth along with professional marketing representatives. Make sure you get the companies contact information for their main office or hiring managers. Typically each regional office will have a hiring manager or a manager who makes the final decision on a new recruit or intern. Don't just leave your resume, get the contact information for your follow-up.

Many large Private Investigative Companies use job boards like indeed.com or job banks like Monster. Query "Private Investigative Jobs" on the internet to see any job postings that may come up.

If you are interesting in learning more about the industry, I would suggest visiting the online national publication of the magazine CLAIMS at http://www.propertycasualty360.com/Claims-Magazine, researching RIMS an organization dedicated to advancing the practice of risk management, https://www.rims.org, the Florida Insurance Fraud Education Committee at www.FIFEC.org and finally the International Association of Special Investigation Units, IASIU at http://www.iasiu.org. All of these sources will provide an insight into our industry and the work we perform.

VI. Private Investigations as a Stepping Stone

If you still have your heart set on the FBI, DEA or another federal government investigative position, I have some really good news for you. The experience you will get on the job as a Claims Investigator will not only be invaluable to building investigative experience, it will satisfy most federal investigative positions pre-requisite of two years investigative experience. As a private investigator your experience has been purely investigative, interviewing, conducting surveillances and locating people. Private Investigations challenges your imagination and resourcefulness. You learn to work with relatively little supervision, write through and concise detailed reports and focus on obtaining results. What can be more attractive to an employer than to hear those accomplished skills. Other private investigators use this experience to pursue law school, but many also remain as career investigators.

Chapter Five
Professional Standards and Ethics

    I.   Understand the Client/Investigator relationship
    II.   Recognize the importance of the initial client interview
    III.   Understand Whether a Client's Intentions are Legal and Ethical
    IV.   Establish a Clear Understanding of Clients Goals
    V.   Working a Case in a Timely and Cost Effective Manner
    VI.   Provide Regular Updates and Reports
    VII.   Confidentiality
    VIII. Potential Conflicts of Interest
    IX.   Providing a Quality Work Product
    X.   Providing Detailed Reports and Invoices
    XI.   Truth in Advertising
    XII.   Agency to Agency Billing
    XIII. Investigators Pledge

5. Understand the Client/Investigator Relationship

According to the Private Investigations Licensing Statutes, your relationship with your client and your assignment is confidential and no one other than your client should be privileged to your investigation or the result thereof. You cannot go into a neighborhood and say, "I'm investigating Joe Neighbor, tell me what you know about him". You must be discreet and always remember entering and exiting a neighborhood without anyone even knowing you where there is the best possible scenario of your investigation. At the very least, when a direct inquiry is necessary and you are instructed to identify yourself during the inquiry, always show respect for the subject you are inquiring about and keep your questioning professional. Never cast a false light on your subject, don't make it sound like he/she did something wrong. You are no the judge and jury so don't interject your personal feelings in the case regardless of what you think you can prove.

I always approach a case thinking that blending in is an important tactic to getting people to willingly provide information. I have heard of instances where an over bearing PI tries to use his credentials to get information and the witness says I'm busy or simply states they don't know anything or doesn't want to get involved. The investigator ends up walking away without any information. Conversely, a respectful, friendly PI who approaches the house under the pretext that he is thinking about moving into the neighborhood may have a better chance of getting information. I have had woman at the door tell me to hold on while she reduces the heat to her stove burner and then invited me into the house for a soft drink and talk about where I am from and what brings me to the community. This may be the same woman that told the obtrusive investigator that she didn't know anything and was busy cooking dinner. Your approach to gathering information and how you handle people is crucial!

Recognize the Importance of the Initial Client Interview

During your initial contact with your client make sure you understand exactly what they are looking for and realize they may not address or have all the information you may need. After all they are not the professional investigator and may not know what is important or critical to your investigation. You may need to review the information provided at the initial contact then conduct some preliminary efforts before re-contacting the client with some additional questions. Make sure you have a plan of attack so that the client is confident in their decision to hire you. Don't say, "what would you like me to do or what do you think I should do?" At the same time don't let an overbearing client tell you how to conduct an investigation. You are the professional and should develop a plan of action after reviewing all the information provided by the client.

Client's Intentions- Legal and Ethical?

Just because a client calls you to perform an investigation doesn't mean you don't have a moral and perhaps legal obligation to make certain the clients' intentions are legal and ethical. Exactly, why are you being asked to perform a specific service? For what and how is the information going to be used. I had an insurance adjuster tell me to sit right in front of the claimant's house so that he saw me and to sit there and watch the guy for 3 days. The adjuster stated that they wanted him to know he was being watched and that we were going to keep watching and let all of his neighbors see us watching him as well. I told the client that surveillance has to be conducted discreetly, with the claimant privacy in mind. We were not allowed by law to imply he did something wrong as this was shedding a false light on the subject. Furthermore, by sitting directly on his house and him knowing we were there and not leaving was harassment.

Sometime in our profession we also get requests from our clients to perform other services not always associated to claims investigations. For instance, I worked for a large trucking company investigating their injured drivers and when the owner of the company was going through a divorce, he called me to surveil his wife and identify her lover. You may also be asked to locate someone, but you need to determine why and for what purpose you are locating the subject. You need to consider the possibility that the other subject doesn't want to be found due to domestic violence issues or perhaps even an Order of Protection granted to the other party to keep the client away.

When I first started in the business my territory was South Florida and the Keys. I was sitting on a WC surveillance assignment when I noticed a male subject exit a house on the same block I was parked. I was well away from my target house and actually sitting off of them because I knew the subject's schedule having worked it several times before. I was merely sitting down the street a couple of blocks waiting for my subjects car to leave the driveway, when the male subject on my block approached my passenger's side window and places a small firearm at the side of my head. He asked me what I was doing and without hesitation I told him I was doing surveillance. After things calmed down, I immediately called the Hollywood Police Department and reported the incident and requested he be arrested. After my assignment I spend two hours in the PD being talked out of filing charges by the DEA. The subject who had pulled the gun on me was a DEA agent supposedly on leave of absence after an incident in Mexico where his partner was captured, tortured and killed. What I also learned is that Private Investigators where being used by the drug cartels. Unbeknown to local PI's they were being hired by the cartels representing themselves as local businessmen wanting to investigate their business partners. Since the DEA often used undercover locations in unmarked office suites in ordinary strip plazas throughout south Florida, there was no way to know who was actually using the space. The hired investigators were told to go to the business location and take a picture of each subject exiting the office, identify their car when they leave and perhaps even follow them home to identify their address. The investigators were told that once the information was gathered, the client would then take it from to analyze the information. What was thought to be an internal corporate security or business intelligence operation, actually turned out to be intelligence supporting a criminal enterprise. As a young investigator, I quickly realized the complexity of my current issue with the DEA agent who over reacted but was in fear of his family who was at home at the time. Not wanting to blemish his years of service, I dropped my charges.

Many states have adopted, a Drivers Privacy Protection Act (DPPA) protecting the privacy of peoples state motor vehicle record information. However in many states this information is still available to the professional investigator, but we need to understand why our clients need this information, because the abuses are real and well known.

In California, the Driver Protection Act DPPA was passed in reaction to a series of abuses of drivers' personal information held by the DMV and other government bodies. The 1989 death of actress Rebecca Schaeffer was a prominent example of such abuse. In that case, a private investigator, hired by an obsessed fan, was able to obtain Rebecca Schaeffer's address through her California motor vehicle record. The fan used her address information to stalk and to kill her. Other incidents around the US and cited by Congress included a ring of Iowa home robbers who targeted victims by writing down the license plates of expensive cars and obtaining home address information from the State's department of motor vehicles.

Senator Barbara Boxer, of California who sponsored 103 S. 1589, a version of the DPPA, cited other examples where stalkers were able to find victims by simply visiting a DMV. She argued that in 34 States, someone could walk into a State Motor Vehicle Department with your license plate number and a few dollars and walk out with your name and home address." Senator Boxer also said:

"In Tempe, AZ, a woman was murdered by a man who had obtained her home address from that State's DMV.

And, in California, a 31-year-old man copied down the license plate numbers of five women in their early twenties, obtained their home address from the DMV and then sent them threatening letters at home. I want to briefly read from two of those letters.

I'm lonely and so I thought of you. I'll give you one week to respond or I will come looking for you.

Another one read: *I looked for you though all I knew about you was your license plate. Now I know more and yet nothing. I know you're a Libra, but I don't know what it's like to smell your hair while I'm kissing your neck and holding you in my arms.*

When they apprehended this subject, they found in his possession a book entitled `You Can Find Anyone' which spelled out how to do just that using someone's license plate.

Americans are in favor of laws protecting their personal information and privacy. Without these laws Americans are not secure in their own homes. It is easy for anyone anywhere to access information as personal as your address and phone number, even if they are not listed in the telephone directory. Even your Social Security number is available. Many Americans are infuriated and, more importantly, they are vulnerable to these violations of privacy.

Recently, a woman in Virginia was shocked to discover black balloons and antiabortion literature on her doorstep days after she had visited a health clinic that performs abortions. Apparently, someone used her license plate number to track down personal information which was used to stalk her.

In another case in Georgia, an obsessive fan obtained the home address of a fashion model from the State Department of Motor Vehicles and assaulted her in front of her apartment.

These are just a few examples of how information gathered can if in the wrong hands be misused. As Professional Investigators, we need to understand that our privileged access to information sometimes restricted to others can be used to harm others if the intent is not clearly understood.

Protect Yourself; Establish The Client's Goals and Contract

Make sure you ask; what is the information going to be used for and have the purpose clearly defined in a written contract between you and the client. Indicate on your contract that the information may not be used or disseminated to a third party or for any reason not stipulated in the contract.

Timely and Cost-Effective Procedures

Competition today is brutal as more and more investigators offer services. Clients expect a swift turnaround time with a case usually handled within three days of the assignment and a full written report within a week to ten days time. Clients also want to know up front what the case will cost them. I try to Flat Rate my charges so the client knows exactly what my services will cost them. This is a pretty accepted practice if you think about it. Most industries do the same thing, an oil change $35.00 and brake job $199.00. These industries have refined their services and know the amount of time each task takes. You should do the same thing, people are put off by investigators that ask for large retainers or can't tell the client what the case will cost. Learn to break up or package your services so they are affordable. Offer a Flat Rate day of surveillance which includes all travel time, mileage and expenses. The going rate in 2012 is around $550.00 a day. For Domestic Cases you may charge less or reduce the amount of time you spend per day on a file. A flat rate of $250.00 is manageable and should get you business. For Domestic cases packages you will need to shorten your day to keep the costs down and utilize the spouse to set up a *sting operation*.

Provide Regular Updates and Reports

Like any profession communication is important to stay on the same page as your client so that there is a clear understanding of what is expected and what has been promised. Results can not be promised but with a solid plan they are usually produced. Give your client regular updates and follow-up your investigation with a full written report and invoice. The target turnaround time to complete an investigation and submit your written report should be two weeks.

Confidentiality

Clients don't always understand the legalities of matters so explaining them is important. Your work is confidential but then the work you generate may be sensitive as well and must be handled accordingly.

Dissemination of Information

The product you create should be turned over to your client. If it is sensitive then indicate so. Criminal and other background records may reflect information not readily available to the public. You would not want a disgruntled worker hiring you so he could spread damaging information around the office about the subject. Divorce cases can be equally ugly with child custody battles and reputation wars. One says things about the other, but when a Professional Investigator is hired, the innuendoes become searchable facts if developed are reported on with ample evidence and corroborative support. However used outside the courtroom for more sinister reasons may violate your dissemination guideline or even damage your adverse parties' reputation and become libelous. Let your client know the criminal record you provided is to be used for court not copied and sent to his boss or co-workers at the office. Making sure you have a clear dissemination policy and understanding with your client will keep you out of trouble.

Identify Potential Conflicts of Interests

When we chose a specialty we also in some cases choose a side. If you work Insurance defense you can't also work for a Personal Injury Attorney. Imagine being the investigator that was given a surveillance assignment then asked by the a plaintiffs attorney firm to video "a day in the life of the claimant", something plaintiff attorneys like to do to show the difficulties the plaintiff lives with on a daily basis. Obviously the investigator would be providing conflicting documentation. We wouldn't also want to represent both a husband and a wife

Provide a Quality Work Product

Well, let me put it to you this way, your name goes on the bottom of the report. As with any business, the cream rises to the top and you are only as good as your last report. Building a reputation in a highly competitive industry is only possible through sustained and maintained quality. You can maintain a business working for different people all of the time but maintaining a corporate client requires hard work and diligent efforts. Substandard work has no place in our industry but unfortunately it exits and a lot of it. I am embarrassed sometimes when I read or review an investigation that was referred to me. My only solitude is that the client recognized the poor quality and lack of results and has sought out a different vendor and now I have the opportunity to satisfy another client and continued to build my client base. Longevity in the industry can only come about through maintaining high business standards and wanting to deliver results to your client. Sometime this takes more time than authorized, but if you're committed to getting results you're not counting hours you're gauging your progress. My dad use to say, my time is worth nothing, focus on your product and everything else will fall in place. Lets face it this is not a cookie cutter job; you never know what you may have to do get the job done so stay flexible. Your effort is only limited by your imagination.

Detailed Reports and Invoices

It may be hard for you to justify your bill or explain in detail what information you uncovered or the efforts that went into the case if you can't write a detailed report. Typically a report may have a synopsis or conclusion that can relay facts quickly, but in a courtroom setting, you must have detailed notes that are transcribed in report form and show your efforts in chronological order by date and time. Your invoice also needs to look professional and should contain your EIN, address and of course a detailed account of your billing, usually by day if you use the flat rate system. The invoice should also contain a notice to the client that they have 30 days to pay or payment due upon receipt and then a [penalty of an interest for late payments. I give my corporate clients 30 days to pay but then add a penalty of 2% per month if not paid on time.

Truth in Advertising

We have all heard the terms of bait and switch in which a client is offered one thing then given something completely different. When you are first starting a business or entering the world of entrepreneurship, you suddenly realize there is more to running a business than just conducting great investigations. Most State Agencies will not permit superlative like "The Best PI Firm in the County", because it is difficult backup a claim like that. Simply put the Federal Trade Commission specifically outlines three basic rules which it applies in determining if an advertisement is truthful or in violation of the set standards for Truth in Advertising". These rules are as follows:

- Advertising must be truthful and non-deceptive;
- Advertisers must have evidence to back up their claims; and
- Advertisements cannot be unfair.

What makes an advertisement deceptive?

According to the FTC's Deception Policy Statement, an ad is deceptive if it contains a statement - or omits information – that is likely to mislead consumers acting reasonably under the circumstances; and is "material" - that is, important to a consumer's decision to buy or use the product.

What makes an advertisement unfair?

According to the Federal Trade Commission Act and the FTC's Unfairness Policy Statement, an ad or business practice is unfair if it causes or is likely to cause substantial consumer injury which a consumer could not reasonably avoid; and it is not outweighed by the benefit to consumers.

How does the FTC determine if an ad is deceptive?

The FTC looks at the ad from the point of view of the "reasonable consumer" - the typical person looking at the ad. Rather than focusing on certain words, the FTC looks at the ad in context - words, phrases, and pictures - to determine what it conveys to consumers.

The FTC looks at both "express" and "implied" claims. An express claim is literally made in the ad. For example, "ABC Mouthwash prevents colds" is an express claim that the product will prevent colds. An implied claim is one made indirectly or by inference. "ABC Mouthwash kills the germs that cause colds" contains an implied claim that the product will prevent colds. Although the ad doesn't literally say that the product prevents colds, it would be reasonable for a consumer to conclude from the statement "kills the germs that cause colds" that the product will prevent colds. Under the law, advertisers must have proof to back up express and implied claims that consumers take from an ad.

The FTC looks at what the ad does not say - that is, if the failure to include information leaves consumers with a misimpression about the product. For example, if a company advertised a collection of books, the ad would be deceptive if it did not disclose that consumers actually would receive abridged versions of the books.

The FTC looks at whether the claim would be "material" - that is, important to a consumer's decision to buy or use the product. Examples of material claims are representations about a product's performance, features, safety, price, or effectiveness.

The FTC looks at whether the advertiser has sufficient evidence to support the claims in the ad. The law requires that advertisers have proof before the ad runs.
What kind of evidence must a company have to support the claims in its ads?
Before a company runs an ad, it has to have a "reasonable basis" for the claims. A "reasonable basis" means objective evidence that supports the claim. The kind of evidence depends on the claim. At a minimum, an advertiser must have the level of evidence that it says it has. For example, the statement "Two out of three doctors recommend ABC Pain Reliever" must be supported by a reliable survey to that effect. If the ad isn't specific, the FTC looks at several factors to determine what level of proof is necessary including what experts in the field think is needed to support the claim. In most cases, ads that make health or safety claims must be supported by "competent and reliable scientific evidence" - tests, studies, or other scientific evidence that has been evaluated by people qualified to review it. In addition, any tests or studies must be conducted using methods that experts in the field accept as accurate.

Are letters from satisfied customers sufficient to substantiate a claim? No. Statements from satisfied customers usually are not sufficient to support a health or safety claim or any other claim that requires objective evaluation.

My company offers a money-back guarantee. Very few people have ever asked for their money back. Must we still have proof to support our advertising claims? Yes.

Offering a money-back guarantee is not a substitute for substantiation. Advertisers still must have proof to support their claims.

What penalties can be imposed against a company that runs a false or deceptive ad?

The penalties depend on the nature of the violation. The remedies that the FTC or the courts have imposed include: Cease and desist orders. These legally-binding orders require companies to stop running the deceptive ad or engaging in the deceptive practice, to have substantiation for claims in future ads, to report periodically to FTC staff about the substantiation they have for claims in new ads, and to pay a fine of $16,000 per day per ad if the company violates the law in the future. Civil penalties range from thousands of dollars to millions of dollars, depending on the nature of the violation. Sometimes advertisers have been ordered to give full or partial refunds to all consumers who bought the product.

Advertisers have been required to take out new ads to correct the misinformation conveyed in the original ad, notify purchasers about deceptive claims in ads, include specific disclosures in future ads, or provide other information to consumers.

Agency-to-Agency billing

Only an "A Agency" can advertise for business. Typically when one agency calls another for assistance, they are looking for assistance at a discounted rate. If the agency charges $75.00 hour then typically will offer their investigators out for around $50.00 an hour. This usually takes place among smaller sized agencies that need to share workers to cover a greater territory. In today's market with so many Nationwide Agencies, companies that can't cover an entire state are consider almost too small to compete and retain large business accounts. So having a good network of agencies that will offer you a discounted rate so you can still profit on your client relationship is a very important element to running a successful business. The discounted rate is important to the business owner and referring agency because they will also have to supervise the referral as well as make sure the report is prepared to the referring companies standards. The reports either done in house or through subcontracted agency, still needs to look the same as the referring companies normal product they deliver everyday. This takes time which is paid for through the up charge of the referring agency normal billable rate. For example, a case referred to another agency for an eight-hour surveillance will cost $50.00 X 8 or $400.00. Based on the average charge of $550.00 per day this leaves $150.00 for the referring agencies bottom time and effort.

Investigators Pledge

We will extend the effectiveness of our profession by cooperating with other investigators and relate professionals by the exchange of information and experience, so long as the interests of our clients or employers are not violated.

We will not advertise our work, skill or merit in an unprofessional or misleading fashion and will avoid all conduct or practice likely to discredit or do injury to the dignity and honor of our profession.

We will, when the appropriate opportunity presents itself, explain to the public the role of our profession in the furtherance of the administration of justice.

We will not knowingly violate any right or privilege of any individual citizen which may be guaranteed or provided by the United States constitution, any state constitution, or the laws of the state and federal governments or any subdivision thereof.

We will make all our reports based upon truth and fact and will only express honest opinion based thereon to serve our clients.

We will not disclose, relate or betray in any fashion that trust or confidence placed in us by either client, employer or associate, without his consent.

We will not suggest, condone or participate in any fashion or degree, for any purpose whatsoever, entrapment.

We will refrain from accepting an assignment or employment if a personal conflict of interest lies therein.

We will deal fairly and equitably with our client or employer, and will clearly explain our duties and the basis for our charges in undertaking such duties.

We will not allow personal feelings or prejudices to interfere with factual and truthful disclosures on the assignments in which we have been employed or consulted.

We will further an honest and legitimate manner of operation and will preserve a client's confidence beyond the term of employment of any private investigator, or other employee. We will not accept other employment which involves the disclosure or use of such confidences whether for the private advantage of the member or his employees, or to the disadvantage of the client without his knowledge, consent, even though there may be other available sources of information.

We will respect the rights of our clients and refrain from divulging information to newspapers or other publications in the protection of our clients and will work to prevent interference in the administration of justice or a fair trial in the courts.

We will endeavor to provide the opportunity, education and skill for the professional development and advancement of investigators in the profession.

We will not directly or indirectly injure the professional reputation, prospects or proactive of another investigator. However, if we consider that an investigator is guilty of unethical, illegal, or unfair practice or design, we will present the information to the state licensing authority for action.

We will uphold and never abuse the principle of appropriate and adequate compensation for those engaged in investigative work.

We will not criticize another investigator's work except in the proper forum for technical discussion and criticism.

We will not compete illegally with other investigators in the solicitation of work. If we become aware of another investigator's illegal solicitation of work, we will then no longer be a party to another's improprieties.

We will not engage in the unauthorized practice of law.

At all times, we will remember that the private investigator business is a profession and all financial dealings with clients should be handled on that basis.

We will labor diligently and unceasingly to elevate the standard practices of our profession and report any unlawful or unprofessional practices so that disciplinary action may be taken.

Chapter Six
Legal Issues in Investigations

   I. Introduction
  II. Law enforcement notification requirement.
 III. Invasion of Privacy
 IIV. Legal Parameters of Trespassing.
   V. Falsification of Information in Reports
  VI. Misrepresentation of Authority.
 VII. Proper Release of Information.
VIII. Chain of Evidence Procedure

6. Introduction

When surveillance was first introduced to the corporate business environment it raised concern to those that felt it could affect or hurt their cases. In particular Personal Injury Attorneys saw this rising technique by insurance companies as an invasion of their client's privacy. They went as far to threaten Insurance companies that its use would cause intentional infliction of emotional distress of their clients. Soon letters threatening the above started going out to many large insurance carriers. Since the letters were suspiciously similar it was apparent that the statewide plaintiffs' bar organization conceived this scheme to frighten insurers away from using surveillance.

This prompted immediate research and study of case law to make sure surveillance was available option. Many large Private Investigations firms hired attorneys to investigate the law. At that time, I was a rising manager in one of these firms and we too took on the matter so as to defend our future business plans.

Simply put, our research indicated that reasonable surveillance activities do not give rise to causes of actions for invasion of privacy or intentional infliction of emotional distress by plaintiffs.

There are other concerns as well the Private Investigator must be aware of. This chapter will address some of the Criminal and Civil Liabilities we are faced with.

Law Enforcement Notification

When you are conducting surveillance in a community it is a courtesy to notify the local law enforcement officers by checking in with dispatch upon arriving on the scene and providing your specific location. You are also to provide your vehicle tag number, type and color of vehicle, your name, and your agency name and telephone number.

There are some grey areas to this rule as you will find that not all municipalities reciprocate the hospitality. In fact, I have been in Counties in which the Sheriff has told me he does not allow surveillance in "his" county. So in this case, you could understand why I didn't want to check in and why I made darn sure no one ever knew I was there when I came to work. So things are not always as cut and dry as they seem. Moreover, although we are encouraged to check in, if you ask any dispatch officer, okay now that I have checked in, what is your policy for handling calls in reference to my vehicle? You will find they may not have much loyalty as their priority is always to their community, but hopefully asking this question raises their awareness to how they respond to a neighbor calling in and asking about your vehicle. Instead of simply stating "He's a Private Investigator" hopefully they will say, yes, we know he's there, he has checked in with our office. But there is no uniform policy on how they will react and while most are professional, there have been some less than helpful. So given these scenarios, understand the risks and know it is to prevent unnecessary visits by patrolman to come check us out and prevent blown covers. At the same time if we parked far enough away from our subjects to avoid this and if we are doing what we are supposed to do; chances are no one even knows we are there. As you will find and hear many times over in this course, a good investigator is to enter and exit the area without anyone every knowing her/she was there.

Finally, I will relate one other issue that you must take into consideration when you are considering checking in. Many people in small towns listen to police scanners and when they hear, "Sgt. Bob, this is control, I just wanted to let you know we just had a Private investigator check in at the corner of Main and Fifth" The next thing you know the who neighborhood knows you are there and you might not of done anything wrong.

The Right of Privacy

The right of privacy actually consists of a number of separate but related rights arising from a variety of legal sources.

A constitutional right of privacy has been found in the U.S. Constitution. This right is currently the subject of much debate because of the nationwide controversy over abortion. Article I, 23, of the Florida Constitution expressly recognizes a right of privacy. The right of privacy under both constitutions protects the individual against governmental intrusions into privacy, but not against intrusions by private individuals or businesses.

Florida and most other states recognize a common-law right of privacy. In some instances, this common law right of privacy has been incorporated into statues and governmental regulations, some of which have enlarged its scope. If plaintiffs do possess a tort cause of action for invasion of privacy resulting from an insurer's surveillance activities, it will be found in the common law right or privacy.

Essentially, the common law right of privacy is the right to be let alone and to live in a community without being held up to the public gaze against one's will. The common law tort actually consists of four distinct privacy interests, which, if invaded, give rise to four distant but related causes of action. These causes of action are called appropriation, intrusion of true privacy, public disclosure or private facts, and false light in the public eye.

Appropriation occurs when the defendant appropriates a person's name or likeness for defendant's commercial advantage. Intrusion of true privacy occurs when the defendant invades plaintiff's private affairs or seclusion in a way that would be objectionable to a reasonable person. The intrusion must be into something that is private – taking pictures of someone in a public place is not actionable. Public disclosure of private facts occurs when the defendant publishes private information about the plaintiff that would be objectionable to a person of ordinary sensibilities. Finally, the tort of false light in the public eye occurs when the defendant publishes facts about the plaintiff, which place the plaintiff in a false light in the public eye. The false light must be something that is objectionable to a person or ordinary sensibilities.

Surveillance and Privacy

Generally, one who seeks to recover damages from another must expect that his claim will be investigated and, therefore, waives his right of privacy to the extent of a reasonable investigation. Because of the public interest in exposing fraudulent claims, reasonable investigation and surveillance of a claimant's activities to determine the validity of a claim are generally not held to be tortuous. Thus, defendants have the right to investigate any and all claims which may have been filed against them and to make such investigation, as they deem necessary.

Similarly, it has been held that insurance companies have the right to investigate any and all possible claims which might be filed against them or their insured's. If the surveillance is conducted in a reasonable and unobtrusive manner, the insurer will incur no liability for invasion of privacy. However, if the investigation is conducted in an unreasonable and obtrusive manner, a defendant may be liable for invasion of privacy. A Georgia court has held, for instance, that a defendant does not have the right to make an investigation in a conspicuous manner sufficient to excite the speculation of the plaintiff's neighbors. An Alabama court has held that there may be an actionable violation of the right to privacy where the person is watched, trailed, shadowed or kept under surveillance in an offensive or improper manner.

Generally, however, courts have upheld a defendant's right to conduct reasonable investigation and surveillance. Thus, in one Florida case where the investigator accidentally exposed himself while trailing the plaintiff on a public highway while trying to investigate the validity of her personal injury claim, the court held that the investigator was not liable for invasion of privacy in the absence of facts showing that the surveillance was intended to harass or intimidate her into involuntary settlement.

A Pennsylvania court held that surveillance films of the plaintiff did not constitute invasion of privacy. The films did not contain embarrassing pictures of the plaintiff, and the sole purpose of the film was to record the plaintiff's movements and daily activities. The court noted that if the films disclosed inconsistencies in the plaintiff's claim "any embarrassment suffered by her would be justified."

Legal Guidelines for Surveillants

The basic legal principles on which surveillants operate are those that do not violate an individual's constitutional rights. There are some principles that serve as general guidelines in this area.

A subject in public view cannot successfully contend that his actions are secret, or that any surveillance of those actions constitutes an invasion of his privacy. Privacy pertains to places where the subject has a "reasonable expectation of privacy", (such as behind a stockade fence), not to public places or movement. To view and observe a subject traveling a public thoroughfare, on a public street, in a public or commercial building, on a golf course, in a public transit vehicle or even in his own garden or public business place would not violate his right to privacy.

Once a subject has entered a private building and the "curtains are drawn" and no easy view is presented to the outside public, and no view of him can be had without using a "Peeping Tom" type of surveillance, then it could be an invasion of privacy.

The courts have recognized the use of optical aids for the extension of human vision in physical surveillance, such as binoculars and telescopes, and admitted the evidential value of photographic evidence, and thus the use of still and video camera equipped with telephoto or zoom lenses. Use of such aids is not considered a violation of the subject's Fourth Amendment rights. Minnesota court, for example, held that the defendant's claim that the "use of a telescopic device" was a form of "unreasonable search" was "without merit". In another case, the court said, "the use of binoculars did not change the character or admissibility of evidence or information gained". If, however, optical aids were used to peer into a subject's home, the courts would tend to rule that this violated the intent of the Fourth Amendment. The use of photographic evidence has long been accepted in courts of the land, and therefore, the equipment that produces such evidence is recognized as a legal aid in investigation.

Each investigator should have on his person a copy of the statues governing Private Investigators. In Florida this would be Florida Statutes 493.6100. This statue states that investigators are authorized under Florida Statutes 493 to conduct surveillances and investigation anywhere in Florida with reference to any matter or any person, including the following: "The identity, conduct, movements, affiliations, association, transactions, reputation or character or any person or group or persons".

No licensee or employee of any licensee shall divulge or relate to any person other than his principal or his employer any information acquired as the result of any surveillance in investigation. Many states consider divulging information a criminal offense and in Florida it is a first degree misdemeanor. Most of the states throughout the US have similar statues.

Trespassing

When "No Trespassing" signs are posted this is your initial warning and should you be caught violating or trespassing you will be cited or arrested.

If the area is no posting, you are entitled to ONE warning.

Most private properties such as apartment complexes, condominiums, private clubs, and golf courses have signs posted stating this is private property. They may not state no trespassing however and you are entitled to one warning or request to leave the premises. After this warning is given you should immediately leave and figure out another way to perform your investigation.

On the other hand a grumpy neighbor cannot ask you to leave his neighborhood or move your car away form his house if you are parked on the side of a public roadway. A public roadway is any paved or concrete roadway that is maintained by the state or local government.

Trespassing is usually not a problem or an issue if you use good judgment. I can say that in my 30 years as a PI, I have never been trespassed, cited or arrested for trespass (knock on wood).

But be aggressive, the worst thing to hear from an investigator is that he couldn't get video because of the area or was afraid to enter the woods, man-up! What you may be too timid to do, another competitor will and you'll lose a client.

Falsification of Reports

Simply put, our investigations are used in legal proceedings that effect peoples lives. Falsifying a report is not only a crime it will get you stripped of your license to be a private investigator and livelihood. In the industry, "Ghosting" is when a person makes up parts of a report usually during surveillance because they weren't there. For example, the investigator is to start his surveillance at 6:00 a.m., but he never gets there until 9:00 a.m., yet in his report he writes he got there at 6:00 a.m. and proceeds to state what he saw. This is usually done when the investigator has worked the case before and knows the persons vehicles or pattern of activity and upon arriving notices the vehicles present so figures or reports no activity took place up until the time he actually arrived. I had an employee once who never shot any film in the mornings and when he did finally shoot some film, he usually then just immediately left. I started to get the impression he was not getting to his surveillances on time in the morning and then when he did arrive if he shot some film of the subject getting the mail or running to the store, he would then just leave. This was not what he was being paid for. He was being paid to conduct eight hours of surveillance usually from 6:00 a.m. – 2:00 p.m.

Based on my hunch that he was 'Ghosting", I assigned him a typical case in Lakeland, Florida, approximately 30 minutes from his house. I then had my assistant manager, go to his house and sit and watch to see what time he left. On that day, the investigator left, but with his wife who he took to the mall where she cut hair. This was at 9:00 a.m., and the investigator got back to the house at 9:30 a.m. The investigator then finally left by himself at 10:12 a.m. having loaded up his camera gear.

I wanted three days for the report on this surveillance to hit my desk and upon reading the report the hours worked read 6:02 a.m. – 2:04 p.m. I had my assistant manager print out the time and date stamped still pictures of his car at the house at 9:00 a.m. and of him entering the vehicle with his wife and then when he returned to the house at 10:12 a.m. I immediately told him he was being fired and to turn in all of his equipment. I subsequently wrote up the matter in detail along with the still pictures, an affidavit from my assistant manager and forwarded the Investigator's report and my investigation to DOACS. A hearing was subsequently held at which time I testified on behalf of the company and as a witness for the state in the revocation of the investigator's license.

No company wants a rogue investigator jeopardizing the reputation of their firm. After all businesses are just groups of people with a common purpose providing a service or product. While the business may be the brain child of one, it supports many other people and their families. No mater how bright and ambitious an entrepreneur may be, he must have good people around him with a common goal. No one should allow such a practice to take place and any direct knowledge or suspicions of ghosting should be immediately reported to your supervisor.

<u>Misrepresentation of Authority</u>

As provided in the statute, misrepresentation of a Court, State, Federal or County employee is expressly prohibited. Moreover misrepresenting yourself as a Police Officer of any type is a Felony.

Investigator must be very careful when using pretexts not to use those that suggest you are a court appointed officer, Police Officer or acting in some other official capacity that would make the civilian think you are an agent of the government on any level. Typically, I say I am an investigator when I really need to get some information, but this is as far as I go. I show them my State Private Investigators License and I don't carry a badge of any sort. Depending on the impression or conclusions they draw that's their own concern. If questioned I state I showed them my ID and again show this same ID to whoever may enquire. The person recalls me showing them my ID and since it states I am a Private Investigator, they are the ones that failed to review the document close enough. In other instances, if I am working an Insurance case, I say I am an Insurance or Claims Investigator.

Proper Release of Information

The dissemination of information is always a concern to the Professional Investigator. You are developing information for your client and typically it is for their eyes or the courts only. Some of the information is sensitive and may involve criminal records. If we run a FDLE criminal records search, the Criminal History comes to you with a paragraph reading this information is sensitive and should not be disseminated to any "third party". In other words the information was not meant to be photocopied 10 0times and dropped all over town. More specifically, your client who may have an axe to grind, may want to share the information with her ex-husband's employer or co-workers to embarrass him. This type of bad judgment is what gets Private Investigators in problem situations. Make sure your reports state that the information is sensitive and was prepared for your client only and should not be shared or disseminated with any third party.

As Investigators and owners of agencies, we get requests for video content and reports, sometimes from people or companies who were not our clients to begin with but who are involved in the same litigation and may also be defendants. Before, providing them with any information you must call your client and if you have a release, have them sign the release clearing you to share the evidence they paid you to develop. Keep in mind that this release does not bar you from charging a retrieval fee, copying or administration charges.

In other unrelated matters, you should not release any information until you are served a subpoena or received a signed release from the person who is or was the subject of the inquiry.

If a client requests a copy of the investigative report, video and evidence this should be done as a matter of practice and procedure, usually within a week's time of the conclusion of your investigation. Every client should receive a written report and invoice for service. They should never have to ask when they will be getting the report because you are behind in your work.

If evidence is being release from the office to be used at a hearing or trial then the investigator involved in the matter should submit a chain of custody form to the custodian of records.

Chain of Evidence Procedure/ Evidence Tampering

Documenting the source of the evidence and keeping it safe is a high priority. Surveillance video is not edited or it may create the appearance that the evidence was tampered with to unfairly misrepresent the subject. Lets say you shoot video of a subject working and every time he stops to rub his back or take a break, you stop the video and back up to record just activity of his working and it appears he never took a break or was bothered by his injury.

Learning how to secure and not contaminate evidence is very important and will pertain to the type of cases you work. Items that are biodegradable should be stored in paper bags sealed and marked appropriately. Other items may be stored in sealed plastic bags. How you pick up and handle items is also important and gets a bit more complicated than this course is prepared to go into. Evidence collection is an entire area of study and many police department have crime scene investigators and evidence collectors.

Knowing your industry and how to prepare and control the evidence is crucial. In claims investigations, the evidence is submitted by the investigators immediately following the investigation and is marked with the subject name, file number date of collection and length of video. The video is then logged into the evidence locker of the agency and secured from any tampering. This record of transfer from the investigator to the office is called the chain of evidence or chain of custody. A letter of the chain of evidence may need to be produced when the case goes to trial and the video is produced as evidence.

Below is a real sample of a letter prepared by Claims Resource for an actual trial.

December 1, 2008

Video Evidence Chain of Custody letter

REF   Subject : Edward Murphy File

The following original video tapes have been removed from the evidence locker and hand delivered to Michael Martof for the hearing on December 2, 2008

As the evidence custodian the following six tapes are in their natural unedited state handed in by the investigators after each surveillance date and logged into our evidence locker. As the custodian of this evidence none of the tapes have been altered in any manner.

Videotape Log #	Investigator	Format
03-335	Clint Shonrock	8mm
03-409	Wendy Crane	8mm
03-452	Wendy Crane	8mm
05-172	Chuck Tiedman	miniDV

(The above four tapes have been copied on CD #1)

CD #2 contains Mr. Martof's videotape for both days. The CD copy is an exact duplicate of the originals.

07-183	Michael Martof	miniDV
07-190	Michael Martof	miniDV

The videotape evidence submitted above, original (format) & prepared CD have not been edited or manipulated in any manner.

Sincerely

John Bilyk
Custodian of Evidence

Chapter Seven
The Private Investigator

I. Work Environment
II. What Makes a Good Private Investigator
   a. Personal Qualifications of Successful Investigators/Surveillants
      i. Ability to Function Unnoticed
      ii. Physical Stamina
      iii. Good Eyesight and Hearing
      iv. Patience and Perseverance
      v. Acting out a Role
      vi. Good Judgment
      vii. Self Confidence and Self Reliance
      viii. Ability to Remember
III. What Type of Training is Available
IV. What Types of Advanced Training and Professional Certifications are there within the Industry?
V. How Does a Private Investigator Dress for Work
VI. How Do I Break into the PI Industry

7. THE PI

Work environment

Many Investigators spend time away from their offices conducting interviews or doing surveillance, but some work in their office most of the day conducting computer searches and making phone calls. When the investigator is working on a case, the environment might range from plush boardrooms to seedy bars. Store and hotel detectives work in the businesses that they protect.

Investigators generally work alone, but they sometimes work with others during surveillance or when following a subject in order to avoid detection by the subject. Some of the work involves confrontation, so the job can be stressful and dangerous. Some situations call for the investigator to be armed, such as certain bodyguard assignments for corporate or celebrity clients. In most cases, however, a weapon is not necessary because the purpose of the work is gathering information and not law enforcement or criminal apprehension. Owners of investigative agencies have the added stress of having to deal with demanding and sometimes distraught clients.

Private Investigators often work irregular hours because of the need to conduct surveillance and contact people who are not available during normal working hours. Early morning, evening, weekend, and holiday work is common.

A recent 2013, survey in a PI industry magazine looked into classifying the most common areas of the Private Investigations business. The author's survey suggested the industry is broken down into ten specialty groups. These groups of specialties were further ranked by their percentage of business in the surveyed investigative firms. The most common assignment was reported as Background Investigations, followed by Civil Investigations, Surveillance, Other, Insurance, Fraud, Corporate Investigations, Accident Reconstruction, Domestic Investigations and Infidelity.

It should not be surprising that Background Investigations lead the list of most popular assignments. It is an investigation that anyone with just about any background can learn and conduct. I would also point out that Criminal Defense Investigations was not identified as a specialty group but was included in the "Other" category with other less often sought assignments.

The most common types of investigations in the survey are supported by the corporate and insurance defense industries. The largest investigative agencies will conduct most all specialty group investigations routinely except for Domestic and Infidelity cases. The large professional investigative agency will be devoted to training their investigators to perform all of these specialties as it may be required as part of one single investigation. Only the "Other" and "Accident Reconstruction" categories may require specialized training, but then again it would depend on the background of the investigator. Most all categories identified by the survey would be within the scope and expectation of the private investigator looking to establish a career in the Private Investigations Industry. So, regardless of your experience or lack of it, your training would be designed to make you skillful in most specialty areas so you are a fully rounded investigator with complementing skills in all areas. After all, being an investigator means you are engaging in an effort to search out and examine or learn the facts about something unknown or perhaps complex. You can't adequately perform satisfactorily lacking some important skills or knowledge. Making sure that you learn these skills will be the responsibility of your trainer and a constant effort of your manager.

While we may debate the skills needed to perform any one of the mentioned specialty areas of investigations, a non-technical professional, aiming for a career in private investigations needs to start with the understanding of four basic building blocks of investigative activities. These principle parts are Surveillance, Locate Procedures, Database Resources and Records Searches and Statement Taking. Building experience in these four areas will enable you to tackle many common place investigations in the private sector and build more experience while doing so.

Depending on the assignment the Private Investigators will determine the method in which the above activities are used or reported. We use the same investigative activities over and again for many different types of cases. We constantly rely on the enormous amount of information that can be gained quickly using a computer to educate ourselves about different topics. The computer is a huge teaching tool to investigators who need to learn a little about many different topics. The computer will be such an important learning tool that it will play an important role training you as an investigator. The information available on the web from private and public sources is infinite with the ability to research just about any topic. You need to understand a subject matter before you can adequately investigate it and the computer will support this educational process. It may not only be a subject matter that you research. You may need to investigate a person as part of your investigation. Information such as a subject's prior arrest history, convictions, civil filings, telephone numbers, motor vehicle registrations, property transactions, associations, club memberships, photographs or personal profiles and activities from social media are all accessible on-line. Social Medias can even help track or find people as they upload content to their Facebook or send out Tweets. In 2009, five teens called the "Hollywood Hills Bunch" used the Internet as their accomplice in tracking celebrities. The teens tracked the movements of stars such as Lindsay Lohan and Paris Hilton then broke into their houses, making off with millions of dollars in stolen possessions in a spree that lasted almost a year.

The Police reported that the teens scoured celebrity blogs and web sites looking for pictures of the celebrity's valuables. The teens then used the Internet to find where the stars lived and raided the homes while the celebrities were away. The operation used by the teens to assist their criminal escapade, are some of the same activities a PI utilizes when hired to locate or track regular individuals. The PI will also have other sources of information which is not accessible to the public, such as credit report information, propriety database sources and other time saving specialized programs that "mine" information from both public and private sources. Because this information can be used to find and track people, it is often regulated by States and Federal Statutes as well as safeguards put in place by the provider through vetted subscription applications and secure access. It is not unusual to perform these searches and obtain personal identifying information such as a person's home address, date of birth and social security number. All such information can be very sensitive if released to the wrong party. This same information if improperly discarded or in the wrong hands can be used to steal someone's identity or for a more sinister matter such as finding a person who purposely doesn't want to be found and has court ordered protection in place.

Personal Qualifications of Successful Investigators/ Surveillants

The qualifications of good investigators/surveillants cover three areas: Physical, mental and resourcefulness, all of which enable the investigator to adapt to different situations.

Ability to Function Unnoticed

There should be nothing outstanding about the surveillant's appearance that would tend to attract attention. Blending with the environment in which the surveillance is to be conducted is one of the initial objectives of the investigator. The ability to blend in with and feel at home in a variety of environments and situations requires a high degree of adaptability and conformity.

Physical Stamina

Endurance is often a major factor in surveillance. Investigators may need to follow a person who is in excellent physical shape and moves rapidly without seeming to tire. In addition, surveillance operations are frequently prolonged, and they often involve tedious periods of waiting. Nonetheless, the investigator must remain on the alert; ready to act quickly when something finally does happen. The ability to put in long hours, to move quickly when necessary, and to do any one of a number of things over a long period to keep from losing track of a subject, all require stamina.

Good Eyesight and Hearing

Visual observation is the heart of surveillance, and therefore, good eyesight is essential. When viewing at great distances, binoculars, telescopes, and night viewing devices can assist the investigator. But always they must have keen eyes so they can quickly perceive and observant minds that can intelligently record what the eyes see. Investigators must register unanticipated movements of the subject so that they can take necessary counteraction.

Surveillance puts investigators' powers of observations to test. What the camera cannot record, the eyes of the investigator should register.

Keen hearing is also a definite plus factor. Occasionally, investigators may be close enough to overhear an informative bit of conversation, in a bar, restaurant, store or office, or on the street. When sitting on surveillance, the investigator should be listening for significant sounds such as sounds emitted from the subject's residence which would indicate that he may be inside working or working somewhere on the premises.

Driving Skills

The driver's eyesight, coordination and reflexes are all important. They determine the difference between immediate and delayed action. Surveillants' vehicles, like the surveillants, should blend into the general flow of traffic with nothing about them to cause them to stand out from other vehicle. Mental alertness and good judgment are the keys to driving adaptively in vehicular surveillance operations.

Resourcefulness

Resourcefulness is one of the most important qualifications for investigators. An investigator who is resourceful can quickly adapt to and successfully cope with changing conditions, unforeseen circumstances and direct challenges.

Patience and Perseverance

In this business, patience is a virtue. There are often tedious waiting periods before anything happens. Investigators must persevere—if one day's effort fails to bring the desired results, they must go at it again and again spite of outside influences and opposition.

Acting out a Role

In some type of surveillance, particularly in undercover work, the investigators have to become actors and take on the role of a corporation employee, secret organization member, salesperson, or other role they must assume to conduct a specific surveillance. They may pose as a telephone serviceman, brush salesman, cab drivers, corporate executives, drug addicts or simply fellow workers on the production lines. Whatever role is assumed carries with it the necessity of acting out that role so effectively that the surveillance activities go completely undetected.

In a disguised outdoor surveillance role, the surveillant investigators must appear to be what they purport to be in dress, manner, and performance. They should appear to be conducting business, delivery or repair service without revealing their interest in what others are doing. Investigators should be able to give a plausible, acceptable reason for being in a given place at a given time should their presence be challenged. With this type of setup, the investigator should have uniforms, I.D.'s, or other documents to support their claims.

Role-playing also includes the ability to talk one's way out of potentially embarrassing situations without creating suspicions should such explanations become necessary. The more effectively and inconspicuously the investigator is able to play the role, the less likely he is to arouse suspicion or be burned.

Knowledge and Good Judgment

All forms of investigation call for good judgment based on knowledge and common sense. Surveillance often puts good judgment and common sense to a real test. Such judgment is based on the background knowledge obtained in pre-surveillance preparation, on personal knowledge of surveillance techniques, and on the logical decisions to be made in different circumstances. Only knowledge can determine the most appropriate technique. Good judgment can tell when and how to apply it.

Self Confidence and Self Reliance

Self confidence and self reliance are good psychological attitudes and traits for investigators to have, enabling them to take on assignments with confidence and rely on their own abilities to cope with any situations that might arise. The more competent one becomes, the more confident one is.

Ability to Remember

Investigators need a good memory. This is especially true on a foot surveillance or when conducting an activities check. Undercover investigators never record information while in the presence of a fellow employee or associate whom they have been assigned to observe. During mobile surveillance and during the observation of a subject who is extremely active, it is not always possible to record information simultaneously. The longer the interval between gathering and recording the information the greater the recall problem. While observations and evidential information should always be recorded at the earliest convenience, some situations are such that this cannot be done until a later time. It is then that the memory and recall ability are very important. Memory can be continually improved by constant exercise and practice.

What Type of Training is Available

Most companies will train you the way they want you to do things. You need to know the basics which will mean practicing, and reading up on whatever type of specialty you decide on pursuing. If your specialty compliments a former vocation then you will just need to learn the formalities of transitioning your talents to offer then in the private sector for a fee. If you have no talent other than pure ambition then you will most likely be a quick learner and study ever aspect of this and any other how to manual you can get your hands on. The simple truth is that private investigation work is a lot of common sense and problem solving put together one piece at a time. Common sense is not something you learn and many investigators will tell you they never stop learning as each case is different. The benefit new investigators have to day is the internet. Just about everything you may need to know about a particular type of case may be at your finger tips in a Google search. For example if you are investigator to try and find out of a guy is an over the road trucker, you can Google, what does it take to be an over the road trucker. What licenses do I need to have and what certifications do I need. These searches and the answers will start your investigation off in one direction or another and upon being thorough, you will most likely get all of the information you need to prove your case. At one time, I needed to refer to a how to guide and if that type of case was not in there I was on my own. With the Internet you are never really on your own.

Advanced Training and Professional Certifications

Continuing Education is always recommended and should be sought out through a local statewide or national association for reputable training and certification. Most states have their local or statewide organizations like CALI, The California Association of Licensed Investigators, TALI, the Texas Association of Licensed investigators and in Florida, FALI, the Florida Association of Licensed Investigators, and FAPI, the Florida Association of Private Investigators. There is also a very well-run organization called NALI, the National Association of Legal Investigators. There are also international associations and of course WAPI, the World Organization of Professional Investigators.

It is also more common to gain expertise in your particular field of interest. If you are working in Business Risk Mitigation, Workers Compensation and Insurance Claims, then participating in Risk Management, WC and Claims Educational Conference will be very helpful. These industry specific educational conferences will also put you in a position top actually come face to face with potential clients.

Some of other national designations available are CFE, Certified Fraud Examiner, Certified Legal Investigator CLI, and Board Accredited Investigator BAI . These l Certifications are usually recommended for investigators with at least three years of experience. There is also the Board Certified Criminal Defense Investigator, Insurance Fraud Investigator, Legal Investigator, Fire Investigator and Certified Surveillance Investigator.

While many states do not **yet** have mandatory Continuing Education Units (CEU's) many investigative associations offer great resources at their conferences for obtaining continuing education and information about updated products.

Dress for Work

If you are out doing SIU or statement work and meeting people, then business casual is required. If you are taking statements from other professionals, then you should dress up to their level. I once had a doctor who I wanted to take a statement from and he was offended that I was not wearing a suit coat and tie. So understand that your attire is important and may stand in the way of getting your job done. During the initial appointment setting ask them if it is okay that you will be dressed in a company polo shirt and slacks or whether they require a suit and tie.

On surveillance the dress is comfortably casual and you should even bring a backup set of clothing. You may sweat through the first set but the second reason for bringing a change of clothes is so you have them incase the subject heads out of town while you're following him. Never leave your subject when he is on the move. In thirty years, I have never been stiffed with the costs of travel or extra time when I followed a person out of town In fact to the contrary, I have been given cart blanche. I once followed a claimant from Tampa to Nevada and onto California, where the claimant took his family to Disney land over Easter. Needless to say, I hadn't packed for the occasion, but I had been in this situation before and it's always nice to know you can get a complete change of clothes at Wal-Mart for about $15.00.

Anyway, clothes are important as are the shoes you are wearing. Many companies prohibit the wearing of flip flops which have been very popular of late. Unfortunately they just don't protect your feet if you need to go into the woods or move quickly to run after someone. To have a pair in your bag is fine but if you work near the beach, but the preferred shoe is a rubber soled shoe or sneakers.

The investigator's clothing line does not stop here though. There should be a camouflaged bag in the truck that contains more essentials of the investigator on the move. This bag should be filled with camouflage clothing. A camouflage hat, possible mosquito hat and even a large camouflage net to be used as a blind.

You should also have bug spray in the bag, toilet paper, pepper spray, and a pair of pruning clippers in case you need to build a blind where one is sparse or doesn't exist. And finally the most important item, a seat. Many hunting supply stores and even Wal-Mart sells a three legged stool or folding chair with a small collapsible cooler underneath in the sporting good s/hunting section of the store. For the clothes and back pack and netting get these from your local Army Navy Store. Also don't forget to bring your monopod and tripod and if you know before hand you are going into the woods, stop for drinks, food and some snacks.

Our goal in surveillance is to get in the best position possible to watch our subject. This may mean a position in the hot son. There are those investigators who constantly look for shade trees to sit under and seem to be more conscientious of their comfort rather than the results of their efforts. If results are your number one priority and they should be, then you will in fact find yourself sitting in the sun. We need to learn to stay cool. Avoid using your air-conditioning in your car to and from cases. This will help acclimate your body to the outside temperature. Get a fan that runs of solar power can be put in your window. Use deodorant not antiperspirant, you want to sweat this is your body's natural cooling system. An antiperspirant blocks your under arm sweat glands prohibiting them from releasing sweat to cool the body, not the most ideal situation .

How do You Break into The Industry

As previously stated the need for more professional Private Investigators is continuing to increase. The ideal candidate is being recruited out of college as a career investigator going to work for one Investigative Firm where he or she will spend their entire career. Many Investigative Companies are large Nationwide Agencies that employ hundreds of full-time field investigators. So entry level positions are readily available to the recent college graduate or honorably discharged military personnel just entering the profession without any experience.

It's important to learn how to identify the types of agencies or firms that offer careers. Over the last generation (25-30 years), the Business Risk and Insurance Claims Industry has offered the most stable employment and grown the most nationwide agencies. These Professional Investigative Firms market businesses and the insurance industry. So no matter what state you may be query the Internet for your states annual Insurance Claims Conferences; Workers Compensation, Property and Liability, Adjusters Training Conferences, Human Resource Managers Conferences and Self-Insured Conferences. There are also associations like:

RIMS - Risk Management Society
IASIU – International Association of Special Investigative Units
FIFEC- Florida Insurance Fraud Educational Conference
WCI Workers Compensation Institute (Florida)

At these conferences, you will find that the vendors and sponsors are exactly the types of professional organizations you want to work for.

For example, at the recent 2014, Florida WCI Workers Compensation Conference, there were approximately 27 Investigative Firms present with booths catering to their clientele. There were another 23 related firms who also employee investigators and estimated another 20 investigative firms represented by conference attendees. Just by walking around the vendor area, a jobseeker could have handed out 50 resumes! I pulled the list of vendor exhibitors for the show to highlight the investigative agencies attendees as well as those know personally to me.

The Industry Professionals

Abacus Research, Inc.
ABI Document Support Services
Absolute Solutions
Advantage Surveillance, Inc.

Archangel Investigations & Protection
Bonnamy & Associates, LLC
Claims Resource Inc.
Claims Verification Inc.
Combined Investigators
Command Investigations, LLC
Conroy, Simberg, Ganon, Krevans, Abel, Lurvey, Morrow & Schefer
CoventBridge
DataPath, Inc.
Delta Investigation
Detect South Inc.
DJO Global
FCI Investigations
G4S Compliance & Investigations
Gold Investigations, Atlanta
Identifax Investigative Services
Investigation Specialists, Inc.
ISO
J.P. Investigative Group, Inc.
J.T. Becker & Company, Inc.
Kelley Alliance Investigations
Law Offices of Robert Dixon
Lemieux & Associates, LLC
Levy & Levy, LLC
Lewis Brisbois Bisgaard & Smith, LLP
Litigation Solutions
Marshall Investigative Group, Inc.
MasterTrace
MKRS Law
Quintairos, Prieto, Wood & Boyer, P.A.
Rainey Kizer Reviere & Bell
Raul T. Aparicio, II, P.A.
S.K.I. Investigations
Schumacher Auto Group
Sedgwick
Selective Investigations Inc.
Semmes, Bowen & Semmes
Shepherd Professional Investigations
SIU Central Inc.
Social Intelligence
Titan Investigative Alliance, LLC
Tower MSA Partners
Veracity Research Co.
Wilson, Jones, Carter & Baxley, P.A.
Windham Group
Woodall & Broome, Inc.

Of course, I would also recommend having your resume on various job boards such as Monster.com and also checking the website, www.Indeed.com for advertised jobs. The International Association of Special Investigative Units IASIU also has a job for investigative candidates.

*During your job search be leery of small agencies where their specialty is advertised as domestic investigations, cheating spouses. We know statistically that a firm relying solely on domestic cases may have difficulty providing a steady work flow to build a career or career path.

Chapter Eight
Database and Record Searches

    I. Before Computers and the Internet
        i. Father of Data Fusion
    II. Typical Background Records Check

8. Before the Computer and Internet

Before the Internet or even a very powerful workplace computer, research was done in person at the courthouse or over the phone. If you were doing a locate investigation, you could expect to spend hours in the courthouse reviewing property records, tax rolls, voters registration cards, hunting, fishing and driver's license information as well as driving records, vehicle registrations, parking tickets and criminal records. This  meant time in the field, gas and miles on your vehicle. To save time, many Investigation Firms had an account or access to reports from a major credit reporting agency. The accounts were usually set up in a "merchant" business name. This enabled access to a person's Credit Report and "Identifying Information", social security number, date of birth, address and perhaps employer. It also identified their "Trade Lines" which were the businesses the person had lines of credit with along with the names of the creditors, the account numbers and contact numbers for the creditors. These reports were like gold, they contained a ton of information useful for working a locate investigation over the phone. Collection Agencies and Skip Tracers had been using these same methods for years tracking down people who "skipped out" or fail to repay a loan and left their former address. So if my target had a Burdines Department Store credit card, it wasn't uncommon for me to call Burdines and ask for the collections department. I would get a person accustomed to doing collection work over the phone and I would merely act as another merchant's agent doing the same job. I would read information off the credit report which would legitimize who I was or alleged to be and would advise that I was trying to find our account holder. Without going into too much detail I would ask if the subject possibly recently reported a change of address. After all it's not uncommon for someone to call the store or business that they have a store credit card with and notify them first of their move and new address. Keep in mind that businesses may only report information to the credit agency periodically or monthly when payment histories are reported and balances change. So the information we got from the merchant, bank or lender was usually the most updated information possible before going in the field. And once you built up a rapport with the merchant, I would go on to ask them if they had any employer information or co-applicant on file.

Hank Asher, the Father of Data Fusion

The blossoming of the Internet in the 1990's brought on-line record search access. Information that had only been available at the courthouse suddenly could be accessed on-line. The Department of Motor Vehicles (DMV) started to release their information in digital format, either directly accessible with a direct user account or through a third-party. The only problem was that you had to search the Internet for all the different sites and sources to find bits and pieces of information. And, the true Holy Grail of information was still the subject's most up to date address history. This information could still only be obtained from one of the three major credit reporting agencies, Experian, Trans Union or Equifax.

This would all change when a man named Hank Asher created a computer generated comprehensive report that would not only data mine all the public sources of information but also contained information from a credit reporting agency known as the "Credit Header". This information included the subjects identifying information, Name, Address History, SSN and Date of Birth. This enabled us to verify the subjects spelling of their name; confirm the name was valid by the linked SSN and of course get the most reliable current and former address history information. The address provided was where the subject had their bills sent. It was the address they put on applications, apartment rentals, car loans, mortgages. We didn't need the merchant account information, the credit scores or payment history we just needed the address and enough other identifying information to confirm we were tracking the right person. Hank Asher delivered that product and is considered a legend in the investigative community.

In 1992, Hank Asher started a business called Database Technologies (DBT) which provided the investigator with the first comprehensive report.

In 1999, DBT Online bought Asher out for US$147 million after the FBI and the Drug Enforcement Administration suspended their contracts following revelations that in 1982, Asher was involved in drug dealings while he was living in the Bahamas. The DEA reported concerns that the company could potentially monitor targets of investigations.

In 2000, Choice Point, an Equifax Company bought DBT for $462 million dollars and won many government contracts back.

Choice Point would later suffer several security breaches which led to the theft of personal information which facilitated a reported 750 cases of identity theft. The scam came to light when a 41-year-old Nigerian citizen, Olatunji Oluwatosin was arrested in October 2004 with five cell phones and three credit cards that belonged to other people. The substantial breach in 2004 led to a $10 million dollar class action settlement and calls for new national privacy laws in the U.S. to protect the personal data of Americans.

In 2008, Lexis Nexis bought Choice Point for $775 million dollars.

In 2011, Mr. Asher returned to the industry he originally created and formed a new company called "TLO". He boasted that TLO created a faster, more accurate and more thorough database report better than any of his previous products.
In January 2013, the Father of "Data Fusion", Hank Asher dies and TLO goes into Bankruptcy.

In December 2013, TLO was purchased by Trans Union for around $166 million dollars and launches Hanks database report called TLOxp, which is touted to be the "most powerful database for background research on people, assets and businesses". TLOxp is reported to be designed to get you the exact information, even in cases where you only have partial source data, such as an incomplete SSN or address. It is also possible to search for a subject using a phonetic name spelling, location radius, or age range.

According to the South Florida Business Journal Lexis Nexis was also interested and prepared to offer $180 million but was too late as Trans Union's offer had already been approved.

If you go on the Internet you will find dozens of companies offering up people searches for a fee. You probably never heard of TLO or LexisNexis, but in the PI's world these are the primary database powerhouses with dependable verified sourced information. Keep in mind that an account with either of these two companies will require significant vetting, verification of licenses, training requirements and possibly a site visit.

Typical Background Records Check

If I were going to do a background check on a subject I would consider all the "source data' I had available to me. Some investigators may have (private) sources that others don't but let's consider what is readily available.

In Florida, I can go to the Florida Department of Law Enforcement (FDLE) website and for $25.00 dollars buy an immediate statewide criminal history check for any subject. Most other states also have similar statewide agency sites that sell this collected information to the public. I can also get a seven-or twelve year driving record from the county courthouse traffic division.

I can run my TLO or Lexis Nexis report and get your SSN, DOB, address, cellular phone number and carrier, your property ownership records, address history for about 20 years, vehicle registration records and driver's license number, name address, type, issue date and height (no picture). Depending on your age, your SSN will tell me what state you were born in or perhaps came of age to start working. Also depending on your age, if I look far enough back in your address history and it matches with your SSN, I will probably determine the house you grew up in. An address search of just that house address should show me other people with your same last name who used that address. These people would be your parents and any siblings. Separate searches could be done on each one of those names to determine where they are today in case I need to speak to them to find you.

TLO now has a new search where you can access license plate recognition data. This feature is called their Vehicle Sightings report. It can show you recent sightings or sighting dating back a year. On a recent case, I had no solid address for the subject and my attorney client told me the subject doesn't work. I ran the vehicle sightings report and found a solid pattern of visits to three locations. The first was a beach front city parking lot where she apparently parked to go to the beach in Sarasota. The second was a real estate agency where I determined she had several friends and use to work there. The third was a non-profit organization where on the day of my investigation, I found her car present while she was inside working as the Marketing Director.

I can go on-line in the county where you live or based on your address history review all of the counties you previous lived and search on-line county civil and criminal records in each county for any reference to you. This will tell me if you have ever been involved in a civil suit either as the plaintiff or defendant in those regions.   Have you ever sued anyone or been sued? Is there a criminal arrest in which you were not charged or convicted and therefore not on your statewide criminal record? I can check each Police Department in each town where you lived and search for any incident reports under your name. I can also search for any incidents that occurred at your address and determine the nature of the incident, what people were involved and whether there is a separate report under another name.

I can go on-line and check Workers Compensation Claim records to see if you have ever been hurt on the job, the nature of your injury and how long you were off from works.

I will check County Property records to determine the value, size and location of the house you live in. It you don't own it, I will determine who your landlord and property owner is by the tax bill receipt. This will also give me their mailing address and if I need more information, I can refer to my TLO database account and most likely get a phone number for your landlord. If you owned the house, I will look at your tax payment history to see if you had problems paying your taxes and a tax certificate was issued. I will look at the value you paid for your house versus what it is worth right now to determine if you are underwater or have a gain. I will look at the houses you owned and sold in the past to judge your possible wealth and financial situation. By the documentary stamp tax on the deed, I can determine the purchase price of the property and deduct your recorded mortgage amount to determine how much was put down in cash.

I can use Google Earth and conduct a street view to possibly see an image of your house which may include the cars in your driveway, boat in the back, camper or RV. An image solely of your house may also be available during my perusal of the County Property Appraisers Office's records. I can check building and zoning records to see if there has been any contractor's work done on your house where a permit was pulled. The contractor listed could possibly be you, the homeowner indicating that the work was done by you. If sub-contractors are listed and you, the homeowner, were acting as the General Contractor than the subs most likely interacted with you and may have information pertinent to my investigation.
I'll go on Facebook for an ID picture of you or check Twitter and other Social Medias to see if you have any uploaded content I can use to form my assessment.
I can contact your neighbors, employer, work associates, references and relatives.
Based on the information I was able to gather, the type of car you drive, the house you live in, your employment, home rental or real estate purchase transactions, criminal, civil and social media information, personal interviews, you would be surprised to see how close of a personal profile I can generate that tells a lot about you.

The above search I outlined is very typical of a background investigation. I have conducted these types of searches for business partners, insurance companies, landlords, employers and Attorneys. I have even been provided juror's names to research so that counsel has a better understanding of the jury.

Over the years, PIs develop contacts that become vitally important to their work. A friend who works at a hotel reservation desk can be helpful in identifying a room number or reservation date for a case. If your town has a large taxi company a source there can tell you where people are picked up and dropped off. So building business relationships is vital and protecting your sources is equally important. I wouldn't put the name of the Taxi Company or even how I obtained the information in my report. The best investigator will have many sources and know how to access different types of information.

<u>My Own Data Mining</u>

My understanding of exposing and following paper trails has served me well over the years not only on cases I was paid to investigate but also in building my own personal wealth. Early in my career, I realized the importance of information and knowing how to find it and use it. I think between the research and pressure to get results your work ethic doesn't allow you to overlook an opportunity. I have always been competitive and have a drive to always do something more. What I have done so far is not good enough and I need to do more or find something else to accomplish. I don't think we can instill that same motivation if we just praise kids at all level regardless of their performance. Some people contend that kids will do well as long as they have a strong sense of confidence, but I can see this leading to complacency. To me it's similar to those that feel they are entitled to free services or assistance. How can you be hungry for something if you feel you're entitled to it or it comes to you without effort?

Being around the courthouse doing research made me keen on how real estate transactions are recorded and the various stages or actions taken with property. For instance, if I saw a transaction of a property using a Quit Claim Deed, I knew by the very nature of the instrument that this was most likely a property transferred between family, friends or associates. A Lis Pendis filing signified the onset of a mortgage Foreclosure. A Tax Deed Certificate meant the property owner was unable or unwilling to pay their property taxes. So if I wanted to I could contact these individual to see if there was any possible business solution that could benefit both of us. Let's say you owned your home for 10 years lost your job and the bank was Foreclosing on your property. Maybe at best if you sold it you would break even but then you would have nothing. You may be ready to walk away because you need to start over again somewhere else, perhaps another city. It could be that five thousand dollars provided the homeowner with enough money for a new start. Or perhaps this payment was for a business agreement where the owner stays in the property as a tenant and agrees to sell the house later when the real estate market improves and then split the profit with the investor.

You never know the possibilities until you are involved in these types of situations, but knowing how to find the properties is the first step.

For about two months, I drove past a house that had a fallen tree lying on its roof as the result of the 2007 hurricanes which came through Central Florida. After noting the house to be vacant every time I drove by I decided to research the property and found the owner had passed away. The house had been empty for over a year and he had no heirs. I found the taxes were being paid by a local investor through a process known as buying tax certificates. Tax certificates are basically notes, offering investors the opportunity to earn an attractive rate of return for paying the property taxes of another individual or entity. When the property is sold, the investor recoups his money plus the interest he charged for paying the taxes. One way to force an owner to sell their house is to file a tax deed foreclosure. Once the investor has a tax certificate that is two years old, he can file for foreclosure. This doesn't mean that he automatically owns the property, it just means the property is forced to a tax deed auction, unless the owner is able to repay the investor the taxes paid plus the attractive interest and costs associated with the foreclosure filing. If the owner does not come forth to settle the tax issue, then the house is sold to the highest bidder. The proceeds from the purchaser of the property are used by the county to pay the investor and the surplus is returned to the original owner. Many times tax deed sales are less spoken about compared to regular foreclosures and as a result the attendance of those interested in buying tax deed foreclosed properties is not as competitive. And, if you where the one filing the foreclosure, chances are you know more about the value of the house than anyone else which puts you in a very key position.

With the house I pursued, the owner was deceased so when it went to auction just two people were bidding, me and one other guy. The other guy had no real knowledge of the house, its condition or value. He was just playing in the process and I ended up buying the property for $70,000 dollars or about half of what the house was worth.

Chapter Nine
Locate Investigations

9. Locate Investigations Guideline

Many investigations will require the knowledge of how to locate someone. As soon as I am asked to conduct a locate investigation, I immediately review all the information the client provided. Many times the key to finding the subject will be in the information provided. The client may say they checked the subject former address and they are no loner there. But this address may have been a rental and the client never thought to identify the landlord or owner of the property and call them for a forwarding address.

Do not hesitate to ask your client for additional information after you have reviewed the information they provided. Keep them involved with the investigation and where it's going. You do not want to report something to your client, after several days of hard work, only to discover that a particular fact was already known by your client. Unfortunately, your client won't tell you everything in the first interview. Not that they're trying to hide things from you but, what you may consider important clues in your investigation, they will not. That's why you must make them part of what you're doing and keep them up to date. Also, if they are part of the decision-making process and a given decision costs then more time and money, it is easier for them to accept the extra charges.

Always remember that most anyone can be found. The professional investigator is only limited by time and money- never their imagination. The steps listed in this lesson are part of the methodology of investigation for a locate investigation on a subject whose moved. It is not intended to cover the steps for an abducted person or child.

Pay special attention to this step—by—step locate investigation and you will find that these are very similar to the steps utilized when conducting a thorough background investigation in relation to your subject. Always keep in mind that investigative work is both scientific and artistic in its application. Learn how to use the resources available to you effectively.

Americans move from place to place more than any other nation of people. Twenty-five percent of us move every year. We move to take advantage of new employment or a business opportunity, to change our lifestyle, to continue our education, or to be closer to our families and friends. To think that every locate assignment you get will be like finding a needle in a haystack would be highly incorrect. Most of the times, we are hired because our clients just don't have the time or know where to begin to look.

Although I know I may be forgetting a case or two, it's actually really difficult for me to recall not being able to locate a person my client sought. I would imagine most of my competitors would say the same thing because that's just the nature of our business. Your only limitations are usually time, money and imagination. The fact is, given unlimited resources; a person's face could be plastered all over the TV one evening and within hours of the first broadcast you may find the phone ringing off the hook with where that missing person was two minutes earlier with precise accuracy. After all, remember, most people we attempt to locate as investigators are lost friends, relatives, former employee who witnesses an accident, or our client's client. These subjects are not on the list of America's Most Wanted. Also, there is a high probability that the investigator will be able to locate a good address for the subject just by running their name in one of our national databases.

Again you need to keep in mind that we are typically looking for ordinary citizens. They are not missing person cases, thank GOD. Just in Florida there are an estimated 9,000 Private Investigators and this would be a very sad world if we worked child abductions cases every day. Don't get me wrong, nationally, missing and exploited children is a growing problem. However organizations like The National Center for Missing & Exploited Children have worked hard with Law Enforcement to dramatically increase the recovery rate for missing children to roughly 90% today. Organizations like this have specific procedures in place and work with the missing child's family and local law enforcement.

As a "For-Hire" Investigator most of your casework will come from business clients such as Attorney Firms, Corporations and Insurance Companies looking for witnesses, defendants and former employees.

The following are step—by—step procedures the professional investigator uses in a standard locate investigation.

STEP 1: The first step of your locate investigation is to simply run a database search with a reputable database firm offered by companies like Lexis Nexis, or TLO. Although we are looking for the most current address on file, don't overlook the oldest address identified either. If the newest address is one that has already been determined to be invalid or no longer good, move your attention to some of the oldest addresses. Many times you will find the oldest address is that of a parent or grandparent. In all cases you are looking for telephone numbers verified and unverified that can be called to inquire about the whereabouts of the subject. Remember we want to first do as much work as we can without leaving our office.

STEP 2: Utilizing your same database run just the address and leave the search name blank. This will identify all of the people who lived at that address over time. What you are looking for is the name of a subject appearing during the same time period your subject was also reported to be at the same address. This overlapping information may indicate that our subject resided at that location with a roommate, family member, ex-spouse or friend. Also, always look for any telephone numbers listed for any subject associated to our subjects address and call every number.

STEP 3: Your next step is to cross reference your subject as well as anyone else identified as a possible associate through the sunbiz.org corporate and business database. This will identify any potential businesses your subject or a related person may be involved in. Remember we are not just looking for Corporations, but also fictitious name filings as well. The broadest search tool should be used in each category by searching under Officers and Registered Agents. Once again any business entity should be contacted. Look through the corporate filings or annual reports for telephone numbers listed on the bottom of the pages as contact numbers for the business. Search the Internet for any website under that business name and query the Contact Us Page to send email requests. Google each person's name to identify any other pertinent information that may be available on-line and follow any lead identified. On-line county tax roll records will help you to determine whether your subject owns any real, personal or business property in that county. The Property Appraiser's Office will identify the property address, value and recorded deed and mortgage. Your next search on-line will include criminal records. County Court Criminal records should be available on-line. Here, you are going to check your subject's name for any convictions under both misdemeanor and felony divisions. If your subject has a record, his or her file folder will contain additional information. The full file can be reviewed in-person by making a personal visit to the courthouse. Criminal records can contain vital information such as known aliases, employers and telephone numbers. Court documents will also provide specific information regarding the charges brought against your subject. Don't forget to check the traffic court. Oftentimes, the traffic court is located in the misdemeanor division of the courthouse. If your subject has received a traffic ticket and you can obtain a copy of it, the traffic ticket will tell you what your subject was driving and list your subject's address at that time. They may even have a scanned copy of the envelope he mailed in his payment with containing a return address. Next, the civil division will be of help to you. Here, you are going to check for any suits filed against your subject, or any suits your subject may have filed. The civil division will also record any liens against your subject, the subject's property or any liens that your subject may have filed against others. The civil division also contains records of marriage and divorce. Occupational licenses can also be searched in person or on-line if available to identify any business the subject may have in the county or city. Also, check the Uniform Commercial Code (UCC) filings in the civil division. A UCC filing is for loans secured with collateral, such as machinery, equipment and any asset that may not have a title or registration. Once again, discovering this paperwork may lead you to a better address for the subject you are looking for or possibly even an unknown business he operates based on the type of collateralized equipment he has loans for. Also, check with the probate court in the city where the subject was last known to reside. The probate court will be a source for any wills your subject may have filed or be the executor of and any adoptions or guardianships your subject may be involved in.

STEP 4: By this point we have already located about 90 percent of the people we have been requested to locate. However if we still haven't found your subject we will need to step it up a notch and invoke some help. Without a doubt the social website of Facebook has dramatically changed the landscape of social interaction. We can now not only look for the subject on Facebook, but we can solicit all of his or her friends to have the source contact us. Power in numbers is a great thing and don't be shy about the numbers part! Ask as many of his/her "friends" to tell the source we need to speak to them and to call us or even ask if someone has a contact number or email. I was recently hired to find several former employees of a company who witnessed a slip and fall accident. The employee's personnel files had been reviewed and there were no clues to determine their locations. I found two of the four rather quickly, secured their statements and then moved on to the other two searching them on Facebook. One of the subject's was identified as living in Atlanta but the other subject seemed to have a more checkered address history and still alluded me. He had been evicted from his last two addresses and the landlords of each had no idea of his current whereabouts or were reluctant to get involved. In one of the evictions I found it was an out of state uncle who actual owned the condominium and evicted his nephew. I elicited the help of about ten of his "friends" on Facebook. Prior to this I had already found his mother, uncle and grandfather. I spoke to all of the sources and while I felt they knew where he lived, they were unwilling to assist me. When I did not get an immediate reply from anyone on Facebook, I put the names of each family member and their addresses in my report and suggested that subpoenas be directed to their attention as they had indicated to me several times that they were in occasional contact with the subject I needed to locate. I considered this a completed assignment 3.5 out of 4 until four months went by and out of the blue, the subject calls me as says, "I heard you are looking for me". The real truth was that I had long closed that file, but wanting to improve my record to 100 percent, I took down his current address and telephone number and sent it to my client!

STEP 5: In more difficult cases a post office box may be the only address you find. In these cases, I usually go to the counter and advise I am attempting to serve the subject or locate them for pending litigation. I simply show my private investigators ID and let them do the rest of the assuming. In these cases, the less you say the better. In order to maintain a Post Office Box, a physical address MUST be on file. If the Postmaster shows me the address and I already know it is no longer valid I tell them so. I ask the Postmaster if he will lock the mailbox so that when the subject comes to the Post Office he won't be able to access his mail box and is forced to come to the counter to inquire about his mail. Sometimes they just hold the mail and place a card inside the box saying "see Post Office Supervisor". Either way the subject is forced to the counter at which point the Postmaster can advise the subject that they need an updated address. Prior to leaving, I ask the Postmaster if I can call him in a week's time to get the subject's update physical address. While this delays your case for a while, it usually works like clockwork and saves you from needing to stake out the Post Office Box waiting for the subject to come check their mail.

I have also found not to ever overlook the value of the local postal carrier who services the route of your subject's last known address. If they are in the area during your visit of the last known address, make sure you speak to them. They see your subject's mail and if you don't think they pay attention you're wrong. They know a lot about the people they deliver to; some know more than others, but always talk to them. They often know what type of car your subject drives, and possibly where they work. When questioning the postal carrier be polite, sincere and don't forget to say thank you.

STEP 6: If I still haven't found the subject, then I need to get even more aggressive. I need to refocus on what I know about where he used to work and live. The subject's past employer or employees the subject worked with are all valuable sources of information and may still be in touch with the subject. The subject's previous landlord or apartment manager may provide valuable information as to where they are. They may have a copy of a lease application filled out by the subject containing information such as references or a nearest relative's contact information. Any known friends or associates of the subject may have the key to where the subject is hiding. If the subject has an ex-husband or wife, and you can locate them, they may be very willing to give you a current address or provide information that will assist you.

STEP 7: Make a personal visit to the physical neighborhood of the subject's last known address. The subject may not have left a forwarding address at the post office for his mail but, most likely, he made friends with some people in the area before moving out. These neighbors may have maintained contact with the subject and know where he or she is living at this time. When conducting this type of face—to—face canvas; don't forget the children that you see in the area. Children have a habit of being very honest and forthcoming with information when questioned in the right way. Now, when I say question the children in the neighborhood, keep in mind that you must exercise extreme discretion when attempting to do this. Don't drive down the streets of suburban America in your black sedan, roll down the window and ask children to come over to your car. Use your head and let common sense prevail.

I was once assigned to locate a subject and after reviewing the subject's file, I initiated a neighborhood canvas at the subject's last known address. The residents at this address turned out to be the subject's family members, his mother, father, brothers and sisters. As I approached the residence, there were several young children, approximately nine or ten years old, playing baseball in the front yard. I walked up to the front yard, picked up the baseball and started playing catch with the kids. After five or ten minutes and a couple of pitches later, I asked one of the children if Johnny, my subject, was home. The child stated to me that his brother Johnny hadn't lived at home for over a year. The child then continued to tell me that his brother, Johnny, had moved out to Colorado and was a cook at a ski lodge called the Big Bear. Moments later, I proceeded to the residence and knocked on the door. The door was answered by Johnny's mother. Using an appropriate pretext, I asked the subject's mother if Johnny was home or if she knew where I could reach him. She stated to me that she hadn't seen her son for well over a year and that he was nothing but trouble. For the next five minutes, she continued to tell me what a disappointment her son had been, repeating she had no contact with him and had no idea where he was. Keep in mind that when you question sources close to your subject, such as relatives or friends, they may try to cover up the truth. As I got back to my office, I looked up the Big Bear and found a Colorado Resort by that name on the Internet. I obtained a telephone number for the resort, called up and asked for the restaurant. I spoke with a hostess at the restaurant and asked for Johnny. The hostess told me that she didn't think he was in yet but to hold on and she would check the schedule. She returned moments later and informed me that Johnny was scheduled to begin work that afternoon at 4:00 p.m. She told me that Johnny was a cook and worked Tuesday through Sunday from 4:00 p.m. until closing.

Following a specific plan of action, I made a personal visit to Johnny's last known address to conduct a thorough canvass of the area. I found this residence to be Johnny's parent's house. Here I discreetly question Johnny's little brother who gave me the information I felt was valid. Had I not gotten the information from Johnny's brother, I would have been much more aggressive with his parents. Parents, despite their differences, usually know how to reach their children.

STEP 8: You may have a list of cases, you need to further investigate and the actual files can only be reviewed by making a personal visit to the county courthouse. Each county courthouse is different and while most are on-line, the record you see online will only be a brief fraction of the information you can get by pulling and reviewing the actual paper file. If you are in a small county be extremely polite and courteous you will get more assistance with a pleasant attitude. You should also be thinking about developing a friend on the inside you can call to obtain information instead of making the drive. The best investigators are always developing their sources.

STEP 9: Hopefully, by following this step—by—step location guide, you have found your subject by now. Remember that the subject's social security can establish which state your subject applied for his or her social security account. It is usually your subject's home state, a state your subject may return to, especially in times of trouble. Your subject may have friends or relatives to stay with or be near or from which to receive assistance. Somewhere during your investigation, a city or town in that state may have been uncovered or mentioned in passing that will help lead you to your subject.

STEP 10: A motor vehicle registration or MVR record search can usually be obtained on the subject at the County Tax Office. These records are also part of the typical database search run through Nexis Lexis or TLO. This information is generally available to the public, although it is considered protected information by a handful of states. Any license plate numbers associated to your subject should be ran to identify the owner. You may have a tag of a car your subject was seen driving in or obtained a ticket in for speeding. The Tag can be cross—referenced to identify the owner's name, date of birth and address.

STEP 11: State driver's license, or DL information, is also commonly accessed by the professional investigator. Driver's license information can be obtained in virtually every state, with a few exceptions. Certain states restrict access by requiring that you have your subject's driver's license number before they will give you any information. This number can be obtained from the database report ran in STEP 1. With the driver's license information, you can determine whether or not your subject has a valid license. It may also show tickets from another state indicating he has moved. Many county courthouses throughout the state sell 7 & 12 year DL records. Call ahead and make certain you are not wasting a trip to the courthouse. These records are also available online through your database source or another on-line specialty search company for a fee.

STEP 12: The local or city utility department is also a good source for locating your subject. Many times these utility services are county run businesses and as such their records are available for review. If the information from the local utility department is not readily accessible to the general public then consider developing an inside source whenever possible.

STEP 13: If you've followed all these steps and are still unable to locate your subject, don't overlook the Department of Corrections, the DOC. Your subject may be receiving three square meals a day, safe and sound in a state correctional facility. With your subject's name and social security number, you can query the supervised population database of the Department of Corrections (DOC) in virtually every state across the country and determine whether your subject is incarcerated at this time. The same holds true for the federal prison system.

STEP 14: If you still have not found the subject of your investigation, call the Bureau of Vital Statistics or double check your database to see if you see DOD after his name indicating the Date of Death. This information is obtained from the SSN Death Benefits database usually part of most national comprehensive databases.

Chapter Ten
Breaking the Cellphone Cover

I. Pre-Paid Phone Cards

10. Prepaid phones have become the most popular type of consumer cellular phone account today. You can juggle the reasons why between affordability, privacy and the fact that you can pick one up at Wal Mart while you're buying baby diapers. It's also an obstacle to overcome for most of us who have a prepaid phone number and need to figure out where it sleeps at night and with whom.

Postpaid phone numbers are so much easier to reverse with databases such as TLO, IRBsearch, Skipsmasher and Delvepoint but only if its owner has had the number for a while and actively uses it pushing their information into mainstream marketing data which our favorite databases will ultimately include.

Insurance purchases, debt collectors and payday loans, along with any other type of service which caters to the under-banked sector of consumers, add to the list of strong data aggregation making it fantastic combination for verifying information on a prepaid cell phone number.

Alternately, social media delivers another source to link an identity to a number. Search the phone number as you would a name in the search bar Facebook. You could find public posts which include the phone number even if you don't find an account linked to it. If you find a profile linked to a phone number, don't jump for joy yet, you still have to confirm that person is the current owner of the phone.

If a phone number is ported from a cell provider to Google Voice, open source and professional databases won't show the date of porting until those sources update their own records. This could take months, or over a year to happen. I'm looking for dates to compare to other reports I've pulled so I can rule it out or confirm who it belongs to. This matters because a number can be ported to a free VoIP service and continue to be used as a cell to set up two step authentication on sites that otherwise would reject a VoIP phone number for registration.

If you locate your target's Twitter account, you can use some nifty Twitter tools such like Tweetpaths and Geosocialfootprint to locate places they've been and surmise a future location. I've found some really good info by searching a phone number in the top search box on Twitter. You'll find mostly younger folks who don't use any part of their real name and tweet publicly about their lives along with some nice pictures of where they really live or stay, "Hey bro call me at 555-555-5555 n letz go 2 da new club 2nite." Don't forget to remove the dashes and search again. Lazy tweeters won't move between two keyboard screens.

Twitter has an enormous selection of third-party search tools which use their oAuth API. A few of my favorite tools have been around for a long time, others are simply a flash in the pan because they violate Twitter's terms and conditions. Twitter's very own search page is found here https://twitter.com/search-advanced

Many social media sites like Twitter and Facebook have included an option for a user to prevent their profile from being found by their phone number. This option is a recent change and is a step in Facebook's Privacy Checkup. If a person has a reason to hide, they may opt out.

Affiliate marketing sites such as Thatsthem and Reversegenie have surprisingly accurate and up to date information. I've been astounded by results on skips that have nothing new in the professional databases but show new home address, phone and occasionally an IP address with a date and a note of the source of info.

You're always going to be referred to a third party company to purchase a report. We refer to these sites as a bait and switch site. If your professional databases can't deliver, I'm pretty sure that the third party sites won't be able to either. Customer discount cards, surveys, credit card companies, sweepstakes entries and even insurance products sell customer data to marketing and lead generation companies and they also sell to Spokeo, Pipl, Zabasearch, Thatsthem and Reversegenie.

Currently the top source of user submitted data is in smartphone games which give an in-game reward for completing an advertiser's survey. Yes, I'll give you my new address and phone number for 100 gold bars. Thank you very much!

Credit card companies you ask? Why yes, American Express sells a list of their card holders who make more than $100,000 a year to companies who want to target their marketing to a particular income range. If American Express does it, then I would believe that Visa and MasterCard do it too.

Numberguru is now owned by Whitepages they offer a product called Whitepages Pro which takes you to a new level of dissecting a phone number. Pro will tell you the name of the app or telecom provider which owns the phone number, dates of porting and if there's any user name and address data, you'll see that too. It will also tell you if the number is in the Do Not Call government registry and has a nice feature of integrating street view if there's an address available. There's a free trial but no batching offered which for me, was a deal breaker.

Pipl has outstanding data and if you use an API subscription, you'll find all kinds of goodies like Amazon accounts, dating site profiles and forum memberships. Their competitor, Spokeo made some changes in the information which they provide after they were ordered to pay a fine of $800,000 by the FTC for selling fake employment records on their background searches and false advertising by using actors to pose as consumers who gave a glowing review on television commercial. Spokeo even had a credit score prediction graphic for each paid search. I'm not at all saying that the Spokeo of today isn't worth trying, but is the data trustworthy?

You'll never find one consistently good source of information. If you fall in love with one and swear by it, just as sure as the sun rises in the morning, you'll eventually be disappointed with results and realize you've sold yourself short because you've limited yourself to only one or two sources.

If the information exists, I can find it. If you've tried, and tried again, and your investigation has an attorney involved, then you can use the power of the subpoena to get strategic information such as how the service is paid, when, account numbers, addresses and phone numbers. A debit card from a personal checking account? What about a reload card purchased at a retail outlet with cash? Each source is a potential piece of information to get you to closer to pay dirt.

The numbers on the prepaid phone refill card are specific to a retail store which stocked it and will also be connected to the cash register which activated it and loaded the funds. An exact date, time, cashier name and a video of the person who purchased it, video of them walking to the parking lot and video of the vehicle they leave in with a possible license plate too.

Some may recall a Texas death row inmate named Richard Tabler who was secretly given a prepaid cell phone by a prison guard. Tabler, who had mental problems, called Texas Sen. John Whitmire to let him know that even though he's on death row, he can still get information, and then proceeded to give the names of the senator's daughters and names of other state prison official's family members. All Texas prisons went on lock down and over 1000 smuggled cell phones were seized from inmates.

Richard Tabler's mother and sister were immediately charged and arrested for buying the refill cards which kept the phone in operation. The Texas Department of Corrections investigation swiftly identified them from a video of the sale by tracing the refill card number.

Our options for getting the good info keeps getting better. If one thing doesn't work, something else will. You just have to keep trying to find that something else.

II. The phone Trap

And one day it happened, without any notice, causing an upheaval in my regular cell phone routine. Apple quietly changed all the rules that applied to iPhone caller ID lingo and left me in the lurch while juggling Starbucks, an armload of mail, and an UNAVAILABLE incoming call.

I never pay any mind to unavailable calls because they're usually robo-calls initiated by telemarketing companies. If someone anticipates a service repair call or appointment reminder then the average cell phone user could answer this type of call, which I carelessly did. A valuable opportunity lost forever and an avoidable situation had I known that the UNAVAILABLE caller ID was actually blocked.

Trapped predictive dialer calls will show as 999-999-9999. Also it's good to know that these programs will display any phone number that the user sets. So when you receive a phone call and return it only to hear that the phone number isn't in service, it's either a predictive dialer with an old number or a scammer deliberately using a fictitious phone number to shield its true identity.

I've been a faithful user of Trapcall in years past. but something with the iPhone 6 release made their reliable service completely wipe out my voice mail allowing callers to hear that my phone, "can't be reached at this moment." Two weeks into the malfunction I simply gave up the service and moved to a toll-free provider which routes all calls to a chosen number.

Toll free numbers have always been trap lines.
A very quick fix made me realize that most folks in our line of work don't realize exactly how toll-free numbers work and why.

How: toll-free numbers don't allow blocked incoming calls.
Why: the U.S. Government says that toll-free number owners who pay per-minute tolls have the right to see the incoming call data. Another very interesting bit of information here is that no call spoofing software will work to spoof a phone number to a toll-free number. I've read other investigators write instructional chapters on using this strategy to carry out an investigative pretext. Apparently those author's have never actually tried to test the theory themselves because it's impossible. It simply won't work.

Trapcall works by using conditional call forwarding (CCF). These codes can be obtained with your cell phone carrier. Using the same method of forwarding your home number to another phone line, you'll dial some codes that tell the phone company provides to you (nearly all cell companies have different codes) to only forward the phone call if you reject it, miss it completely or if your phone is turned off. Your phone company can help you set up CCF.

A few toll-free number providers to consider for trapline phone service are Kall8.com and Ureach.com.

There are also Agencies that speacialize is phone service

Chapter Eleven
Surveillance

I. Surveillance
   A. Covert and Overt Surveillance
   B. Types of Surveillance
      1. Fixed or Stationary Surveillance
      2. Mobile or Moving Surveillance
         a. Loose Tail
         b. Close Tail
   C. Pre-surveillance Preparation
      1. Positive Identification
         a. Photograph
         b. Description
         c. Observation
      2. Personal Data
      3. Subject's Lifestyle
      4. Purpose of Investigation
      5. Surveillance Territory
      6. Plan the Surveillance
      7. Equipment

II. Observation Posts and Stationary Surveillance
   A. Selecting Observations Posts
      1. Surveillance Movements
      2. Equipment
      3. Inside Surveillance
      4. Outside Surveillance Post
      5. Surveillance Rural Area

III. Automobile Surveillance
   A. Selecting Surveillance Vehicles
      1. Avoid Vehicles that Attract Attention
      2. Good Operating Condition
   B. Conducting Surveillance
      1. Initiating Surveillance
      2. Surveillance Do's
      3. Surveillance Don'ts

IV. Daily Surveillance Check List
   A. Preliminary Surveillance Investigation
   B. Arrival, Subject's Residence
   C. Canvass Neighborhood
   D. Take up Surveillance Position
   E. Observations

11. SURVEILLANCE

Any investigator will tell you that surveillance is one of the most important skills to learn. It can be used in almost any type of case and over time, your experience, like any art, gets perfected over time. Due to the importance of this subject, I have attempted to get very detailed with the subject.

Mobile surveillance is the covert (concealed), and constant watch of a subject while following the subject on foot or in a vehicle. Stationary surveillance is the observation of a subject or location from a fixed vantage point. Many times this position is concealed in the woods where camouflage clothing is worn or a natural "blind" is made from the surrounding tree branches and debris to blend in with your surroundings. The goal of course is to remain undetected in your position to afford the greatest opportunity to observe your subject in their natural state.

The key to any successful surveillance is to enter and exit the area without anyone knowing you where there.

The investigator who functions, as a covert observer is known as a surveillant. The "subject" is the person, under observation. <u>The art of surveillance is the investigator's ability to conduct observation of this nature without the subject ever being made aware of the surveillance.</u>

Surveillance is a form of direct observation. The investigators personally and directly observe the activities of the subject and any information thereby disclosed.

1. **Stationary/Fixed Surveillance**

In fixed surveillance the investigators (surveillants) observe from a fixed observation post. Fixed surveillance is used in the surveillance of places and of persons who frequent those places. In our business, fixed surveillances are usually conducted from a parked vehicle or from a surveillance position on foot, which affords a better view of the residence where our subject resides.

A fixed or stationary surveillance can very suddenly become a moving surveillance if the subject decides to leave the area, either on foot or by vehicle. However in many instances, an investigator may need to decide whether the surveillance will remain stationary or whether mobile surveillance will even be an option. In some instances it is not practical to attempt to do both. This is sometimes the case in very rural areas where the only discreet position will be a stationary one in the woods. In these cases it is advised to park your vehicle at a busy location where other vehicles are parked or be dropped off in the woods by a second investigator. A car parked in a remote area too close to your surveillance position will surely tip off any savvy subject.

2. Mobile or Moving Surveillance

Mobile surveillance occurs when both the subject and the surveillants are on the move by foot, in a vehicle, or in public transportation. Obviously moving surveillance makes great demands on the resourcefulness of the surveillant.

In a moving surveillance the investigators follow the subject, either on foot or in a suitable vehicle and tracks their every move all while observing any significant events, contacts, or activities, or any bit of evidence that the subject may inadvertently disclose to the surveillant.

3. Degrees of Moving Surveillance

Various degrees of moving surveillance are indicated by such terms as loose tail, close tail, open tail, rough tail. The nature of the case, the type of information needed, and the importance of continuous surveillance are all factors that help to determine the degree of persistent observation maintained.

a. Loose Tail

A loose tail, or loose surveillance is a cautious procedure that is performed to obtain general information about the subject's activities, associates, and habits without running great risk of being detected. In other words, the subject is followed loosely; it is not as persistent as the close tail.

b. Close Tail

Close surveillance tends to pursue the operation at any cost, within reason. The subject is kept under close observation at all times, even when the risk of discovery is high. The importance of the information to be learned may warrant that risk.

In our business the degree of surveillance should fall somewhere in between the loose tail surveillance and the close tail surveillance.

B. PRESURVEILLANCE PREPARATION

Success or failure depends largely on the surveillant's ability and resourcefulness in preparation for, and performance of surveillance activities. Maximum preparation paves the way for maximum performance. The adequately prepared usually succeed; the unprepared are almost sure to fail.

Too many times surveillants have relied on old information or addresses provided by adjusters, attorneys and others who are not completely in the know. This results in wasteful valuable and embarrassing hours of hanging around watching a house from which the subject moved two or three weeks ago. A quick phone call to the individual's home the night before, a check with directory assistance or a spot check or some pre-surveillance work during the week before is well worthwhile in avoiding such a catastrophe. It is usually not necessary to visit the neighborhood before a surveillance or call, however, if other pre-surveillance investigation leads the surveillant to believe that the subject may not reside at the address, then further pre-surveillance investigation is necessary.

The more information one has about the person to be followed, the more likelihood there is of the investigator being able to adjust intelligently to the subject's activities and unexpected moves. Knowledge of the subject's habits, associates, appointments, favorite places to go, business and social ties and friends and relatives can help the investigator pick up the subject's trail after temporarily losing it.

Whenever a surveillant has been detected he has not only wasted his valuable time, he has alerted the subject to the fact that he has been placed under observation.

Surveillants should have a prior knowledge of the following if possible:

1. The subject, the specific person or place to be surveilled.

2. The area in which the surveillance is to be conducted.

3. The specific objective of the surveillance.

4. The circumstances under which the investigator will have to function.

5. The type of surveillance.

    1. <u>Positive Identification</u>

Certainty of the subject's identification is obviously the first rule of surveillance. Investigators must be sure that they positively know the identity of their subject so as not to waste time and effort following the wrong person.

There are three procedures for securing a subject's appearance identification. As far as it is possible to do so, investigators should have:

1. A recent photograph of the subject provided by the client or previous investigation done by another agency.

2. A complete description of the subject.

3. Close personal observation of the subject.

Recent photographs, when available, can be very helpful, particularly full-length photographs that allow examination of the posture, build, height and weight of the subject. It is unusual that our clients provide us with a photograph of the subject. However, if the case was worked by another investigator in the office, it is possible that video or still images or available to review. It is best to obtain a complete description of the subject from more than one person. Good descriptions are sometimes hard to come by; however, they are essential and when more than one is obtained comparison of the descriptions may prove helpful. Descriptions of a person one has never met are especially valuable when they include a significant personal characteristic or habit that distinguishes the subject from others.

Quite often the client does have a full description of the subject, however, if they do not the information is available through other sources. If there is an attorney representing the insured, he may have taken a deposition and had the opportunity to observe the subject. He then could describe the subject. If neither the client nor the attorney have a physical description, it is possible to obtain a physical description from the insured or a rehabilitation worker. However, before contacting either one authorization should be gotten from the client.

Please be aware that it is not always possible to get a physical description though the surveillance has to be initiated in spite of it.

A casual introduction to ID the subject is a more sensitive situation. The surveillant must never be obvious about it. If at all possible, it is best to have someone else point the subject out to the investigator so that the investigator does not have any personal confrontation with the subject. When it is necessary for the investigator to personally contact the subject, it should be done in a casual manner, very natural, and the investigator should make every effort to identify the subject without creating suspicion on the part of the subject.

An investigator should always try to avoid any personal confrontation with a subject during the early stages of the investigation.

Most observations will be made while looking at the subject from behind. Any physical characteristics identifiable from behind are excellent tailing identification factors. Surveillants can watch the subject from behind after they have identified his face in person. Check for characteristics of appearance and movements. Is there anything about the subject's posture or build or in the way he carries himself, gestures he makes, or the way he holds his head? What about his gait, the speed and manner of his walking? Other things to look for are as follows: Does the subject usually go bare headed? What is the color of his hair? How does it appear from the back? Or does the subject wear hats, or caps? If so, what type, style and color are they? Is the subject bald or partially bald? What, if any, portion of his baldness can be seen from behind? Is his hair long or short? If long, does it reach his shoulders? Or is it cut high up the neck?

If the subject is a woman, the style as well as the color of the hair should be noted. Investigators should compose a complete mental image of the subject as he appears from behind. Are his shoulders massive with his head set close to them? Or does he have narrow shoulders and a long neck? Is there anything unusual about the way in which he walks, stands or moves? Is his walk quick and firm, or slow and hesitant: Is his carriage erect and straight, or does he sway from side to side? Does he lean forward or is he stooped over: Is there anything unusual about the subject's appearance? What actions, gestures, or habits are noticeable? Analyze the subject's entire form and movements from behind and note carefully and clearly visible identifiable physical or moving characteristics that can be readily viewed and quickly detected from behind. Some subjects will have more pronounced identification clues than others.

    2. <u>Personal Data</u>

In addition to knowing what the subject looks like, it is particularly important to know who the subject actually is. A second rule of preparation is to get all available personal data on the subject:

1. Full name, nicknames, and any aliases.

2. Residence, address and telephone number.

3. Where the employed: Company name, address and telephone number.

4. Means of transportation: Owns car, public transportation, rides with someone else, or walks.

    3. <u>Subject's Lifestyles</u>

The third rule of preparation is to learn as much as possible about the subject's lifestyle. This covers a wide area of relevant factors such as:

1. The subject's family, associates and friends.

2. Places he frequents.

3. His most noticeable habits.

4. Characteristics of his neighborhood.
5. Is he a family man, a loner, or has a girlfriend.

6. His reputation in the community.

It is always advisable to have the names and addresses of the subject's relatives, key associates and friends. Then, when the subject stops at one of their homes, the investigator will know who he is going to see or at least in whose home the subject is in at that particular time. If the investigator has previously looked up or acquired the telephone numbers of the subject's friends, associates, and relative, and places he frequents most and they lose track of him during a surveillance in any of these areas, they can make a "pretext" telephone call and learn if the subject is there and perhaps pick up on the subject again.

If possible, the surveillants should know the cars owned and driven by the subject, their model, year and license number.

The greater one's knowledge of the subject, the more prepared they'll be in following the subject.

4. Purpose of Investigation

Surveillants should know why the subject needs to be placed under surveillance. An investigator receiving a surveillance assignment should be fully informed about its purpose. The investigator should also know what specific information the client wants the investigator to obtain. He should also be aware of the exact instructions received from the client such as any monetary limits placed upon the investigation or limited amount of hours to be placed on the investigation. Usually the client will request whether or not they want videotape, still photographs or both if they subject is involved in any noteworthy activity. If there are any questions in the investigator's mind as to the purpose or the objectives of the surveillance, then the client should be contacted before any investigation is initiated.

5. Surveillance Territory

Familiarity with the areas and with the environment in which the assignment is to be conducted is essential.

There are three major steps to take to become familiar with the areas and locations in which surveillance is to be conducted:

1. Study maps of the areas.

2. Make a preliminary survey of the areas.

3. Closely observe the neighborhood environment.

Maps should be studied to determine the layout of the streets: Alleys and dead-end streets; main travel ways; freeways, turnpikes and their on and off ramps; apparent natural get-away routes and public transportation routes. Being familiar with the area is essential in moving surveillance. Map study, a personal survey and environmental information all combine to create a functional familiarity with the territory that enables the investigators to make quick, intelligent moves as required.

Driving through the street, it helps to take special note of parking and vacant lots, and service stations, fast food outlets and markets at intersections that would permit a quick transition from a street of traveling to a cross street. Driveways connecting two streets also provide useful throughways. The value of such quick bypass from one street to another to keep from being detained at a light or by unusual heavy traffic is quite helpful.

While surveying the neighborhood, the investigator should attempt to identify a point or address in the area where he believes the subject will first appear, whether it be at the subject's front door, car, someone else's residence, place of business, parking place, etc. The investigator should also determine if there are any other addresses in the nearby area where the subject might visit during the surveillance. If so, the investigator should map out the route that the subject is most likely to take.

Before conducting an automobile surveillance, it is advisable to drive around the streets in the immediate area in which the observation is expected to begin. The investigator should select a key vantage point (never in the same block as the subject's place) from which the investigator can readily observe the subject's place and wait and watch for his appearance.

If the subject lives in an area that is sparsely traveled or in a patrolled residential area, the investigator should not make their survey so obvious as to call attention to themselves or their vehicle. Pre-surveillance survey should be done as normally as possible, attracting as little attention as possible.

When establishing stationary surveillance, the survey is confined to a few blocks in all directions that are immediately adjacent to the premise that is being observed.

Primary objective is to select a suitable observation post or place for the surveillance.

If the area is rural, familiarity with the terrain and main highways as well as country roads is important. Nothing should be done to arouse curiosity in the neighborhood, or to get anyone to talk about the investigator's presence there. It is best not to make repeated trips throughout the neighborhood.

Please note that familiarizing oneself with the area is commonly done on the morning of the surveillance. We do not usually have the luxury of examining the area before the actual day of surveillance unless the investigator happens to be in the area. In most cases, it is not necessary to survey the area prior to the morning of the surveillance unless other information indicates different. Reality is that our clients do not want to pay for a special visit to the neighborhood to survey the situation unless it is warranted.

6. <u>Plan the Surveillance</u>

Some effort should be put forth in planning the surveillance such as whether the surveillance is going to be conducted by one investigator or more than one. If there is more than one investigator conducting the surveillance, then the investigators need to get together to go over strategy. The investigators must understand the procedures for the interchange of positions and under what situations or at what times the lead surveillance is changed. Organizational and procedural matters need to be settled, for example, the signal system should be perfected.

The investigator should plan to blend in with the environment in which the surveillance will be conducted. The type of clothing worn and the general appearance and behavior of the investigator should mesh with the area that he will be in so that nothing will appear conspicuous.

Foot surveillants should carry sufficient change for possible bus fares, taxi fares and other incidental costs that might arise while maintaining a continuous watch on the subject. Moving surveillants need to have money for gas and possible automotive emergencies, as well as for tolls and unexpected expenses.

In vehicular surveillance, changeable items of apparel are often carried to minimize recognition. These might include jackets, hats, caps, wigs, different types of eyeglasses, and other items that can be quickly changed. A foot surveillant may wear a jacket that can be reversed. In areas and seasons of frequent rain, it is best to carry a rain slicker to avoid appearing conspicuous walking the street in short sleeves in a downpour. Pens and a notebook should always be carried. Some surveillants carry pocket sized recorders for making notes.

7. <u>Equipment</u>

When conducting vehicle surveillance it is necessary for the investigator to carry all of his camera equipment.

All observation and photographic equipment should be planned and arranged for before the actual surveillance begins. In addition, every piece should be pre-tested by the investigator to make certain that it is in good working order before it is taken into the field. There is nothing more aggravating, more frustrating and more inexcusable than to miss photographic documentation of evidence because the camera will not function correctly on the spur of the moment, or because it is not loaded or because the investigator simply forgot to adequately charge the battery or pick up a tape.

II. OBSERVATION POSTS AND STATIONARY SURVEILLANCE

Stationary surveillance may be a temporary stake out or it may call for prolonged observation of a suspect or suspect's premises. In its briefest and simplest form, it may only be an investigator sitting in the shadows of a doorway or sitting in an automobile watching a place down the street. In its most elaborate form, it is a fully equipped observation post set up in an office building, hotel, apartment house or other location from which a clear view may be had of the subject premises and all its entrances and exits.

A. **Selecting the Observation Post**

The first step in selecting a suitable observation post is a preliminary survey of the area surrounding the place to be watched. This was mentioned previously, however, this section will cover the subject in more detail. As mentioned previously, such survey should consider the character of a neighborhood and its residents, the types of businesses and social outlets in the area, and specifically, the most logical location for the observation post.

Surveillance for observation post selection must provide the best view of the place, including all exits, as well as the best cover for the surveillants. The post should be out of sight of anyone who might be accidentally or intentionally looking at or watching the surveillants. It is best to have an indoor observation post, however, this is usually not the case. Ninety-five percent of our surveillance work is conducted from a vehicle. When conducting surveillances outdoors, inside a vehicle, the surveillants need to find some sort of outdoor cover created by nature or man or operate in an area under some suitable community disguise.

Surveillants should have a reasonable cover story to use whenever it becomes necessary to make an explanation of their presence in the area. The true reason for their being in the area and the identity of the subject premise should never be disclosed to anyone. This includes the subject, business friends, neighbors or social acquaintances. Once the surveillance is completed, no one in the area should have knowledge of the surveillance or who was the subject of the surveillance. Obviously, if the surveillant is in the neighborhood for a few days or even one full day, some suspicion may be aroused on the part of the neighbors, however, it should be those neighbors that are at least one block away from the subject premises and who are less likely to have any dealings with the subject. The secrecy during a surveillance must be maintained.

1. Surveillant Movements

The secrecy of the surveillance depends not only on the extent of the undercover protection provided by the observation post, but also the actions of the surveillants themselves. All movements to and from the post should be routine and as noticeable as possible. In no way should the surveillants attract attention to themselves. Surveillants should be especially careful not to arouse suspicious when they:

1. Establish the observation post.
2. Come and go to and from the post.
3. Leave the post to terminate the surveillance.

Every precaution should be taken when performing any activity that may be observed by others so that the surveillants can remain unsuspected and incognito.

2. <u>Equipment</u>

During all surveillances, the surveillant should be fully equipped in reference to video equipment. The equipment is fairly bulky and should always be kept out of sight of anyone passing by the surveillance position. This can be accomplished by keeping the equipment in cases covered by a towel. Not only should the video equipment be kept covered, but also any notes pertaining to the case. It is not unusual to be on a surveillance and have someone walk up to you surveillance vehicle and start a conversation. If papers are left lying around in a car, they can be easily viewed by others.

3. <u>Indoor Observations Posts</u>

Indoor surveillance enables the surveillant to remain undercover and to set up their equipment and conduct their operation out of view of passers by and persons who may be frequenting the premises under surveillance.

Inside the observation rooms, the surveillants should take positions several feet away from the windows. They should never stand or sit near a window. They should not be observed through the window from the street below or from offices or rooms across the street.

As far as possible, the investigator should eliminate the chances of curious people somehow peering through the glass into their post. Window draperies can be partially drawn and blinds can be pulled completely down to within a few inches of the windowsill. Observations can be made from above or below the window shade, or from a small opening in the drawn draperies.

4. <u>Outdoor Surveillance Post</u>

As in most cases, indoor surveillance positions are not available and therefore must be conducted outdoors. Surveillants have to find some sort of outdoor cover created by nature or man, conduct their surveillance from an equipped vehicle, or operate in the open under some suitable community disguise.

The nature, extent and duration of the surveillance will affect the type of outdoor role assumed by the investigator.

Surveillances conducted by our agency are usually conducted from an automobile. It is best to select several viewing points, if possible, so that the surveillant can move from time to time and is never in one place for a prolonged period of time. This is not always possible, and in some cases it is best to stay in one position if there is good cover. Discretion must be used in this area.

When conducting stationary surveillance from an automobile, the following are effective guidelines:

1. Never park in the same block as the place to be watched. The next block is the closest that an investigator should get to the subject's place.

2. Always drive to and from the position in a normal manner, like one of the residents of the area.

3. When moving form one vantage point to another, do so as inconspicuously as possible without any unusual activity.

4. After parking the car the surveillant should sit in the passenger seat rather than the driver seat. It will appear as though the surveillant is waiting for the driver.

5. An alternative to the above is to have the surveillant sit in the back seat, lower the sun visors, raise the headrests and put up a sun shade to make the surveillant's presence less easily detected. The sun shields that stretch across the front windows serve as a good cover in appropriate situations. A coat or shirt on the hanger in the back seat can also help a great deal.

6. Always use a car that is inconspicuous in make or color (like Magnum's red Ferrari, right!) and one that is so average that it will not draw attention to itself or to its occupants. The vehicle should be parked out of site in a position so that it is not in direct view of anyone that may be peering through the subject's windows or in the direct view of any close neighbors. More importantly, the surveillant should not be visible to anyone at the subject's residence or close neighbors.

7. When it is necessary to park along side the road in front of a residence, park between two properties so that either resident doesn't feel as though they are being watched or that you are on their property.

Vans are effective observation posts. Various methods have been used to camouflage vans to hide the surveillance observations.

Some vans use one-way glass through which observations can be made; other use curtains that are partially drawn. Others have the appearance of a delivery truck with boxes stacked inside equipped with camouflage peepholes.

Some investigators follow the practice of getting people accustomed to the presence of the van by driving it to the area and leaving it there part of the day several days before starting actual surveillance. Each morning the driver locks the van and leaves to return later in the day. On the morning the surveillance begins, he drives as usual to the viewing site, parks the van, locks the surveillants and their equipment hidden inside.

As with the automobile, the van should be positioned so that it is partially hidden from the view of anyone at the subject's place.

5. Surveillance, Rural Areas

Trees are among the most useful natural covers: Large bushes, brush piles, tree stumps and the like provide suitable cover. Nature provides other possible surveillance points in its rock formations, ravines, gullies, crops, hillside brush, and similar cover.

Surveillants can also take advantage of manmade or man provided barriers to help to hide them from easy view. Fences and outdoor equipment for example can help hide at least part of the human body or the automobile.

Whether a surveillant should move into his rural observation post on foot or in some sort of vehicle depends on such factors as:

1. The kind of natural cover provided by the area.
2. The extent of large open spaces to be crossed.
3. The need to avoid the curiosity of residents of the area.
4. Importance of being able to return to the vehicle quickly.
5. The importance of keeping the subject premise under direct observation as opposed to a block or two away.

When the surveillant finds it necessary to move in and out of a site on foot, he should:

1. Avoid regularly used footpaths where he is more likely to meet other persons. They may realize he is a stranger in the area and wonder why he is there.

2. Always try to keep some object between yourself and the subject's premises. By doing so, you create a blind spot for anyone who might look your way, trees, clumps of bushes, straw stacks or haystacks, farm equipment, stone piles, etc., can be used. Any one of these objects between the investigator and the subject's premises will reduce the likelihood of the investigator being seen, as he will naturally focus in on the closer objects.

3. Walk on hard surfaces as far as possible. Hard surfaces do not leave footprints, but soft surfaces do. Certain surfaces are noisy by nature and must be walked over with greater care.

4. Always walk quietly and unhurriedly. An investigator should never rush in or out of an observation post.

5. Pause frequently to look around discreetly and listen carefully for sounds and movement.

6. Always walk below the crest of a hill.

7. As far as possible, avoid crossing large open spaces.

8. When possible, walk into the wind or across the wind. This tactic makes it more difficult for dogs to pick up an investigator's scent. It is usually better to try to quiet an approaching dog and make friends with it rather than create the added commotion of trying to scare it away.

9. Use a somewhat different route each time when entering the observation post. Do not create a pathway that can be used as others by a tracking method.

10. If possible, move into the observation post at night under the cover of darkness. When traveling during the daylight hours, schedule comings and goings at different times so as not to create a regular time schedule for the investigator's activities in the area. Also, coordinate traveling time when there is less activity in the subject's neighborhood.

11. When leaving the post, the investigator should make certain that he has left nothing behind that would create a suspicion of surveillance or identify the investigator.

III. **AUTOMOBILE SURVEILLANCE**

A moving surveillance, a tail or shadow may be on foot, in a vehicle, or may use a combination of walking and riding.

B. Selecting Surveillance Vehicles

1. Surveillants should avoid attaching any features to surveillance vehicles that would attract attention to them. There should be no observable distinguishing features or decorations, outside or inside the cars that could attract the attention of other motorists or pedestrians. This includes no decorations of any sort on the hood, wheels, bumper, or windshield. No bumper stickers, fancy wheel covers, or attention attracting objects dangling form the rear view mirror. The only exception would be objects or stickers that

are used to alter the appearance of the surveillance vehicle while the surveillance is in progress.

2. All surveillant vehicles should be in excellent operating condition. They should be kept tuned, filled with gas, and the ignition system should be working at optimum level. The cars must be capable of any quick maneuver and set for any road condition.

C. Conducting Surveillance

It is important to know that rear vision views often have blind spots, which means there are areas behind the subject's car where it is more difficult for him to get a good look at who may be following him. Cars with two side mirrors have better rear vision than those with only one. The best place for the surveillant car to drive is to the right and behind the subject with another car between,. The lane to the subject's right usually falls within his greater rear vision blind spot. Blind spots are located outside the view area covered by the rear vision mirror and the left side mirror. On a three-lane street with the subject's car in the middle lane, the blind spots would be the right land and part of the left inside lane. The subject's best view is of traffic in the lane directly behind him, with a partial view of the lane to his left. Blind spots should be taken advantage of whenever possible when tailing another vehicle, and also when the investigator approaches an occupied parked vehicle on foot.

As in all surveillance situations, the two primary risks are being detected and losing the subject. The closer one is to the subject, the greater the detection risk. The farther one is from the subject, the greater the risk of losing him. To achieve the delicate balance between the two, calls for considerable driving skill.

The driver must stay close enough to keep the subject in view.

As mentioned previously, when following someone for a long period of time, it is advisable to change disguises. Elaborate disguises are not recommended. Simple disguises such as putting on or taking off a cap, hat or wig, or changing sunglasses is advisable.

Some investigators carry items that can be used to make the interior of a car appear different. These changes can all be made while the subject is turning a corner or during any time when the surveillant car is not within view of the subject's car.

1. Initiating Surveillance

During the preliminary survey, the surveillant selects a good starting point, a position of advantage from which they can watch and wait for the subject to appear.

The traffic in the area affects the location of the surveillance position. If it is an area of reasonably heavy traffic it can be closer to the subject's place. If it is an area of very little traffic the surveillant's car must be located at a greater distance from the subject's place because movement in the area will be more readily noticeable and identifiable. In such instances it is best to have a pair of binoculars available so that the surveillant can be certain it is the subject entering and leaving in his car and not someone else. Also, when starting out it is best to determine the most likely route that the subject would take on leaving the residence and take up a surveillance position accordingly. It is best to take up a position where the subject is less likely to pass by the surveillant.

If the subject travels towards the surveillant vehicle then the investigator must react quickly by slumping down in the vehicle to avoid being detected. A window open an inch or two will greatly help you hear the cars go by. The best alternative is to leave the surveillance position quickly to a position where the subject's vehicle can be observed. Pulling into a driveway, parking lot or other location can reduce the chances of the subject taking notice to the investigator's vehicle or the investigator. Look for such turn around spots <u>before</u> starting the surveillance.

When the surveillant is sitting in his vehicle, it is important to watch for close neighbors passing by or neighbors on foot or bicycle. The same maneuvers should be made as mentioned above. It is essential that the surveillant avoid being noticed by the subject, the subject's family or any close neighbors.

It is also important for the surveillant to keep in mind that anyone leaving the subject's residence or close neighbors could return to the neighborhood at any time. If at all possible the surveillant should attempt to make himself and his vehicle less noticeable.

2. <u>Techniques of Vehicle Surveillance (Surveillance Do's)</u>

For speedy reference, techniques of vehicle surveillance are as follows:

1. The surveillant's vehicle, usually an automobile but perhaps a van or truck should blend naturally with the vehicular traffic of the area. Its model, make and color should be inconspicuous.

2. When more than one surveillance car is used each should be of a different color and make.

3. Drivers should alter their driving techniques from time to time but should generally take advantage of the subject's rear vision blind spots. They should try to make it difficult for the subject to observe the surveillant's car(s) while at the same time keeping the subject's car in view. Surveillants' cars must be driven by drivers with quick reflexes who can think and act on the spur of the moment.

4. If there are two surveillants in the vehicle one should drive and watch the traffic and the other should watch the subject's car. The observer can also keep the surveillance log and function as the jumper should temporary foot surveillance be required.

5. Automobile surveillants should drive normally and blend in with the flow of traffic. They must avoid quick spurts of speed and if they need to speed up do so gradually. They should try to abstain from running red lights in pursuit and from other irregular moves that attract attention. It often requires considerable skill to negotiate traffic and keep the surveillance from becoming obvious.

6. In vehicular surveillance a man and a woman in a car would usually arouse less suspicion than two men. If you are two men keep one in the back seat so they are less obvious.

7. Distance behind the subject's car is always a key factor. It varies according to circumstances. It would be less in crowded city traffic and greater on the highways and in rural areas. On downtown streets, in large cities, the usual procedure is to keep one car, not more than two cars between the subject's car and the surveillant's vehicle. In residential areas, the surveillant vehicle should stay at least one block behind the subject's vehicle. In rural areas, distances are increased as necessary, but the investigator must always keep within sight range.

8. When using two vehicles the most usual driving position is for the lead car to follow the subject car one or two cars behind it and in the lane to the right of it, unless the subject's car is already in the right lane, in which case the lead car follows behind it. The backup car would follow approximately the same distance behind the lead car in the left lane. These cars can readily change positions in the normal flow of traffic by the lead car slowing down and the backup car speeding up a bit to take over the lead position, each of the cars moving into their respective lanes.

9. When there is only one investigator in the vehicle, the investigator has to watch the street traffic, pedestrians, and the subject's car all at the same time. It is important for the surveillant to be familiar with the appearance of the subject's vehicle form behind as well as the subject so that both can be quickly spotted if surveillance contact is broken for a period of time.

10. When it is a one vehicle surveillance it is best for the surveillant to stay in the lane to the right of the subject to make it more difficult for the subject to see the investigator. If the subject is in the right curb lane and the car between moves out of that lane to the left, the surveillant can move into the left lane also. If there are three lanes, the investigator may prefer the middle lane so that he can negotiate a move to the right or left should the

subject's car turn in either direction. Positioning of the surveillant's car is always a matter of good common sense and judgment in the light of all prevailing conditions.

11. When the subject is stopped at a red light and is in the right lane of traffic the investigator should keep in mind that the subject could make a right turn. If the investigator is one vehicle behind the subject he may be left sitting in the right lane of traffic due to the vehicle in front of him having elected to go straight instead of right.

12. It's important for the investigator to maintain visual contact of the subject's vehicle at all times if possible. Don't let the surveillance become routine, even on a turnpike or interstate. It is very easy for the investigator to lose sight of the subject in traffic if the investigator's attention is elsewhere.

13. When the subject leaves it is very important that you waste no time in getting on him. The most likely time that you will lose the subject is in the beginning. With that in mind, watch his taillights for when he steps on the brakes to shift the car into reverse or drive. Backup lights should be watched. Exhaust can often be a good indication that the car has been started. Keep the motor vehicle in view when it is parked at the subject's home whenever possible.

14. Always be looking ahead. Look for upcoming stop signs, cautions signs, curves, the timing of stoplights. Keep an eye on the subject's directional if he uses them and keep a mental map in your mind of the general direction that the subject appears to be going.

15. When traveling on an interstate or turnpike, surveillance should be tightened up when exits are coming up and loosened up when exits are some distance away. Always prefer the right hand side since to get off the highway the subject will have to take the right hand lane with very few exceptions.

16. When the subject stops at a light, stop sign, or in traffic, the normal distance whether you are following someone or not is to have the license plate of the vehicle in front resting on the top of your hood. When you have stopped, this is the normal distance to wait behind the other person. Any closer or further is abnormal and will attract some attention.

17. Do not let more than two cars come between you in city traffic. Avoid allowing vans, buses, trucks and pedestrians come in front of you. Try to evaluate the driver that is trying to come in between you.

18. When you enter the highway behind a subject check your watch immediately when the subject heads onto the ramp. Calculate in your mind what delay has been made from the time that the subject entered the ramp

to that point in time that you finally got on. This is extremely important since the distance that the subject will gain on you is incredible once he gets on the highway. For example, if the subject is forty-five seconds ahead of you and travels sixty miles per hour, the subject will gain three-quarters of a mile in the time it takes you to enter the highway. You would then travel seventy miles per hour for four and a half minutes' time (or about five and a half miles) just to catch up to the subject. Needless to say this means that you should avoid any excess delays in following the individual onto the highway, but when it occurs expect to do some driving before you see the subject again.

If it is forty miles to the next exit you have nothing to worry about, but if the exits are only a couple of miles apart you can be in serious trouble with even a half-minute delay.

19. Be aware of the general direction in which the subject appears to be traveling. For example, if the subject is traveling in a general northeasterly direction and you lose him, you may come to a fork in the road where the choice is northeast or northwest. Obviously, you take the northeast direction.

20. Remember that people do not usually go very far from their home. People seldom go more than a couple of miles from home, so if you lose them check the area where they were last seen. Don't go off onto a highway and travel for an hour's ride expecting to pick up on the subject. Stay where you lost the subject and check that area with extreme care. Ninety percent of the time you will relocate the subject. Make sure the check is systematic. After checking the area, return to the subject's house or other likely locations that were identified through surveillance up to that point or on a previous occasion.

21. Do not get overly nervous when following a subject. This will eventually take its toll on your alertness and abilities to stay with the subject. If you go into a surveillance with the attitude you are going to be "made" you eventually will be, or you will lose the subject. Do not go into a surveillance with the attitude that if you lose the subject you can "get the subject another day". Even though this is true, it is a waste of the investigator's time and the client's money. As your experience grows you will find that you seldom, if ever, lose anyone and most of the times that you did lose a subject it was because of your own self-consciousness. <u>When confronted with a choice to either stay on a subject or possibly attract attention, or loosen up and possibly lose the subject, take the choice of staying with the subject.</u>

22. In business areas when the subject enters an establishment or home for any length of time and you have to remain in the area and you are on foot, try to get off the sidewalk and wait in hallways of office buildings or apartment

houses, etc. Look through the front door and thereby attract no attention from any passersby except people entering or leaving the building. Have a good excuse ready for hanging around, be it for the benefit of the tenants or anyone else. Indicate that you are "waiting for a girlfriend" or grab a paper bag filled with trash, which might look like a lunch bag and indicate that you are waiting for a ride to a new job.

23. When there is a school crossing guard or other live obstruction anywhere near where you are taking a subject out of an area on a surveillance, it is sometimes smart to approach that person, explain your problem, and ask for their cooperation in letting you pass quickly when you leave. Most school crossing guards and security guards will cooperate with you and try to help if they know what you are doing.

Needless to say, you never tell them or anyone else exactly who you are watching or why.

3. <u>Surveillance Don'ts</u>

1. Don't be afraid that you are going to get "made" by the subject. Without exception every beginner doing surveillance makes this mistake and loses people because he thinks he has been made. Although you are important and very noticeable to yourself, you are just another face in the crowds to everyone else and if you dress normally, drive normal and look reasonably normal you should never have any problems.

2. Don't try to second-guess what the subject is doing. It is absolutely impossible to try to explain why people go where they go, do what they do, etc. Avoid thinking about why the subject is making particular movements and avoid thinking that the subject's activities are affected by your presence. Merely follow the subject, note what the subject does, where they go, and try to figure it out later on.

3. Don't travel all over the world. If you have lost someone, proceed immediately in that general direction that you last saw them headed and after you have exhausted that possibility reasonably, stop, and turn back. Then check the immediate area in which they were lost. If you do not find them go back to the last place that they were seen, their house, or any other location that you suspect they may have gone to within reason, based on earlier surveillance reports or background knowledge. Do not travel long distances hoping to get "lucky" because you will not. If you are unable to find them return to their house and await their return. Get the best vantage possible for the most absolute best film. When they return home and have dozens of brown plastic bags in the trunk of their car saying "Wal-Mart" there's no longer any doubt where they had gone. Our goal now is to get the best video of them unloading the car to document their physical capabilities of bending over, lifting and carrying heavy bags of groceries in each hand.

4. Don't forget that three pictures are necessary in a person's mind to begin to become suspicious of you. This means that the subject must have three good, clear, lasting looks at your face before they become suspicious that you are following them or that they're running into you too often. This doesn't mean passing glances while you are driving by at thirty miles per hours in a car and they merely look at the vehicle. This means three good full looks at you where your face registers. After you have had two of these happen to you where the subject just looks at your face, etc., try to delay the third one happening as long as possible, or change your appearance, vehicle, etc., before that third picture is taken in their mind. At that point, if you're relatively certain that you've been "made" discontinue and come back at a later date.

5. Don't check in with the police department unless necessary. Do not broadcast to the police or other officials that you are conducting surveillance in that certain area unless you feel that it is absolutely necessary. The less people that know about your activity, the better, and if something does go wrong you will not be blaming the police unfairly just because you checked in with them.

6. Don't get ahead of the subject. Never pass the subject's vehicle or pass him on foot unless it is absolutely necessary. This is a terrible mistake to make and a very bad habit to get into, which will cause you many wasted hours.

7. Don't leave your car unless absolutely necessary. If you do have to leave your automobile make sure you are able to get back to the automobile before the subject leaves in his vehicle. Many times an investigator will be caught too far away from his vehicle and the subject drives out of sight. The investigator should leave his surveillance position only when he is relatively certain that the subject will not be leaving the area or when he knows that he will be able to return to his vehicle in time to follow the subject.

8. Never throw trash from your car when sitting on a surveillance. If you are questioned by the police and they see such a mess they will not be convinced that you are a professional and to be taken seriously. This may seem like a small point but you need all the goodwill you can get and littering is no way to get it.

9. Don't get into an interesting book or other reading material when you are on a surveillance. The next thing you know, three minutes have gone by and during the time the subject has left. Try the radio and various am and fm radio stations so as not to get bored.

V. **DAILY SURVEILLANCE CHECK LIST**

A. Preliminary Surveillance Investigation

Prior to arriving in the area, you should have already printed out your database background report. I usually run this and review it the night before my surveillance. I would have also used Google Earth to see if I can actually see a picture of my targets house. If a picture is not available there, I will check with the County Property Appraiser's Office on line as they also sometimes have a picture of the house. This search also verifies who owns the house and what the value of the house is. A value of a house can tell you a lot about the neighborhood and what to expect.

B. Arrival, Subject's Residence

On an initial surveillance assignment I will routinely arrive at 6:00 a.m. on a weekday and 7:00 a.m. on a weekend day.

Once I arrive in the neighborhood, I will look to see if I see the cars identified in the database I reviewed. This will be the first indicator that my subject still lives at the reported address.

C. Canvass Neighborhood

I will circle the area to look for the exits so that I don't get caught off guard when they leave the area. I should have a general idea of which way they will depart and which way leads to the closest store or business area.

D. Take up Surveillance Position

The surveillance position you choose will be the most important decision you make and could make or break the investigation. Too far away and you risk missing activity, too close and you risk being spotted.

1. As a rule of thumb, the subject's front door and or car and driveway should be observable form your position. You need to see if they are picked up by someone else, leave on foot or leave in their personal vehicle. '
2. I prefer to have my car pointed away from the subject's residence and off to a wide peripheral spot usually affording some obstruction of my car.

E. Observations
1. My first notes in the case will be a complete description of the house and cars and any special characteristics which make my subjects house stand out or seem pertinent to the case.

2. I will continue to make hourly notations throughout the day until my subject moves then those notations become specific to my subject, where they went and how they moved in reference to their reported injury.

Chapter Twelve
Private Investigator Equipment

    I.   Basic knowledge of specialty investigation equipment.
    II.   Basic knowledge on the proper\legal use of audio recorder/audio recording.
    III.   Basic knowledge on the proper\legal use of video recorders/video recording.
    IV.   Basic knowledge on the proper\legal use of still cameras\still photography.
    V.   Understand when to use photography on surveillance.
    VI.   Video Software and Agency Management Software

12. Equipment For the Professional Investigator

One of the most important objectives of any surveillance is to obtain video of your subject. As a rule of thumb, you should know that any video taken of your subject during surveillance which has an elapsed time of less than ten or fifteen minutes of your subject's activities will, for the most part, be considered inadequate for most investigative purposes. The first thing we should talk about is the use of your camcorder. When you're videoing, you must train your camera on the subject of your investigation and leave it there. Taking fifteen minutes of video during the course of your investigation, ten minutes of which is nothing but your subject's home or car will never be sufficient. In surveillance, it's important to remember that your goal is to objectively document your subject's movement and behavior through the use of video. That means obtaining video of the activities your subject is engaged in. Video of residences, vehicles or persons not directly pertinent to your investigation will not be of any help to you. It's up to you as a professional private investigator to take this untrained video camera and teach it to perform to your specifications by recoding the subject under surveillance.

Video cameras have come a long way and I can recall the early days when the video recorder was a reel to reel machine with an attached camera on a cord. Cameras especially surveillance cameras, were two—piece units where the camera was separate from the actual recording device. Of course, this situation created a cumbersome problem in that the moving of the two individual pieces, which were connected by a cable, was not only a difficult job but extremely conspicuous when used in the field situation. With the introduction of the one piece camera and recorder combination called the "camcorder", the ability to conceal your video camera was increased tremendously. The camcorder is readily concealable and extremely portable so it can be used in a variety of hidden applications. Today, microchip technology has created pin hole cameras that enable covert videoing on flash cards or mini hard drives half the size of a pack of cigarettes. Considering their size the options that you have in concealing such units are almost limitless. Companies like Super Circuits out of Texas, have the ability to hide a surveillance camera in a clock, radio, fire alarm, emergency light systems, stereos, books, briefcases, garbage cans, fence posts, power transformers, picture frames, loose—

leaf binders, lamps, radar detectors and even mailboxes. Some organizations even specialize in hiding video cameras in stuffed animals. Because of advanced chip technology and the miniaturization of the video camera, or surveillance camera, the possibilities for the concealment of your camcorder are almost limitless.

As a private investigator, your camera is your weapon. You must be comfortable and knowledgeable in its use and applications. Practice shooting video by going to a busy shopping center or grocery store and video people coming and going form their car to the front door and from the front door to their car. Most camcorders are also equipped with a red, flashing LED light mounted on the front of the camcorder. This light called the "tally light" and can be turned off in the camera settings mode. If it cannot be turned off you will want to put a small piece of black electrical tape and cover the LED light on the front of your camcorder before conducting any surveillance investigation. This, once again, will allow you to video your subject without anyone around you being aware of the fact that you're recording their movements. Before utilizing your camcorder or any advanced video surveillance equipment, we strongly recommend that you read, in detail, the instructions accompanying the equipment. Once again, it is important that you familiarize yourself with any video surveillance equipment before ever attempting to utilize it in the field. Your comfort level with this equipment is fundamental to your success in the field as an investigator. Practice, practice, practice.

The stock camera battery can always be upgraded with an extended life one a standard upgrade is a two hour battery. Remember to remove the battery from your camcorder during periods of inactivity when the camera is not in use. If you charge your battery to its full capacity the evening before conducting the surveillance and attach it to your camcorder, by the time you begin your surveillance the next morning, you could lose some of the battery's capacity. Remember, leave your battery unattached until you're ready to use it. Always have a second and maybe even a third fully charged battery as part of your accessories. You never know when you will may need to shoot a full day's activity so be prepared. Always bring your charger with you so that you can be recharging a battery while using another.

A professional private investigator will also want to invest in a camcorder cigarette lighter battery cord. In this manner, the camcorder can be operated via a cigarette lighter battery cord, using your automobile battery as your source for power. Your camcorder batteries can then be utilized when you leave your vehicle, giving you the maximum benefit of portability. Using your power sources in this manner will increase your effectiveness as an investigator in the field by prolonging your opportunities for video surveillance. Most cameras also serve as chargers now so with the cigarette battery cord, you can charge a battery in between shooting or carry a second camera of the same make and model, which is also highly recommended.

Never, use the automatic focus functions on your camcorder when filming. The automatic focus should be used before you actually film just to set the correct focus for the distance you are shooting. Once the auto focus is set, turn it OFF. This is important because the automatic focus function on your camcorder automatically focuses on the nearest object to the camcorder. This means that if a person or a motor vehicle, a leaf, a bush, a fly or even a speck of dust comes between you and the subject that you're attempting to video, the camcorder will refocus on this interference until it passes and then again attempt to refocus on your subject. Time and time again, valuable and irreplaceable video has been lost by professional investigators who become lackadaisical and forget to place their camcorder on manual focus or know how to turn it on and off quickly.

The quality of the lens your camera has is an extremely important part of your choice of which camera to purchase. Most camcorders come equipped with an 8:1 or 12:1 zoom capability. However, for surveillance situations, this won't allow you to get close enough to your subject in all cases. Look for a camera with at least a 22/1 optical zoom capacity. If you're attempting to take video from a distance of one or two blocks, or in some cases further than this, you may find it advantageous to utilize a telephoto lens. The telephoto lens will significantly multiply the effectiveness of your camera's inter telephoto optical capabilities. Using a telephoto lens also gives you the ability to distance yourself from the subject of your surveillance. The use of a camera with a standard 22/1 optical lens will effectively create a buffer or safety zone of around 100 yards during your surveillance. Never consider the Digital Zoom capability of a camera as we do not use Digital Zoom technology during surveillance. This technology merely takes the pixels of an image and enhances them electronically splitting them and filling in the pixels to make the image look larger, but the quality is greatly depleted. This poor quality image, coupled with the necessity of needing to stream it over the internet will make your efforts look more like a mosaic piece of art rather than a surveillance film. So remember, we NEVER use the digital zoom technology and shut this feature off in the main camera settings.

Your camera should also be equipped with a color view finder to make spotting the subject in a diverse background quicker. Many inexpensive cameras cut corners by having a black and white view finder since they expect the camera user to use the flip open screen. While we use both in surveillance, we use the view finder more as it enables the investigator to more quickly locate the subject and steady the image simultaneously using both hands and your head.

Finally your camera should come equipped with "image stabilization" technology. This cuts down on any minor movement caused by free holding the camera.

<u>Camera Make Model and Specifications</u>

3. Lens capacity with at least a 22/1 Optical Resolution.
4. Image Stabilizer
5. Color Viewfinder
6. Manual Focus Button

<u>Tripods/Monopods</u>

1. Standard six foot tripod
2. Standard Monopod

3. Jo Mount specialty equipment

The tripod is another important piece of equipment. One of the most common complaints about surveillance videotape is the fact that it is often so shaky that the viewer is unable to clearly identify the subject of an investigation or the activity that the subject is engaged in. A tripod can help to alleviate shaky videotape. There are several factors that can cause shaky video. First, you may be taping your subject for an extended period of time, often as long as an hour or more. It's very difficult to hold a camcorder still for ten minutes, let alone an hour. A tripod or single pod extending from the base of your camera will allow you to take clear and steady video. Secondly, if you're conducting surveillance from your vehicle, make sure that you turn your engine off while taping. It won't always be comfortable without air conditioning, but the vibration caused by your engine will significantly and adversely affect your video recording. If for some reason, you don't have a tripod, it's very important to use good video technique. Shooting steady videotape can also be accomplished by using a rest, or supporting the camera with both hands. Both elbows should be parallel to each other and tucked towards the middle of your chest. By holding the camcorder in this manner, you're allowing your skeletal structure to support the weight of the camcorder, instead of your muscles and tendons. If you hold the camcorder with one hand, flaring your elbow out to the side, your arms will inevitably become tired and start to shake, especially when you're taping for long periods of time. Using the proper recording technique that we've discussed will allow you to obtain clear and steady videotape evidence in almost any situation. However, you should always have and use a tripod for any extended vide recording.

If you are still using an older style camera with videotapes, then one videotape should be used for each subject you are surveilling. Never attempt to obtain evidence for another investigation on the same tape. Don't ever reuse an old tape or attempt to tape over old video. The risk of getting an old contaminated tape caught in your camera is not worth the $5.00 cost of a new tape. It is also extremely dangerous to review the videotape of your subject and then continue to use the same tape on a subsequent day. It's dangerous because most camcorders will automatically cut out a portion of the video when reactivated after playback. You may erase or lose valuable evidence by doing this.

Remember that the camcorder is one of the professional investigator's most important pieces of equipment. Cameras have come down in costs tremendously but are still an investment and need to be taken care of properly. Your camcorder will be affected by moisture, extreme heat, extreme cold and sudden temperature changes. Therefore, your camcorder should never be left in your vehicle in the sun and heat for the entire day. Treat it like your pet — it'll die if improperly cared for or subjected to abuse and neglect. Never ever leave your camcorder in your vehicle overnight. Your vehicle is never a safe or secure place to leave expensive equipment or valuable evidence.

Let's recap the operation of your camcorder.

1. Always charge your batteries before leaving the house and don't leave a battery in a camera which is not in use.

2. Know your camera before you attempt to use it in the field.

3. Always turn your camera to manual focus before filming.

4. Paranoia has no place in securing video. Remember that your camera is pre—trained to record dashboards, floorboards and trees. You must train your camera to stay on the subject under surveillance, no matter what happens, keep the subjects head at the top of your view finder screen and his feet at the bottom of your view finder screen.

5. Don't attempt to review your video in the field until your entire investigation is complete, so as to ensure no accidental erasure takes place.

GPS

When I initially started I recall doing investigations without a GPS. In fact for years I argued with my wife that I did not need a GPs because I had map quest on my phone and before that because I printed out directions to my surveillance or investigation prior to leaving the house. I just couldn't justify why I should pay money for a device I really didn't need. But I couldn't have been more incorrect, after almost three years of refusing the device, I received one from Santa. I didn't realize how much time I had wasted following a map or driving directions. And in those cases were I would go to one address and find my subject no longer lived there and then needed to follow-up visiting several other addresses the GPS was incredible of getting me from one location to the next. And even in surveillances when I was following someone on a day of errands and then entered their address as we headed back, I saw I could foresee all of the subject's turns. And then there were those cases when I thought the claimant was purposely taking me into a quiet residential area in order to detect a tail, but my GPS re-assured me this was a short cut back to the claimant's house. And then there are the special investigation days when I would set out to interview one person only to find this subject identified two more witnesses and just by calling them I could enter their address in my GPS and let the witness know exactly when I would be there to secure their statements.

I am now the GPS markets biggest advocate, it is a must have tool for the mobile investigator.

Equipment List

    A. <u>Covert Camera</u>

        1. Small Comfortable item with ability to hook in video capture device.

    2. Button Camera with hard drive, preferable hard wired with viewing monitor.
    3. Date and Time compatible
    4. Reliable! No cheap Glasses, Pen Cameras

B. <u>Camouflage Clothing and Backpack</u>

    1. Full gear obtainable from army navy store
    2. Binoculars
    3. Bug spray
    4. Pruning clippers
    5. Collapsible Stool
    6. Tri –pod
    7. Duct Tape

C. <u>Statement Recorder</u>

    1. Hard drive USB
    2. Ear bud Microphone for Two Way Statement Recording

D. <u>Lap Top</u>

    1. With-in last three years model

D. <u>Smart Phone</u>

    1. With internet service w/e-mail set up
    2. Notes Application

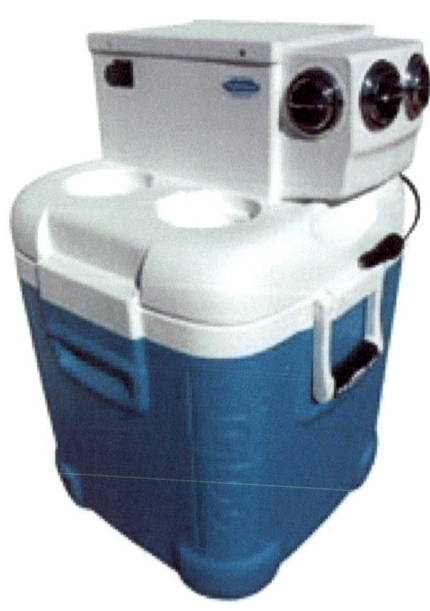

E. Pinnacle/Dazzle Video Capture and Video Compression Software for uploading and streaming video.

F. In-Car Cooling Unit- Swampy.net

There is only one cooler that will really work in the Florida heat and this is made by swamy.net. You can buy just the top part and use your own cooler. This is the ONLY cooler I will recommend. The MK3 ($600) and MK4 ($650)

VI. Video Software and Agency Management Software

During an investigation, securing video of a subject may be your key piece of evidence. In any personal injury case this is usually the key piece of evidence and initiating surveillance is all about getting that most valuable activity on video. Once it's on your cameras hard drive or memory, it will need to be downloaded to a computer, copied to a DVD and marked as evidence for storage. A copy will need to be delivered to your client. Today, most firms use software or websites that host powerful backend databases created to effectively manage the Agency's operation and deliver content to its clients. This content is the final report, an invoice and the video obtained. The software also acts as a virtual filing cabinet with all documents associated to the case stored electronically. This way it becomes an archive of all cases and accessible 24/7 from any Internet connection.

CaseFacts, www.casefactsonline.com is one of those Agency Management Software companies. They have integrated an embedded HTML5 player in their software that any video or audio statement uploaded can be STREAMED and not have to be downloaded first. CaseFacts shared with us how this works. An investigator will copy the video from his/her camera onto their computer making a copy in a DVD format and making it as evidence to logged in and stored and a material piece of evidence. Secondly, the original copy on the computer now needs to be  uploaded to the PI Agency's website using the CaseFacts backend system. Typically the video may be in a .AVI, Mpeg4 or WMV. With CaseFacts software the embedded player requires the video to be in an HTML5 h.264 format. This will enable the HTML5 Player to stream the video. If the video is not already in this format which it may not be, then available converter software is readily accessible. There are hundreds of such brands but two that come to mine cover both ends of the financial spectrum. Sorenson Squeeze www.sorensonmedia.com for instance can be upwards of $800.00 while www.freemaker.com is $9.99. Once the video is in the proper format it is ready to upload to the Agency's website for delivery to the client. The client will get a link when the file is ready for viewing.

In the CaseFacts system, the client gets a link to the entire electronic file. Here the client can access and view, the report, invoice and video from any Internet location. This enables a client to view the results of an investigation from their home, office or on the road. Inserted below is a typical screen a client will get once their video and report 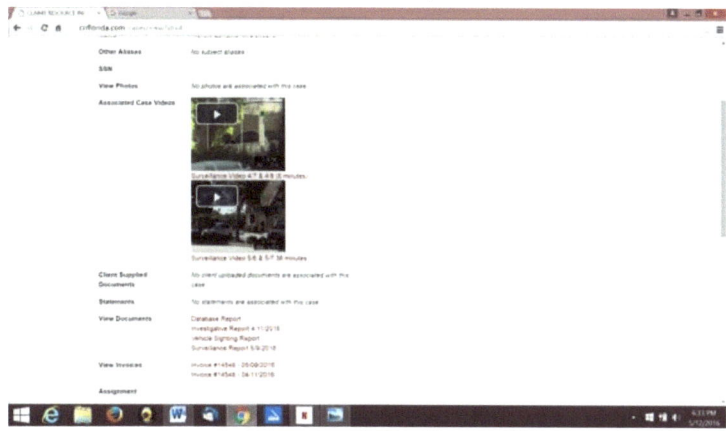 has been uploaded. The pictures in the screen are the surveillance video evidence uploaded and which streams directly from the site. Many large Clients like Insurance Companies don't allow their employees/adjuster to download files so a PI Agency being able to stream a video is very important to furthering their business practice.

Whether you're a single PI or managing a small firm, management software can make a huge difference in your organizational process and it certainly makes a statement about your level of professionalism. Many Investigators spend most of their career continually educating themselves in investigative techniques and developing that sixth sense that enables them to see things others don't and complete investigations instinctively. But now as a business owner the learning and educational process significantly changes. You're expected to know everything about investigations but developing your business sense is now your new objective.

A good case management system can cost upwards of a half million dollars to develop. To buy the system, you'll pay a tenth of that but that's still outside many start-up PI's budget. But there is NO EXCUSE not to have the same system as a SaaS (Software as a Service). Many PIs bundle or use several different software tools like Excel for case tracking, Outlook for emails, Quick Books for billing, DropBox for videos or routinely mail out CD's and DVDs to clients with report, invoice and video.

Most large companies invest heavily in software application development, and they do so for a compelling reason: their future might depend on it. Today, IT Strategy is considered Business Strategy and if you don't invest in technology and move ahead, then you're just going to fall behind.

Software spending in the United States has risen significantly, as software gradually became critical for almost every company's performance. Yet for most small PI Firms, the cost of acquiring a profession Internet or cloud based office application was out of reach or those products available fell short of accurately capturing a firm's requirements.

More than 40% of the respondents to a Computerworld Forecast survey said that their organizations will spend more on Software as a Service (SaaS) in 2015. This is not only a corporate trend, but one that enables the smaller firms to compete on a grander scale.

The bottom line is that we need to invest in our businesses and PI Agency Management Software is exactly that, an investment NOT an expense. Any company big or small that incorporates technology to enhance operations saves money. If it wasn't true, we wouldn't have computers.

Chapter Thirteen
Safe Guarding and Restricted Information

    I.   Gramm-Leach-Bliley Act
    II.   Fair Credit Reporting
    III.   NCIC

13. Gramm–Leach–Bliley Act (GLB)

The Gram-Leach-Bliley Act (GLB) also known as the Financial Services Modernization Act of 1999, was signed into law by President Bill Clinton opening up the market among banking companies, securities companies and insurance companies. The Gramm–Leach–Bliley Act allowed commercial banks, investment banks, securities firms, and insurance companies to consolidate. For example, Citicorp (a commercial bank holding company) merged with Travelers Group (an insurance company) in 1998 to form the conglomerate Citigroup, a corporation combining banking, securities and insurance services under a house of brands that included Citibank, Smith Barney, Primerica, and Travelers. This combination, announced in 1998, would have violated previous laws by combining securities, insurance, and banking. The law was passed to legalize these mergers.

Changes Caused by the Act

    Many of the largest banks, brokerages, and insurance companies desired the Act at the time. The justification was that individuals usually put more money into investments when the economy is doing well, but they put most of their money into savings accounts when the economy turns bad. With the new Act, they would be able to do both 'savings' and 'investment' at the same financial institution, which would be able to do well in both good and bad economic times.

What Does the GLB Act have to do with being a PI?

    With peoples personal information becoming more condensed and available at one location, the fear of Identity theft becomes a concern. Now a criminal may only have to access one major bank or insurance company and get personal information on thousands of account holders. So with the more relaxed freedoms GLB brought to businesses it also created a greater need for security and securing the information businesses maintained.

As a Private Investigator we also accumulate data and have access to databases that permit us to obtain a person's personal identifying information such as their date of birth and social security number. Our investigative reports will often contain information about a subject's daily activities, work place, vehicles and other profiling information. These reports, in the wrong hands could result in Identity Theft. Therefore, it is crucial that the information and files a Private Investigations Firm creates is held in a safe and secure manner.

Fair Credit Reporting Act (FCRA) is a United States Federal Law that regulates the collection, dissemination, and use of consumer information, including consumer credit information. Along with the Fair Debt Collection Practices Act (FDCPA), it forms the base of consumer credit rights in the United States.

Consumer Reporting Agencies – Credit Bureaus

Consumer reporting agencies (CRAs) are entities that collect and disseminate information about consumers to be used for credit evaluation and certain other purposes, including employment. Under the Fair Credit reporting Act, CRAs have a number of responsibilities including the following:

1. Provide a consumer with information about him or her in the agency's files and to take steps to verify the accuracy of information disputed by a consumer.
2. If negative information is removed as a result of a consumer's dispute, it may not be reinserted without notifying the consumer within five days, in writing.
3. CRAs may not retain negative information for an excessive period (typically seven years from the date of the delinquency with the exception of bankruptcies (10 years) and tax liens (seven years from the time they are paid).

The three big CRAs — Experian, TransUnion, and Equifax — do not interact with information furnishers directly as a result of consumer disputes. They use a system called E-Oscar. In some areas of the country, however, there are other credit bureaus. For example, in Texas, if a consumer tries to dispute information with Equifax directly, they must go through CSC Credit Services which is linked to the Equifax database. Nonetheless, errors made by CRAs and reflected in an individual's report are to be fixed and standard procedures are in place for consumer the opportunity to correct a mistake.

Nationwide Specialty Consumer Reporting Agencies

In addition to the three big CRAs, the FCRA also classifies dozens of other information technology companies as "nationwide specialty consumer reporting agencies" that produce individual consumer reports used to make credit determinations. Under Section 603(w) of the Fair Credit Reporting Act, the term "nationwide specialty consumer reporting agency" means a consumer reporting agency that compiles and maintains files on consumers on a nationwide basis relating to

1. medical records or payments;
2. residential or tenant history;
3. check writing history;
4. employment history; or
5. insurance claims

Because these nationwide specialty consumer reporting agencies sell consumer credit report files, they are required to provide annual disclosures of their report files to any consumers who request disclosure. This list of companies includes some of the database companies investigative firms have access to like TLO who is owned by Trans Union, Insurance Services Office (ISO) which Insurance company claims professionals use, Tenant Data Services and LexisNexis, another excellent investigative database resource.

Any time an Investigative Firm accesses a specialty reporting agency they will do so through a subscription agreement that requires vetting and strict access and use guidelines.

The reports we obtain through our database companies are not credit reports and should not be used to determine someone's credit status or financial ability to purchase a business or even rent an apartment. So be careful not to misuse this information or misconstrue this information for credit worthiness determination which should be done with a release and the roper credit report accessed.

Likelihood of Errors on a Credit Report

A large portion of consumer credit reports contain errors. A study released by the U.S. Public Interest Research Group in June 2004 found that 79% of the consumer credit reports surveyed contained some kind of error or mistake. However, the General Accountability Office released a study disputing this figure but the fact remains that mistakes can happen and in the digital age this may be the result of an inaccurate reported Social Security Number or address.

For the professional PI, this means that the Database Reports we receive should be used as an **investigative tool** only not factual information until verified by a separate and independent investigation. It's not unusual for a subject and his wife to both fill out a rental application and in the process their Social Security Numbers get reversed. Sop as an investigator we are always conscious of the fact that errors occur and we cross check and double check information to make sure it is accurate and the best information available.

III. NCIC

NCIC is a computerized index of criminal justice information (i.e.- criminal record history information, fugitives, stolen properties, missing persons). It is available to Federal, State, and Local Law Enforcement and other Criminal Justice Agencies. It is not intended to be used by Private Investigators and the access to such information by a PI can be a criminal offense.

The **National Crime Information Center**, or NCIC, was launched on January 27, 1967. NCIC helps criminal justice professionals apprehend fugitives, locate missing persons, recover stolen property, and identify terrorists. It also assists law enforcement officers in performing their official duties more safely and provides them with information necessary to aid in protecting the general public.

How NCIC is used: Criminal justice agencies enter records into NCIC that are accessible to law enforcement agencies nationwide. For example, a law enforcement officer can search NCIC during a traffic stop to determine if the vehicle in question is stolen or if the driver is a wanted by law enforcement. The system responds instantly. However, a positive response from NCIC is not probable cause for an officer to take action. NCIC policy requires the inquiring agency to make contact with the entering agency to verify the information is accurate and up-to-date. Once the record is confirmed, the inquiring agency may take action to arrest a fugitive, return a missing person, charge a subject with violation of a protection order, or recover stolen property.

The FBI provides a host computer and telecommunication lines to a single point of contact in each of the 50 states, the District of Columbia, Puerto Rico, the U.S. Virgin Islands, Guam, and Canada, as well as federal criminal justice agencies. Those jurisdictions, in turn, operate their own computer systems, providing access to nearly all local criminal justice agencies and authorized non-criminal justice agencies nationwide. The entry, modification, and removal of records are the responsibility of the agency that entered them.

Success Stories

Following a speeding-related traffic stop of an individual in Newhall, California in December 2005, the California Highway Patrol conducted a search of NCIC. The search produced a terrorism-related lookout instructing the officer to contact the FBI's Terrorist Screening Center (TSC) for assistance in identifying the subject, who was confirmed to be a positive identity match to the individual listed in the NCIC lookout and was the main subject of an FBI San Francisco international terrorism investigation. Traveling with the subject were two additional individuals who were fully identified. The subject was arrested for possession of methamphetamine, and a female passenger was arrested on two outstanding warrants.

In 2009, an NCIC search on a license plate number revealed the plate was linked to a vehicle owned by a man wanted for the July 2008 murder of his mother in Mississippi. When the Florida sheriffs that had queried the plate approached the vehicle, the suspect pulled a sawed-off shotgun from under a blanket and pointed the weapon at the deputies. The deputies shot and killed the suspect before he could fire.

Perhaps one of the more well-known examples of an NCIC search involved Oklahoma City bomber Timothy McVeigh.

About 90 minutes after the bombing, an Oklahoma State Highway Patrolman had stopped McVeigh and arrested him on unrelated weapons charges. After identifying McVeigh as the renter of the explosives-laden Ryder truck, investigators entered his name into the NCIC computer. They found that McVeigh was sitting—two days after the bombing—in a nearby jail cell on the unrelated weapons charges.

NCIC searches are just another example of how Law Enforcement is leveraging technology and information-sharing to track down criminals.

MIS USE

Federal regulations and NCIC policy have classified NCIC information as <u>sensitive and have restricted access to and use of such information to authorized criminal justice agencies for criminal justice purposes.</u> These purposes include conducting criminal investigations or screening applicants for employment in criminal justice positions.

In December 1991, 20 individuals in New Jersey and Florida were indicted under federal bribery, theft of government property, and computer fraud statutes for selling criminal history information obtained from NCIC.

A private Investigator CAN NOT access this information. Asking your friend who is a Police Officer to run a subject's name through the NCIC database is a Felony!

Chapter Fourteen
Report Writing and Field Note Taking

I. Introduction
II. Adaptation of the Report
III. Taking Notes
IV. Using a Smart Phone
V. Connecting the Dots
VI. Proof Reading
VII. Outline Samples
VIII. Photos and Video Capture

14. Introduction

A report is the communication of information to others. The most important and essential ingredient of the report is "fact". Fact is generally described in reporting as "new information"

The ultimate basis of any good report is facts. That means direct observations, inspections, experience or research. By definition, a report must be more than vague "ideas" and "opinions". The ideas must have solid basis in fact.

The modern report is one of the most interesting developments of the last century. The growth of the technical professional in all industries and the widening activities of those responsible for handling concerns have all led to the increased need for written communication. Due to this extreme growth, the written report has become of utmost importance especially in providing a permanent record.

The report is an account of something heard, seen, read or done. A written report is an account of something heard, seen, read or done expressed in writing. Today, reports play an important part of public and corporate affairs. If no standardized form is furnished, it is often very difficult to develop a logical arrangement for a report to incorporate all of the facts a good report must contain.

Adaptation to the Reader

A good report writer makes his or her reports fit the interests, peculiarities, knowledge and desires of his/her readers. No matter how correct the form of the report, the style is inadequate and poor if it is unsuited to the intended reader.

Therefore you do not want to be too overly technical. Attempt to relay your facts in clear, concise everyday language.

It is a very good idea to write down phrases that you will become accustomed to using often. Also the report, although factual, is more interesting if it tells a story and maintains a logical sequence of events in a commonsense sequence that the reader can follow. Your report should also attempt to answer any question it may present.

EXAMPLE

Upon my arrival at 5:30 a.m., I noticed the gate was open. According to the neighbor I spoke to later, I learned the subject usually leaves the gate open after she leaves in the morning and does not close it until she returns home in the evening.

Be Thorough

All of the facts that have a bearing on the incident must be recorded in an easy-to-read format. All directly connected circumstances must be included and addressed. Include all persons interviewed and steps taken. Remember your memory alone is not sufficient to insure completeness. You will have to refer to your field notes, sketches, pictures, etc. If your report requires any further explanation, then you have not thoroughly answered the questions who, what, where, when, why and how.

Be Accurate

One of the main requirements of a report is that it be accurate. Report on the facts of the incident. If opinions are reported, they must be clearly labeled as such. The information upon which a report is based must be factual.

Taking Notes

The heart of the report starts with good notes. Eventually you will learn quickly what types of notes you will need to compile a good report. By following your investigative outlines, you will not only learn ideas valuable in the investigation, but also to acquire and conduct the steps that would be expected. These field notes are referred to as "work product". They are usually the only notes used in testifying in a case. Your report written later is not considered work product and therefore often not admissible as evidence. If you can remember the O. J. Simpson trial you may recall the investigator who appeared on the stand flipping through his loose leaf note-book filled with his progressive field notes. These were the only notes he used to refresh his recollection of what he heard, saw, read or did at the time.

The better your notes are, the easier the report is to compile when you are done with your investigation. And fortunately, for all investigators the reporting process gets easier over time.

Use Your Smart Phone Note Taking Application

After many years in business, I can say I have learned one thing, which is that I never stop learning. Learn to be a good listener as ideas will come to you if you are paying attention.

Recently, Kristen a graduate student working on a human behavior study project asked me, "if you could change the behavior of your staff to solve a business process problem what would it be?" I thought carefully and said, getting the investigators to spend less time procrastinating about their reports and just get them turned into the office quicker. The sooner I get their investigative reports in the office, the quicker I can bill out their time and get our money.

Cash flow is a big part of any business and your clients need to have their reports before they submit an invoice for payment. When an agency has ten or twenty investigators the work turn-in schedule is very important. There is nothing more aggravating then to one week and then each of them turn in ten reports the following week making the fluctuation in work unpredictable and overwhelming. Getting my investigators to routinely turn in five completed reports a week on a steady basis would not only create a constant stream of income, but also a predictable work load. No investigative owner should ever assume he won't have to review reports. All reports must be reviewed by the owner or manager of the agency, no matter what the skill level of the case investigator may be.

After explaining my business in more depth, Kristen asked if I had considered offering incentives to the investigators. Why should I have to give an investigator an incentive or reward for doing their job. I explained that I had in the past gone this route through a program that rewarded the investigators with the highest bill-outs each week. I also paid a bonus to the investigator who shot the most video each month. Having been there and done that, I now preferred a tool rather than a stimulus. I had used in the past dictation machines and voice recognition software which helped, but still required a lap top or significant editing. Kristen asked me if there was any one investigator that seemed to be more productive or turned in his or her work with more regularity than the others and, there was. By interviewing this person, we found that he would text message his notes throughout the day and email them to himself so that most of the report writing work was already done by the end of his day. Today, I encourage all investigators to use a notes application on their smart phone throughout the day to increase their productivity and reduce report writing time. As a result, we have improved our turn around reporting time, maintained a better case volume flow and consistent weekly bill-out totals.

With this simple procedure, we have adjusted our guidelines to give investigators five days to work an assignment, followed by days to compile and submit the report to the office for processing.

Connecting the Dots

What I am going to say next may go against everything else you have ever heard about report writing. It may even go against prior training you have had as a Police Officer, Military Investigator or Detective. Since many Investigators come from a law enforcement environment, they are routinely told to keep their opinions out of a report and report just the facts. It is typically a supervisor or prosecuting attorney that analyzes your information and develops a legal strategy. However in the private sector, there is only you and your client. In a domestic case, you are the professional who needs to thoroughly explain the value of the evidence you developed. In an insurance case, the claim investigator needs to lead the adjuster through the investigation so important evidence can be gathered for the defense. Think of it this way, an attorney will take a case and in a court room setting deliver an opening argument. The argument will be what they think happened and how they intent to prove it or what the other party contends and how they intend to rebut it. This is where they add their strategy and then begin to submit the evidence to make their argument. A good PI, based on his experience will usually have a plan of action in mind or develop a plan once some information has been developed. The bottom line is that in order to be valuable to our client we need to serve their interests. This means develop information helpful to the reason we were hired.

Whether you like it or not, you are not impartial, you work for your client and are looking to develop information helpful to them not information detrimental to them. This is the business side of being a private investigator. You need to understand that it's not just reporting the facts regardless of what they are. It is your job to interpret your findings and report then in the best light and most favorable light of your client. Throughout your report you need to keep in mind your position and strategy. The Private Investigator hired by OJ Simpson did not look for evidence that pointed to him being guilty. He was developing information to show or imply his innocence.

If my client was reported to have selfishly drank the last of the water in a survivor situation, after my investigation I may write that my investigation learned that the glass of water was left half full. I don't want to give the connotation it was half empty and in fact I may have even learned or secured a statement saying that the glass was never filled to the top. So I present a problem for my accuser in determining exactly how much my client even ever drank. Maybe it was just a sip and it was predetermined that everyone could take a sip each day so my client did nothing wrong. In this simple exercise, I developed a defense once I learned a little about the details. This is the same exercise you must go through with each and every case you work. Your efforts regardless of how they were preformed must be interpreted and reported in a manner beneficial to your client. Sometimes you will need to lake extra steps to prove your point.

Proofreading

After you have completed your report, you should read your report thoroughly to make sure that it says exactly what you desire it to say. A good report writer will be totally objective while proofreading his report; try to imagine yourself as the reader and not the writer. Look for essential things that you may have over looked in the report. Read your report out loud. Awkward phrasing is often hard to read orally. By doing this you should get some idea of how effectively you organize your thoughts. And by all means spellcheck your reports.

Reporting and Investigations Outline Samples

Many Companies have specific reports formats they will require you to follow. The following report formats are just an example or recommendation of a report format. It is important that each investigator be completely familiar with report styles and rules for reporting. It is very important to keep to a format so that all reports conform to a particular flow. This way your clients will get use to where to look for specific information and can resource it quickly when needed.

Follow your report outline as close as possible so as not to leave out any information. Review not only your outline but also <u>any particular requests made by the client</u>. Review any information given to you by the client or by your company. Typically at the onset of an assignment you will receive specific instructions specifying your assignment. This assignment sheet must be carefully and thoroughly reviewed so that all of your client's questions and pertinent information are covered in your report and the report is <u>adapted</u> to your client's interests and concerns. A good report format can keep you on track and emphasize your ability to provide a results oriented product. The following is just an example and not meant to be the best or only option. Your agency will provide you with a report sample to follow. If you are staring out on your own, it is recommended that you design your own report formats and outlines to follow and keep your reports consistent looking. I have provided an example of a surveillance outline report for your review.

CONFIDENTIAL INVESTIGATIVE REPORT
(DATE)

CLIENTS COMPANY	Re:	Your File No. : 000-00-000
CLIENT'S NAME		Addt'l File No. : 0000-00000
STREET ADDRESS		Our File No. : 000-0000-000
CITY, STATE, ZIP, CODE		Insured: NAME OF INSURED
		Employee: NAME OF EMPLOYEE
		SSN: (Partial)
		D/L: DATE OF LOSS

Assignment Received	:	MONTH/DAY/YEAR
Previous Correspondence	:	MONTH/DAY/YEAR *(if letter/memo)*
Type of Claim	:	STATE TYPE OF CLAIM
Alleged Injury	:	STATE INJURY OR INJURIES
Assignment	:	STATE TYPE OF ASSIGNMENT (include number of days assigned to case, evening, daytime, limited surveillance number on hours each day, 4 hours weekend. weekday, 2 man surveillance, surveillance with $ limit, and any other specifics concerning EXACTLY what was requested.

Synopsis

Investigator: Name of Investigator / The Investigative Agency

Date of Investigation: Day of Week / Month / Day / Year; Time
EXAMPLE: Monday, July 7, 2014 (6:00 a.m. - 3:30 p.m.); Tuesday, July 8, 2014 (6:00 a.m. - 3:30 p.m.).

Objectives: Determine Employee's daily activities, degree of disability and employment status. (Be specific. If they want to see how active "on the weekend" say so. State whether it was a rush to see what the employee had planned this day because" he /she cancelled a doctors appointment or therapy visit", etc. If a 2 man investigation state why necessary).

Pertinent Information: *Most Important Category DO NOT JUST SUMMARIZE THE DAY. Dictate the <u>highlights,</u> and special events that specifically portray the employee activity level and physical capability, this is what's important. How does what the employee did relate to his injury and what he is not suppose to be doing? Always indicate how much video documentation was obtained. What significant event or information was developed. Review "assignment sheet" and answer any specific questions the client raised). In most cases it is recommended that he speak to at lease one or two neighbors before leaving a surveillance for the day to* *determine whether there is more information available about your subject that you would not otherwise obtain.*

Then give your recommendation of what needs to be done as a follow-up. Always report this in a separate paragraph so that the reader does not miss it. This is vitally important for us to be able to conduct a complete and thorough investigation. We do not want cases being closed that are not complete.

EXAMPLE
During my day of surveillance .....

1) The employee was very active being first observed at _____ a.m./p.m. as he/she
   (Briefly give a general overview of what the employee did during your surveillance efforts) When describing the Employee's movements, cover the following briefly)
   a. Did the employee exhibit a limp?
   c. Did the employee walk with a cane?
   d. Was the employee observed with any type of orthopedic aid?
   e. Was the employee capable of entering and exiting his vehicle without hesitation or the appearance of stiffness/restriction?
   f. Can the employee drive?
   g. Did the employee partake in any strenuous activity?
   h. Did the employee do any bending, lifting, squatting, sitting or standing for a long period of time.

2) Indicate whether the employee is working? or whether there is any indication that he/she might be?

3) Briefly indicate whether the employee was observed performing, or found involved in any noteworthy activity that may be contradictory to his <u>current allegations</u>.(the specificity concerning movements and physical abilities should be commented on in the actual details. Keep your pertinent information informative, concise and to the point!

In a separate paragraph indicate your efforts to develop NEW or corroborating information about the Employee's activities. What did you determine during you neighborhood contact at the end of the day? This information is necessary to help direct the investigation, utilize time wisely, and focus on obtaining the necessary evidence to defend or verify the claim. **If the employee was found WORKING skip to number 3.**

   a) What did the neighbors have to say regarding the employee's normal everyday activities?

   b) Does what the neighbors say support or contradict your findings?

    c) If the employee is found working...
        1) Proceed to identify co-workers and supervisor.
        2) Verify employment through administration/personnel department.
            a. start date/length of employment
            b. rate of pay/salary
            c. specific job duties/supervisors name

Finally most important, is your thoughts and recommendations on how to proceed. Don't just say I think we need two more days of surveillance. Give your reasons and be specific about what still needs to be done. Review the follow-up suggestions in Chapter 6 or call the office for advise. Any investigator with less than six months of employment should review all verbal reports and follow-up suggestion first with his supervisor before calling a client.

As your last sentence state (Please see page _____ for Details of Investigation).

Physical Description:

1) Race/Color
2) Sex
3) Date of Birth and Age
4) Height
5) Build - Slender/Medium/Muscular/Heavy/Obese
6) Weight
7) Hair Color/Length
8) Facial Hair
9) Eye Color
10) Other Identifying Characteristics

Verbal Report:

1) Date
2) Time
3) How or with who detailed message given? Be specific (voice mail or adjuster/secretary)
4) Full or partial report.
5) Any follow-up instruction by client? If further authorization given was it clearly indicated that additional charges would apply? Was the original limit increased? Is so by what amount? Was a two-man investigation authorized? Is so clearly state so.
6) If **NO** verbal report was requested, state the following:
As requested, no verbal report was made on this file.

BE CAREFUL HOW YOU DOCUMENT ANY DIFFICULTY YOU HAD CONTACTING THE ADJUSTER. WE DO NOT WANT TO OFFEND THE ADJUSTER OR MAKE THEM LOOK BAD TO A SUPERVISOR OR ANYONE ELSE REVIEWING A REPORT.

Do not leave a message asking the adjuster to call the office. Leave a complete message regarding the outcome of your investigation when verbal report is made. Advise that a partial/full report will follow. Advise that you are in the field but if the adjuster should need to reach you they can leave a message at the office for you to call them.

Case Status: Is case open or closed? If the client asked you to diary the case, indicate the diary date when the case is scheduled to do again. Also indicate what may still need to be done once additional authorization is given.

Thank you very much for this opportunity to have been of service. Should you have any questions regarding this investigation, you can contact me at (telephone number of office where you retrieve your messages. Use ONE NUMBER, and NEVER let other Investigator working for you or helping out give different phone numbers. Get use to **branding** and giving out just one number)

Enclosures: List your enclosures. Do not describe in detail, this was done in Documentation caption. Just indicate the number of different pieces of evidence enclosed.

EXAMPLE:

Enclosures: (1) Three still photographs
                  (2) One business card
                  (3) Copy of occupational license
                  (4) Video tape copy (Attorney only)

cc: Joe D. Brown, Esquire
       1289 Tree Limb Lane
       Orlando, Florida 34673

Indicate whether any copy of the report should be forwarded to another party. Instruct your typist to print an extra copy of the report when you are dictating this request. Enclosures should be copies and double prints must be enclosed to send both parties all the indicated enclosures.

If a video tape copy only goes to the attorney make sure this is stated in the enclosure as indicated above.

Details of Investigation

Background Database Internet Research

All surveillance reports are to include this caption regardless of whether a search was conducted. When a search has not been requested, the caption should read "None requested". If there is a search pending, it should then read, "Pending _____ history". (i.e., Criminal, Driver's License, Workers' Compensation, Florida Public Records Search (Nexis Lexis, IRB, TLO, etc...)

When a search has been conducted and the information received address the evidence or enclosures in detail. A few examples are as follows:

Enclosure No. 2 is the FDLE, (State, County) criminal history search requested. This search revealed the subject was most recently found guilty of burglary in June of 2013. According to the arrest information the subject was arrested as he attempted to flee a convenience store at 4:30 am exiting through a broken window in the rear of the store. Unbeknown to the subject the police were on the scene as a silent alarm was triggered some 20 minutes prior to his arrest. Prior to this arrest we also found that in 2009, the subject was prosecuted for Assault, but the charge was subsequently acquitted. The specific details of this case were not available at this time and would have to be ordered from the county archives. Should you require more information of this offense, I would suggest ordering the file, which should take 4-5 days.

The subject's (Employee's) driving history revealed he has had four citations dating back to 2001. The last citation was issued in 2011, for careless driving.

For Workers' Compensation searches report as much information as possible about the claim. Identify the date(s) of the WC claim, lost time, injury, and carrier.

The subject's (Employee's) vehicle history search revealed he currently owns a 2014 Ford Mustang, along with a 2002 Toyota Corolla. The subject's (Employee's) wife (name), is also listed on the registration.

If you have the copy of the search requested (which should always be the case, include the document with the report and refer to it by its enclosure number as indicated above).

After dictating **ANY** DATABASE information always include the following disclaimer: "This information was provided by a third party and should be used as an investigative tool only and should be verified through a separate and independent investigation."

Next go online and check the County Property Appraise to see who owns the house, how much they paid. If the target doesn't own the house secure the landlord/owners name and address in case you need to contact them.

Search all available online county records such as the County Recorder's Office for any civil or criminal filings. Review all available file information on line.

Use your Browser to see what pops up after entering their full name and city.

Any and all information obtained should be listed in your report and captioned prior to initiating the investigation.

A sample of this caption should be as follows:

Internet Search

During a name and address search, I found the claimant and his wife are listed as member of The Villages Dance Club, promoted by Dancers Abound located at 11962 CR101, Suite 101, The Villages, FL 32162. The shop is operated by manager Deb Moss and Jim Shomaker.

On the web the clubs URL is http://danceclub-thevillages.com/index.html. Here I found a picture of the claimant and his wife who are referred to as "George And Martha posing on the dance floor. I found their next event is called the "2014 Dance Off" It will occur in March. Below is a copy of the Clubs Event notice......

EARLY IN YOUR INVESTIGATION YOU MAY ALSO FIND THAT A PRE-SURVEILLANCE INVESTIGATION IS NEEDED TO IDENTIFY THE EMPLOYEE, LOCATE THE RESIDENCE OR DETERMINE A SUITABLE SURVEILLANCE LOCATION. MANY TIMES THIS IS IMPERATIVE ESPECIALLY WHEN A RURAL BOX AND ROUTE NUMBER IS THE ONLY ADDRESS KNOWN.

THE FOLLOWING CAPTIONS ARE **EXAMPLES** OF HOW THIS INFORMATION CAN BE DICTATED.

Pre-Surveillance Investigation - Employee's Residence
<u>Route 5, box 54-A , Ocala Florida 32970</u>　　　　　Thursday, February 1, 2014
<u>4:33 p.m.</u>

On the above captioned date, I proceeded to canvass the Anderson Heights area located approximately 16 miles south of S.R. 55 and Hwy. 247 on Samson Rd. also known as Route 6. The Employee's residence was found to be located in the Samson Mobile Home Park on lot A. Specifically, the Employee's residence is a doublewide mobile home, which is yellow in color with white trim and is in excellent condition. Underneath the carport, which is just to the left of the residence I observed no vehicles.

Immediately after my arrival in the area I observed an elderly female subject, who is apparently the Employee's wife, arrive at the residence on a bicycle. After placing the bicycle underneath the carport, the female subject then entered the residence where her activities were no longer observable.

At this point, having located the residence and familiarizing myself with the area, I elected to depart the area and return on the following day.

Pre-Surveillance Investigation-Employee's Residence
2115 Nottingham Rd., Melbourne, Florida 32935   Thursday, February 1, 2014
4:30p.m.

During the late afternoon hours of the above captioned date, I was in the general area of the Employee's residence on an unrelated matter and elected to make a personal visit to his residence for the purpose of making some general observations as well as familiarizing myself with the area. Upon my arrival in the area, I found that the Employee's residence is located in a middle, working class, residential area with in the city limits of Melbourne, Florida.

Specifically, the Employee's residence is a one story, single family home that is light brown in color with brown trim. I noted that the residence was in very good condition and the lawn was immaculately landscaped. Parked on the swell of the road, directly in front of the Employee's residence was a silver Mazda pickup truck, which was attached to a small utility trailer, bearing Florida registration AI5-62T. I noted the trailer contained various types of lawn maintenance equipment. The side of the trailer stated "Timely Lawn Service".

Also, at the time of my arrival, I was fortunate enough to have the opportunity to directly observe the employee. The employee, who was standing underneath the carport, which is on the southeast side of the residence is a white male, approximately 49 years of age, approximately 6'1" tall, weighs 195 pounds and has brown hair, which is graying. I noted the employee was wearing a T-shirt, blue jeans, and black rubber soled shoes. I observed the employee drinking a mug of coffee while looking about the neighborhood. After just a few moments, the employee turned and entered his residence at which point his activities were no longer observable. Not wanting to arouse suspicion, I elected to depart the area.

WHEN NO PRE-SURVEILLANCE IS NECESSARY THE INVESTIGATION WILL PROCEED ONTO THE ACTUAL SURVEILLANCE.

Surveillance - Employee's Residence
1276 Deer Lake Circle Apopka Florida 32712   Monday, July 7, 2014
6:00 p.m.

The first day of a surveillance is typically started at 6:00 a.m. during the week. Make certain you leave early enough to account for your travel time. Our first objective is to determine whether the subject may be gainfully employed. Once this is determined we then will concentrate on the severity of the injury. What can and can't the employee do? The more activity we observe and document, the better prepared we will be in defending the claim against exaggeration or outright fraud.

01) State full residential address in the caption.
02) Briefly provide driving directions to the residence. If the address is in a metropolitan area just provide directions from the nearest WELL-KNOWN intersection. If the address is a rural area then give more explicit directions.
03) Indicate telephone number and whether published or unpublished.
04) List persons residing with the employee whenever possible (since dictation will occur after the investigation, this information should be known).
05) Describe type of residence (single family/multifamily/condominium/townhouse/apartment).
06) Color and other identifying characteristics
07) Economic status of neighborhood (lower, middle or upper working class)
08) Social Environment (adult community/retirement community; closely knit residential community/rural sparsely populated community)
09) Maintenance (Well maintained/in need of repair/manicured lawn/trash & debris everywhere)
10) Upon arrival were there any lights on in or outside of the residence?
11) Were there any signs that some early morning movement may have already taken place?
12) Identify all vehicles at the residence fully color/make/model/tag numbers. (later you will run the tag and put more information in the report under the caption "Dept. Of Highway Safety and Motor Vehicles"
12) Indicate the position of the vehicles in relationship to the residence.
13) Do any of the vehicles exhibit a registration sticker correlating to the Employee's month of birth?
15) Report any other observations noted.
16) Describe and assume your surveillance position.
EXAMPLE: I assumed a surveillance position approximately 200 yards north of the Employee's property. This position afforded me an unobstructed view of both the Employee's front door and vehicle parked in the driveway.

Always start each step you take with a caption. Your report should flow like a detailed story. Take your time to ensure that your complete thoughts and observations are expressed.

As you dictate your report, remember your focus, concentration should be on the employee and his/her movements. Don't go into detail about the description of neighbors, the milkman or other less pertinent observations. No weather forecasts please (we need to do surveillance in the rain because we can not guarantee the weather. Furthermore many people go to work in the rain! Employment is our primary concern. Case management is also important and if you try to work on only sunny days, you will fall behind quickly with your caseload.)

Details regarding the Employee's identify, conduct, movements, affiliations, associations, transactions, reputation or character are your focal points. Your observations, investigative findings concerning these involvement's need to be documented and well detailed in your report. Dictate in complete sentences and allow the reader to follow your line of thinking.

During your surveillances you will routinely run the registration of the vehicle(s) observed at the residence to determine which one the subject may own or operate. You will also "run" the tag registrations of the people stopping by to visit the employee.

Initially your first call will usually occur around 8:00 - 9:00 a.m. The closest tag agency and telephone number to call can be found in the company handbook and will depend on the area you are working in. Once you make the call you should be aware of all the information available. The following caption is an example of how this information should be captioned. The information listed below the caption should be obtained and incorporated into the dictated paragraph under this caption.

EXAMPLE

Department of Highway Safety & Motor Vehicles
<u>Vehicle Registration Information</u>   <u>Monday, July 7, 2014</u>
<u>8:33 a.m.</u>

Identify make, model and year of vehicle
Subject's <u>full</u> name
Date of Birth
Address that appears on registration
Driver's License number
<u>Lien holder</u>
Anything unusual or contradictory to the information already known

SAMPLE DICTATION

I contacted the above agency to determine the owner of the late model pearl colored Dodge Caravan bearing the Florida registration of 5AB-CDI parked in the driveway. This vehicle was identified as a 1992 Dodge Caravan registered to a Jim F. Brown whose address was listed as 1276 Deer Lake Circle Apopka, Florida 32712. Jim Brown's date of birth was indicated as July 7, 1950 and his driver's license number was B420-678-50-287. Furthermore, the lien holder on this vehicle was identified as Marty's Buy Here Pay Here located at 560 Semoran Blvd., Altamonte, Florida.

<u>10:30 a.m.</u>

By 10:30 a.m., you are requested to determine whether the employee is inside the residence. This is done solely to insure that we are not sitting on an empty house or the Employee's prior residence before he moved to Europe. This is NOT a time to pretext the EMPLOYEE or ANY family member for information. Therefore, information concerning ONLY whether or not the employee is at home needs to be addressed. DO NOT go into any details concerning your contact.

If you are required to leave your surveillance position to make the above telephone call, indicate the time you left the area.

EXAMPLE

10:28 a.m.

Finding no early morning movement by the employee, I elected to momentarily depart my surveillance position to proceed and verify the Employee's presence in the residence.

10:30 a.m.

Although the employee had not been seen, I confirmed that he/she was, in fact, inside the residence. (To determine how to make these discreet findings refer to using pretexts)

10:37 a.m.

Having confirmed that the employee was in fact inside the residence, I returned to the Employee's neighborhood to resume my investigation. Upon my return, I noticed no movement by either vehicle at the residence nor any sign of the employee or any other subject outside. In anticipation of any possible activity, I immediately resumed my surveillance position.

EXAMPLE

10:30 a.m.

As suspected, it was determined that no one appeared to be inside the residence. Apparently either the employee had spent the preceding night away from the residence or he had left prior to my early morning arrival (In this case you would proceed with a thorough neighborhood inquiry to determine why the employee was not home). This would be done BEFORE you leave the area for the day.

Sometimes you need to advise the reader that you are moving onto another step so, follow me. This can be done by first prefacing your move before actually doing it.

Example: It was apparent that the telephone number provided by the employee was not for this Deer Lake Dr. address. I, therefore, elected to contact a Nationwide Database to ascertain what address did correlate to this number.

National Database -Telephone Number Records Search
(407) 933-2010

Through this Database I determined that the telephone number listed was actually for the business, Claims Resource, Incorporated. The account address was identified as 414 Greenbrier Ave, Suite 62, Celebration, Florida 34747.

I proceeded to contact this business in order to determine what if any association exists between the employee and this business.

Telephone Contact - The Business
(407) 933-2010   Monday, July 7, 2014
11:30 a.m.

In the example above, I continued to move the reader from one step of my investigation into the next.

During this conversation let's assume the telephone call developed an address for the employee. Once obtaining this information we then proceeded to the address to verify that the employee did in fact reside at this location.

Employee's Residence-333 Kiwi Court - Casselberry, Florida 32707
12:15 p.m. VT

Once at this location I immediately spotted the employee out side cutting the grass pushing a conventional lawn mower. I immediately began shooting video of this activity. From the on-set it was apparent that the mower was an older model and not self propelled. The employee, who was leaning forward at approximately a 45 degree angle was sweating profusely as it appeared the lawn was severely over grown etc......

(Make note of the **VT** in this caption which denotes Video Taken. Be certain that the time on the tape and the times in your report MATCH. If the times are off for some reason it must be addressed whenever the video is mentioned).

Verbal Report
3:40 p.m.

Subsequent to your surveillance efforts a report to the client needs to be made. This will be your opportunity to bring the client up to date and also advise him/her of your recommended follow-up. Verbal reports are most often given at the end of your authorized investigation.

I HAVE LISTED SOME HELPFUL HINTS THAT MAY MAKE YOUR REPORT WRITIG GO A BIT SMOOTHER.

Quite often we say things in our reports that although occurred exactly as we stated, can mislead the client into thinking that we were not as thorough as we should have been and, therefore, a margin for error appears to exist.

For example, let's say your report goes as follows:

> A white female approximately 5' tall, 140 pounds, blonde hair and appearing to be approximately 42 years of age exited the residence. This subject resembled the description provided by your office, and thus, for the remainder of this report will be referred to as the employee.

In actuality, having read this report, it seems that you immediately assumed that this subject was the employee merely from the fact that she resembled the characteristics of the employee. In a true sense, this is usually how we first identify a subject and then later proceed in verifying that it is, in fact, the employee. Therefore, at no time while you're writing the report several days later, should there be any doubt in your mind whether or not this subject was or was not the employee.

Therefore, this sentence should start out simply as;

> The employee, a white female approximately 5' tall, 140 pounds, blonde hair and appearing to be approximately 42 years of age exited the residence.

This eliminates any doubt that may be placed in our client's mind that the subject we followed was not, in fact, the employee and only assumed to be based on her description.

Later in your report you can also provide other information based on the vehicle's registration and perhaps a discreet conversation with the subject, which further corroborated your identification of the employee.

Surveillance **LOST EMPLOYEE**

It's not difficult to lose a employee during a "tail" as we have all found out. Taking the time to word this misfortune may help ease the reader into what you are about to say. Once I read a report where the investigator had followed the employee all over town then merely stated that he lost the employee at a red light.

Many times intervening traffic, construction and traffic lights are the true demons in this business. Take the time to explain the circumstances that prohibited your continuing efforts. Don't go into detail three pages long but give a simple explanation. Always explain that you continued in the same general area as the employee was last seen and thoroughly canvassed the area in an attempt to relocate the employee. I also think it sounds a little bit better if we refer to our relationship with the employee as "contact".

Example: I lost contact with the employee due to intervening traffic at the intersection of A1A and Boogie Board Rd. I continued south on A1A for several miles, thoroughly canvassing the area, however, I found no opportunity to relocate the employee.

And finally, always remember to **RETURN** to the Employee's residence in case he was only running an errand. Many times you will find that the employee returns to his residence within a short time period. He may also be carrying evidence to provide a clue as to where he was. It's typical to lose someone and observe him return home 45 minutes later with a large bag possibly bearing the green and orange K-Mart insignia on the side. It's doesn't take a Ph.D. to surmise where he was. Make note of this observation and then continue with your surveillance efforts. Then stay an hour or two longer into the day to make up for the time the employee was out of your view. If you have nothing else scheduled for this day, it is recommended you get a good surveillance position and remain in the area UNTIL the employee returns home. This way we will at least get good film of them returning to the residence and who knows what they might unload from the vehicle or do immediately following their return. Chances are this may put off an urgent need to work the case again the following day.

Surveillance **PHOTOS/VIDEO**

Photographic documentation in every report should be an objective of any company reporting requirements. It's easy to tell the investigators who have learned the video capture technique and have it down to a simple and easy process however for those less skilled with PC's it may be a challenge they need to spend more time on to over come. With the ability to make prints from your Video, you should avoid stopping video to shoot from a still digital camera. Digital cameras are really obsolete unless you need very high quality photographs and are not doing

surveillance. In this case the save digital file will be all you need to save and send your client. The digital file can also be inserted into your report.

In order to extract a photograph from a digital video recording you will need a Video Capturing device and software from companies like Dazzle and Pinnacle. These devices are made up of a hardware device in which a cable runs from the device to your computer by a USB cord. The device itself will hook up with your digital camera through an S Cable, RCA Composite Cables or DV Cable.

Remember in order to capture a photo with the time and date stamp called meta data, a video capture device MUST be used. The same holds true for the actual video. You can not simply drag and drop video from your camera to a computer file and still get the time and date stamp (or at least not without some very high tech video programs).

Surveillance **P.O. Box**

Whenever only a post office box address is given, we must dictate the procedures we initiated to obtain an actual physical address. If perhaps a previous report provided directions to the Employee's residence then report this as well. Never merely start a surveillance under the caption of a post office box address because, it's obvious that the employee doesn't live in a mailbox. Whichever is the case, it needs to be clearly indicated in the report.

REMEMBER

The examples are not meant to be complete and comprehensive for all circumstances. Each set of circumstances will demand different actions and reporting. First and foremost be persistent and use your imagination at all times.

Chapter Fifteen
Common Investigations & Reports

> I. Cheating Spouse
> II. Child Custody
> III. Child Support
> IV. Slip and Fall
> V. Wrongful Death
> VI. SIU/Insurance Claims Investigations
> VII. Domestic / Infidelity
> VIII. Computer Forensic

 Examples of Common Investigations & Reports

In this section I have put together a reference guide with several different types of investigations I worked so you can see my procedures, style, wording and format.

Cheating Spouse

Many newcomers to the industry will find themselves working Divorce Cases, Cheating Spouses and Cheating Significant Others. This is an excellent area to begin your career as the clients will be less sophisticated and more likely to assist you. I worked a case where the woman had devoted 20 plus years to her husband who was busy building a successful business with of course the assistance of his wife. But the husband took an interest in the 20 year old office's marketing girl and soon went astray or at least that's what my client felt. She needed surveillance on her husband to see if he was cheating. The husband never gave any indication that he was intimate with the young girl. He insisted that his wife was just being jealous and imagining things. The cheating spouse thought he was too sharp to be caught. He had blacked out windows on his Cadillac and the two would make rendezvous secretly in a busy hospital parking lot. He would even take her to his Cocoa Beach Condominium where he would drive into the building secured under ground parking and take up to unit via an indoor elevator all outside the scope of any tailing investigator.

Child Custody Case

You may find yourself investigating a parent for a Child Custody Case and may be following the subject to show he has personal issues such as drinks excessively, uses drugs or has a lifestyle not otherwise conducive to raising or having minors in his/her custody. In a case I recently worked, the woman stated her husband was basically a functioning alcoholic however she realized that his constant intoxication was putting her children at risk and she wanted supervised visitation. To prove a point she wanted me to pick him up after work and document (through video) his activities. After work he went directly to a local bar for happy hour. I proceeded inside and observed him drink four beers in one hour. I recorded video of him drinking and secured the name of the bartender and the date and time of our visit so that a receipt could be obtained documenting the subject's purchases. After the happy hour he drove to a convenience store to pump gas and bought a beer. I was fortunate enough to get video of him opening the tab and drinking it while still in the gas stations parking lot. He then proceeded across town and stopped at his favorite hangout to play darts and shoot pool. Inside, I observed him drink four more beers and do two shots over a three hour period of time. At 11:30 p.m. he headed outside and got in his car to drive home. The video was used to prove a point that her husband was not capable of restraining his drinking. In fact her husband had two previous DUI's and currently did not have a valid license.

Child Support Case

The subject claimed he was injured and did not have any income to meet his support obligations and wanted the child support reduced. The client knew he was working and stated that his new girlfriend just wanted all the money and was not concerned with the wellbeing of his children from the previous marriage. The client needed to show the judge that her husband was working and that the support should continue and in no way be reduced. (See sample report following page)

Sample Child Support Dispute

CONFIDENTIAL

September 29, 2013

Gary Shady, Esquire	Re:	Your File No.	: Dibson Vs Smith
LAW OFFICES		Addt'l File No.	: N/S
1750 N. Montgomery Ave.		Our File No.	: FL-0410-DOM
Maitland, FL 32751		Subject	: Andrew Smith
		SSN	: N/S
		D/L	: N/S

Assignment Received   : March 2010
Previous Correspondence   : None
Type of Claim   : Domestic
Assignment   : Determine the work activities of Mr. Andrew Smith who resides at 8244 Stark Lane Circle, Maitland, Florida 32751. Mr. Smith reports not working and may have a suspended Driver's License and is not supposed to be driving.

Synopsis

Investigator: John Bilyk/ www.claimsresource.cc / 877-274-2000

Dates of Investigation: Monday, April 5, 2010 and Spot Check Thursday, September 23, 2010.

Pertinent Information: I proceeded with surveillance in order to determine if the subject was working.

Surveillance Subject's Residence -8211 Stark Lane Circle,
Maitland, Florida 32751   Monday, April 5, 2010
5:24 a.m.

Due to the subject's history of working within the construction field, I arrived in the early morning hours to document his activities. At the above time, I noticed no cars or trucks parked in the driveway leading to the attached single car garage. There however is also common parking or extra spaces across for the townhouse units. Located here I observed a maroon Ford King Ranch Pick-up which had been described as the subject's primary vehicle. To the left of this vehicle was a white SUV and to the right of that was a large white cargo van. I observed no detectable lights on inside the residence nor any indication of early morning movement.

7:22 a.m. VT

A blond haired female, appearing to be in her 40's, exited the townhouse through the privacy fence gate leading to the parking area. She entered the white SUV and departed the area.

7:39 a.m.- 7:41 a.m. VT

The subject exited the Townhouse's fenced in entrance and proceeded to walk to the white cargo van parked next to the Ford King Ranch truck. He opened the rear of the cargo van apparently checking the contents inside. He was dressed in blue jeans and a blue t-shirt.

7:50 a.m. VT

The male subject exited again this time with a large dog which he proceeded to walk in the grassy area in front of the parked vehicles. The subject was now wearing a baseball cap and was smoking a cigarette. He then returned to the townhouse.

7:54 a.m. VT

The subject exited again, went to the Ford truck then walked back towards the house then was seen again entering the driver's side door of the white van. The subject then proceeded to drive the vehicle heading in a southeasterly direction, south on Orange Ave., left on Solana, left on Webster, right on Pennsylvania which turned into Lake Sue, right on Winter Park Drive, left on Corrine and right on Osprey Ave.

8:20 a.m.-8:28 a.m. VT

The subject stopped at 3722 Ibis Drive, Orlando. I was advised that the subject reportedly had his driving privileges revoked however he was driving this white van bearing the Florida registration X76-8BB. As he arrived he remained seated in his van as another individual who had been waiting for him walked to the driver's door and engaged in conversation. This subject has a long brown hair he wears in a pony tail. He was wearing a baseball cap as well and a tan shirt with advertisement on the back. He was also driving a tan colored pick-up truck. Our subject appeared to be going over things with him and then the pony tailed male departed.

8:43 a.m. – 8:59 a.m. VT

After conversing with the male in the tan truck, our subject parked his van and walked over to another large male appearing to be around 6'4" tall and weighing around 300 pounds working on the exterior of a private residence. He had a white pick-up truck parked around the other side of the property. His tag was obscured, but it was a Lake County Tag. Our subject then walked around with a large coffee cup in his hand, went inside and spoke to the owner and was observed several times traversing the property and meeting with the large male worker present putting using an impact hammer drill to remove the fake or faux exterior brick from the block house. Our subject was apparently there over seeing this males work. I would later learn that they are removing all the fake brick and then resurfacing the house with stucco.

9:02 a.m.

After spending about 15 minutes at this house our subject then left the large worker behind and re-entered the cargo van's driver's seat and again drove himself out of the area. Traveling right on Glenridge, left on Lakemont Ave., right on Mizell Ave., right on Perth Lane, right on Greene drive and left on Brookshire Avenue.

9:16 a.m. –9:22 a.m. VT

The subject arrived at another private residence this one located at 5230 Fitzwalter Drive. Here the subject first went inside for several minutes then came back outside to remove some tool bags which he then carried inside.

At this point, it appeared the subject was running at least a crew of two. I was unsure if he was working for himself or another company. It was apparent he was working, and while he was in Winter Park, I proceeded back over to the first house.

Private Residence -3722 Ibis Drive, Orlando

I parked my vehicle out of sight of the property and walked up to the large male working by himself removing the fake brick on the house. He had removed nearly all of the brick on the carport side of the house. I advised I had a similar home with the same fake brick and wanted to know what it would cost to remove it. I asked him for his companies name and he stated that he worked for a guy called "blue". I could tell though that he was thinking about perhaps getting my job for himself. I asked for "blue's" number and he gave me his. He said he was Craig and I could reach him at 352.321.5855.

I next proceeded back to 5230 Fitzwalter Drive and as I arrived the owner, a young dark haired female, was just backing out of her driveway in a red compact. Seeing that our subject was now gone, I rolled down my window and stated was there a worker here earlier? Her eyes opened wide like I had just stolen her most precious secret and she said no? I said he told me to meet him here and that he was just at the residence. But she maintained that look and insisted no one was at the residence. At this point, either she was lying or she wasn't awake or home when he got there and already left. But the red car was there when he arrived and she was leaving in the same red car. I am not quite certain about this situation, but the video shows he went into the residence at 5230 Fitzwalter Drive.

Telephone Contact Ms. Lynn Dibson 407.461.6677

I relayed the above details to Ms. Dibson and asked if Andrew goes by the name of "blue" and she said yes, that his nickname. I then told her about the pony tailed male and she said he has been a worker for her ex-husband for some time. I advised that it appeared possible the home on Ibis may have had a new gravel roof and perhaps Mr. Smith is getting leads from his current girlfriend's families roofing business, but I had not confirmed anything about how he is getting his work.

Orange County Property Appraiser

As a cursory effort, I searched the records for the owners of 3722 Ibis Drive, Orlando and found them to be Layton and Lisa Marie Slev. I checked 411 for a phone listing, but found no listings for a Lee at that address. At some point, we may want to contact them to learn how they heard about our subject if by word of month, another job/homeowner, referral from the roofing company or an advertisement some where.

302220033206101 12/04/2006

At this point, having identified two jobs with just one days or 5 hours effort, it appears that our subject is very much in business and also driving.

Continued Spot Check   Thursday, September 23, 2010

I returned to the area and noticed the Mr. Smith now has ladder racks and tow ladders on top of the white van. It appears he has been accumulating tools for his job and further fitting the van to support more tools. I took a photograph while in the area. You can see the comparison pictures between what the van looked like in April to what it looks like in September.

Client Update

In this case, the client reported that her ex-husband had filed a motion to have his child custody payments lowered because he stated that he was not working or working as much as he had been when the child payments had been originally set.

During a limited four hour investigation, the subject was followed to a Winter Park neighborhood where he met a pony tailed worker and seemed to be giving him possible instructions for the day. He then met another worker who was working removing the fake brink from the front a ranch home and was then reportedly going to stucco the whole house. The subject himself then went to another job where he was apparently working by himself and observed carrying his bag of tools inside. So in this one four hour period of time, the subject appeared to have as many as three separate jobs going on.

On the day of the hearing as I prepared to attend the hearing as a witness, I drove past the subject's house in the morning and found his truck has been upgraded with ladder racks and ladders on the top of his 2010 van, so it appears his business may be growing not shrinking.

Finally, please note that the subject does not have a valid driver's license as it has been suspended but is still driving.

Case Status: Closed

Thank you for the opportunity to be of service.

Should you have any questions regarding this investigation, please contact my office by phone or via the internet at cases@claimsresource.cc

****End of Report****

Slip and Fall

I routinely investigate slip and fall accidents and during the course of these investigations, I look for any deficiencies in the floor or interview witnesses to rule out any debris left on the floor. I go so far as to determine the amount of cashier register receipts so I can determine the number of patrons visiting that store a day. I interview the manager and determine the store floor is monitored every 15 minutes. I have even taken statements of people coming and going from the store asking them have they ever felt the store was un-kept or the floors slippery. I take this information along with the statistics that 500 patrons visit the store on a daily basis and that this is the only fall that has ever occurred in the ketchup isle to create doubt about what happened. With no noted debris, a history of no prior accidents and witnesses feeling the floors are safe and not slippery was this really a slip and fall or was this a trip or staged fall. We have all tripped or slipped at one time. What makes this a libel incident is when negligence enters into the situation. But if a person comes into a store and is not paying attention and trips on their own feet, the business owner did nothing wrong.

In my 30 years in the business I have found that there is no shortage of professional con artists out there faking slip and falls. One that comes to mind occurred in south Florida in around 2010. I was given a clam made by a woman who fell in a large beauty supply chain. It turns out that the woman went to the hospital and had a $500 CAT scan done on her head she stated she hit on the floor. The whole bill was around $1200.00. The woman very politely called the insurance company and said just reimburse me the $1200.00. The adjuster ran a claims history report on the woman and found over 15 claims for similar activities. Either this woman was the unluckiest person in the world or she was a professional claimant. What was more interesting was that she had another incident the same day at a large pet supermarket, only a block away from the beauty products chain. I went to the pet supermarket and spoke to the manager who out m in touch with his risk management department. I learned the same woman had allegedly slipped and fell, hit her head and went to the hospital. The bill was #1200.00. In fact the bill submitted to them was the same bill submitted to my client. The scam here is to go to the hospital have some medical attention they send the bill to multiple locations. The other scam is that she never intended to pay the hospital either. During my investigation, I found the address she used was a mail box center. The center had two forms of ID a student ID and a business ID. Both were completely fraudulent. I called the woman several times attending try to get her to meet with me so I could determine her true identity. I even wanted to stake out the mail box location, but she hadn't paid the bill for two months and apparently only used the address to imitate the claim. The mail center was locking her box and the scam artist knew at this point going to that box was not a good idea. This was an experienced professional claimant who just happened to pick the wrong insurance company this time. Unfortunately not all companies have access to the ISO claim reporting system. So those without the resources to check a claimant's prior claim history will continue to support the efforts of these scam artists.

Wrongful Death Suit

I was asked to investigate a suit for wrongful death filed by the decedent's mother. She claimed a wrongful death suit and "damages" for the loss of her son whom she loved dearly. She stated that her son had been rear ended in an auto accident and severely hurt. She stated that he was on pain medication which he did not like to take. She further stated that he was unable to work due to his injury and subsequently became depressed then shot himself all as a result of the car accident.

Well going into this case, I knew I had investigated hundreds of auto accident and injured claimants that had not shot themselves. There had to be more to this case and the adjuster told me that it was suggested that the claimant may have been Baker Acted in the past meaning that someone thought he was a harm to himself and he was admitted and retained for some type of psychiatric evaluation.

I immediately thought to myself, that this guy had some underlying psychiatric issues I had to document. With his address being in Tallahassee, I also thought maybe he was a student. I wanted to determine if perhaps while at college he was known as a heavy partier or drug user. What I found was a history of mental health issues including Chronic Panic Attack and that if left untreated had a documented high rate of suicides. (See sample report following page)

Sample Wrongful Death Suit

CONFIDENTIAL

August 26, 2009

Mr. Steve Johnson	Re:	Your File No.	: UHV8646
TRAVELERS		Addtl File No.	: N/S
7840 Woodland Center		Our File No.	: FL-0809-006
Tampa, FL 33614		Insured	: CLABE & KERRY POLK
		Subject	: Thomas Frashline
		SSN	: 589-32-9442
		D/L	: 5/29/2008

Assignment Received   : August 4, 2009
Previous Correspondence : None
Type of Claim   : Auto
Assignment   : Identify potential witnesses and sources of information pertinent to the investigation. Secure information concerning the reported Baker Acting of the Claimant. Identify information concerning the claimant's past, background and relationship with his mother.

Synopsis

Investigator: John Bilyk/www.claimsresource.cc / 877/274-2000

Date of Investigation: Wednesday, August 5, 2009; Tuesday, August 18, 2009; Thursday, August 19, 2009; Friday, August 20, 2009; Monday, August 24, 2009 and Tuesday, August 25, 2009.

Pertinent Information: On Wednesday, August 5, 2009, I proceeded to the claimant's former address where he lived in off campus housing near the University of Tallahassee. The claimant's building is located in a heavily wooded townhouse community about one mile from campus. The townhouses are occupied by mostly college students and most are privately owned. The claimant's unit is exactly the same as the others in the complex and is a three unit townhouse building with units marked A,B &C. The deceased claimant reportedly occupied the center unit "B". I found Ms. Annie Greco living to the right in unit C and unit A was empty and for rent by Spirit Reality with a telephone number of 850.877.4343. All of the occupants now living in Unit B are new move-ins. I spoke to Ms. Greco whose Dad purchased her unit two years ago. She was aware of the deceased claimant, but never knew him personally and never spoke to him. She stated the house was pretty quiet and she never had any interaction with any of the occupants.

I next expanded my search and found another resident in one building over located to the right in unit 1348-A. This subject Arty Gallegos is a senior at FSU and also lived within 20 feet of the claimant's unit. The two other units 1348-A and B were further away but had occupants that were new to the area.

I expanded my search to the left of the claimant's unit to 1352-B. This subject Amanda Russo is a graduate student and has lived in her unit for 4 years. Her unit is about 30 feet away. She also did not know the claimant nor had she had any interaction with him. She too lived there through the summer of 2008 and stated the residence was pretty quiet and not known as a party house or partying residents.

Background Check - Leon County Civil Records Search Tallahassee, FL

I next proceeded to check County records for any notation regarding the deceased. I searched records from 9/30/1953 to the present 8/5/2009 and found no entries involving our subject.

I did find that the claimant's townhouse was owned by Aaron and Scott Brummett. They apparently purchased the property on March 5, 2008, from Earl and Amanda Simpson. The purchase price was $130,000 and the transaction was recorded in the official Leon County Clerks Office and can be found in Book 3822 Page 1912. The Brummetts therefore would have been the landlords for the deceased.

Criminal Background Check - Leon County Sheriff's Office Tallahassee, FL

I also checked local criminal records and again found no entry for the subject based on his name, SSN and DOB.

Criminal Background - Pinellas County Sheriff's Office, Clearwater, Florida

Here I identified one record for Thomas Michael Frashline, Case # CTC0002447NCPIN. This case involved our subject being charged on August 30, 2000 for Smoking in School.

Pinellas County Civil Records Search

Once again I found no civil records involving the claimant and no notation of a Baker Act.

Criminal Background - Hillsboro County, Tampa, FL

Again I searched the computer criminal county records under the subject's name but found no entry.

Hillsboro County Civil Records Search

Again I found no civil record and no notation of the claimant being Baker Acted.

Locate Witnesses

I next turned my attention to locating the possible witnesses initially identified only as the claimant's mother and ex-girlfriend. Through a background database I identified the claimant's mother as Ms. Mary Ann Frashline, residing at 40 Pelican Place, Palm Harbor, FL.

I next identified the ex-girlfriend as Amber Angelo. Through database searches and address cross reference, I found an address shared by both the deceased and Ms. Angelo. This address was 12239 Country White Circle, Tampa, FL 33635-6279.

Telephone Update

As requested I spoke to the Claims Handler, Mr. Johnson and learned that we can not contact the claimant's mother, but to go ahead and proceed with a neighborhood investigation in Palm Harbor. He also stated that he had more statements from other witnesses on CD and he would forward them to me.

On Monday, August 10, 2009, I received the CDs for the statements of Mary Ann Frashline, Paul Casamiro, Nicholas De George, Jeremy Borders and Eric Vanderlaan. I listened to these recordings but found they contained no personal identifying information on the witnesses. I re-contacted Mr. Johnson who indicated he has requested contact information for the subjects but has not heard back from the Claimant's Attorney. Therefore aside from Ms. Angelo, and the claimant's mother, I had no current address for Mr. Casamiro, De George or Border.

Background Database Searches
Locate Witnesses Tuesday, August 18, 2009

I initiated preliminary efforts to locate the most current addresses for the witnesses and ran background Database searches on each subject. I received the following addresses for each subject:

Jeremy Brantlyn Borderes- SSN 259-67-xxxx DOB 3/23/1987
July 2009 – address 1851 Perimeter Road, Fernandina Beach, FL 32034-1952

Paulo Alexander Casamiros- SSN 037-58-xxx DOB 11/6/1985
135 Dixie Drive, Tallahassee, FL 32304-3018

Eric Robert Vanderlander- SSN 592-64-xxxx DOB 10/19/1984
135 Dixie Drive, Tallahassee, FL 32304-3018
Telephone # 850-597-9179

Nicholas Georges- SSN 493-02-xxxx- DOB 8/5/1984
July 2009- 13738 Bluewater Circle, Orlando, FL 32828-8317
Telephone Number 727-600-6649

Once having addresses identified, I proceeded to contact the witnesses. I first made a personal visit to Ms. Angelo's residence.

Recorded Witness Statement
Ms. Allendina Amber Angelo
DOB 2/5/1986 / SSN 593-32-xxxx / Cellular 727.899.1223
1239 Country White Circle,
Tampa, FL 33635-6279   Thursday, August 20, 2009

I made contact with Ms. Angelo in the evening at her house in west, Tampa. Here she resides wither current Fiancé' Mark Sebben. I discussed my visit at great length with both the witness and her Fiancé before being invited inside to start the recorded statement.

During the statement, the witness stated that she knew the claimant, (Thomas Frashline) for about three years and lived with him for over a year from 2007 – 2008. She stated that when she first met him he stated <u>she saved his life for another year and told her he was throwing a gun he owned in a lake near his house.</u> Apparently, this was not the first time he referenced a gun either. She stated he told her he was arrested for selling a firearm in school or to a school mate. She stated the claimant never finished school or graduated and attended Palm Harbor University High School. According to the witness Thomas stated he experimented with Acid and knew he heavily used Marijuana. He also told her he was involved in a lot of school fighting. She did not know him in H.S. and actually went to another school. She stated that ever since she knew him he smoked a lot of Marijuana. In fact, during the time she knew him he held one job working at Target but lost the job because of panic attacks and throwing up on the job. Prior to his job at Target he sold Marijuana for a living. She stated that he could not function without constant Marijuana use. He smoked to go to Grocery shopping, he smoked to go to Wal-Mart, he even smoked just to play video games. She stated he was the type of person that had a mind that just would not stop and Marijuana seemed to calm him down. He was definitely a handful though and she thought she could change him but found it was just not possible. She stated he was severely depressed probably Bi-Polar and needed medical attention. This was out of the question though because Thomas never liked to take any type of prescription medication. She confirmed that he did not speak to his Mother, Sister or older Brother, nor did they have any thing to do with him. She stated she would be the one that tried to force the family to get together. She stated she made Thomas go to mostly birthday parties where they met at a local restaurant. They did not get together for Christmas or Thanksgiving. She stated that she told the claimant she was ending their relationship around the end of January beginning of February 2008, after the Bucs playoff game and that evening he threatened to kill himself by trying to walk into traffic. This occurred at the intersection of Tampa Road and US19. This was the night that another friend (Jarred) called the Police and the claimant was Baker Acted for around three days. According to Ms. Angelo, the claimant's mother got him out even though she begged her to let him stay there. And once he was out, he came back to Ms. Angelo's home to live and slept on the couch. She wanted the claimant to leave he was depressing, didn't want to work and was costing her money. She was in college taking night classes and working during the day. She was emotionally tired, financially indebt and he was no help. He would have his panic attacks in the middle of the night wake up to walk around the block or throw up. He was a mess and while she initially thought she could help him, she realized she couldn't. She truly cared for him but the toll was too great and she didn't get any help from Thomas, mother. She originally spoke to his mother about him coming back to live with her, but when she tried to call Ms. Frashline she would not answer. The claimant also tried to call her but she did not respond. The witness wanted him gone and found a mutual friend Nicholas Georges in Tallahassee who was going to school there and had an extra room. So the witness drove the now deceased claimant, to Tallahassee and dropped him off. The witness also stated that Thomas told her he lost his job in Tallahassee because of Panic Attacks. The witness told me another person I should contact was Bill Hoyland (727.612.7532. He was apparently present the night the claimant wanted to kill himself after the break-up by walking into traffic.

<u>Bill Hoyland-727.612.7532</u>

I found this number was a pay as you go number and it was currently out of minutes. The witness, Ms. Angelo told me this may happen and to keep trying it.

Neighborhood Investigation – 40 Pelican Place,
Palm Harbor, FL 31790   Friday, August 21, 2009

Here I canvassed the area and spoke to all the neighbors on both side of the claimant's former address. I also determined and spoke to Mr. Foss who bought Ms. Mary Ann Frashline's house nearly 1.5 years ago. In fact, I learned that she moved prior to the claimant's suicide. Mr. Foss did not know anything about the family other than possibly they were having financial problems and needed to sell the house. The Frashline house is located at the end of a dead end cul-de-sac. I contacted all of the residents within close proximity to the residence.

50 Pelican Place

These tenants have two small children and while they knew of the claimant they only saw him occasionally outside. The father, Jerry-stated that he recalls the claimant on the phone outside and remembers he had long hair and looked ruff. He stated he would sometime make his presence known to the claimant because he sometimes would speak loudly on the phone using obscenities or sounding angry. Aside from these brief interactions, he also recalled the neighbor on the other side of the claimant's house, identified as Merilyn Yount telling him Ms. Mary Ann Frashline "has gone through a lot with that boy"

30 Pelican Place

This residence is owned by The Yount's, but they now rent the home and the renters were no at home at the time. I left a note asking them to have their landlord contact me at her convenience.

60 Pelican Place- 727.424.4316

This address is occupied by the McClish's. They had no information to offer and did not have any interaction with the family.

20 Pelican Place

This is an older couple and while they recall a fight at the residence, they did not know which boys were which only that when he went to try top break it up someone said "old man get out of here". Obviously there was a lack of respect for the man which represented to his wife a dangerous situation and she pleaded for his to come back which he did. The woman stated she recalled the police coming to the area afterwards.

Ms. Dorothy Mraz

Ms. Mraz has lived on the corner for the past 20 years and knew Ms. Frashline and her family. She knew the two boys, the claimant and his older brother but did not have much to say about them. She stated they came and went from the area and she really did not know anything about their personal life. She too offered that the closest neighbor to the Frashlines was Ms. Merlynn Yount, but she has moved out of the neighborhood, but was believed to still live somewhere in Palm Harbor. Ms. Mraz stated that Ms. Frashline babysat Ms. Yount's children occasionally.

Notes were put on several more neighbors' homes however I received no further contacts. I did however speak to everyone close the Frashline home with the exception of Ms. Yount.

Database Search - Ms. Yount- Monday, August 24, 2009

I ran a name search and database and identified the subject as Ms. Merlynn Kay Yount SSN- 313-58-0333 DOB 8/27/1963 Address: 3130 Glenridge Drive, Palm Harbor, FL 34685-1723 Phone Number: 727.781.1836 (verified in name of Robert Yount) Alt. Possible Number : 813.964.4055

I called both numbers above and left a brief message asking for a return call. I have not heard back from her as of this date.

Recorded Witness Statement
Nicholas Georges   Tuesday, August 25, 2009

I made a personal visit to Mr. George's address where he currently lives with his brother and another roommate while attending graduate school at UCF in Sociology. Mr. DeGeorge stated that he never meant to get involved in this situation. He stated that he believed Thomas Frashline injured his shoulder and it affected his ability to work and this was why he was fired from Belk's at the Tallahassee Mall. I asked him to clarify what the Plaintiffs attorney seemed to be representing by the statements. I asked him specifically if he felt the accident and the subsequent pain led to the claimant to committing suicide. He stated that he did not say that. He stated that he did not state that the injury or pain caused the suicide. He stated it was a combination of things, a combination of life's difficulties that Thomas struggled with. Thomas thought he would get his life on tract and thought he would get back together with Amber Anthony. He stated you know it is like the Romeo and Juliet effect he studied in Sociology. The witness stated that he took Thomas Frashline to work in the morning, picked him up for lunch and then picked him up to come home. He said Thomas depended on him and while he didn't see anything unusual about his personality, he knew he used drugs/marijuana regularly. The witness advised that he lived with Thomas for around six months before Thomas left to go care for his terminally ill father in NY or NJ. He then lived with him again when Amber Anthony brought him to Tallahassee. He stated that Thomas first started to work at a Cleaner's in Tallahassee, but had a conflict, he thinks it was with the hours they wanted him to work. He stated the claimant then went to Belks.

Mr. Georges stated that he does not know what has been represented by his statement to the Tallahassee Attorney, but he does not want to be involved. He lost a friend and that is it. He can not make any statement about any specific causation of the suicide. In fact, he stated that he gave multiple statements to the Attorney. Mr. Georges stated that he is joining the Military and will follow his brother's footsteps as he is currently serving in the Military. He will only speak the truth and has no agenda with this case nor does he want anyone to use or misrepresent his statements. In his statement he stated that the accident was like the straw that broke the camels back, but perhaps this has been misrepresented. Thomas had a lot of issues he was dealing with the most significant seemed to be his relationship with Ms. Angelo. Thomas felt, as did Georges, that they would get back together. Georges stated that he saw Thomas experience panic attacks when arguing with Ms. Angelo or hearing she was seeing another person. He stated he had no knowledge of Thomas' mental health or prior background and was not that close to him. He stated that he was actually closer to Thomas' brother. <u>He wanted to clearly state though that he never said nor meant to represent that the accident or pain Thomas felt from his injuries caused him to kill himself.</u>

<u>Electronic Update</u>   <u>Wednesday, August 26, 2009</u>

On the above date an electronic update/partial report was sent to the Claims Handler Mr. Steve Johnson and the SIU, Mr. Bill Howland. It appears the claimant became a highly depended person. He needed Amber Angelo to the point when things did not go well he developed panic attacks, threw up and couldn't sleep. The claimant reportedly had trouble sleeping but he also heavily used drugs/marijuana and also was believed to experiment with harder substances like acid. After his girlfriend could no longer handle the situation and dependency of the claimant she drove him to Tallahassee to live with Mr. Georges. The witness Georges described more of the same dependency. He drove the claimant to work, picked him up for lunch and at the end of the day. He too thought he could help the claimant get his life together. But he didn't know that the claimant may have had more serious issues as he knew nothing about his past and stated the claimant was a year older than him. He didn't even know if the claimant graduated from high school. Mr. Georges also confirmed the claimant used Marijuana regularly. Georges also knew that the claimant was supposed to go live with his mother in PA instead of coming to Tallahassee, but didn't recall what happened to change things. The witness, Ms. Angelo reported, she felt the mother knew what a problem Thomas was and didn't want anyone to know. In fact, Ms. Angelo believed Ms. Frashline probably knew Thomas needed medical attention or more serious help. Thomas suffered from Panic Attacks witnessed by Ms. Angelo and Mr. Georges. Panic attacks so severe that he threw up while working at Target. Neither, Ms. Angelo or Mr. Georges had a mental health background to diagnosis the causation or seriousness of the Mr. Frashline's situation. They both thought they could help Thomas, but perhaps they underestimated the severity of his mental health situation.

<u>Internet Research Panic Attacks</u>

Although the claimant's symptoms were referred to as Panic Attacks by the witnesses, they had no medical diagnosis. Ms. Angelo stated that Thomas would wake up in the middle of the night having the attack and would need to leave the house and walk around the block. To better understand this disorder, I conducted a brief search of the internet and found The American Psychological Association states Panic Attacks are often experienced in conjunction with anxiety disorders and other psychological conditions, although panic attacks are not always indicative of a mental disorder, they have a multitude of causations. To name a few though I found it can be heredity, side effects from certain types of medications, or from various substances both prescribed and un-prescribed as part of their withdrawal syndrome or rebound effect. Experiencing a panic attack is said to be one of the most intensely frightening, upsetting and uncomfortable experiences of a person's life (the claimant had them routinely). Sufferers of panic attacks often report a fear or sense of dying, "going crazy", or experiencing a heart attack or "flashing vision", feeling faint or nauseated (the claimant would throw up), heavy breathing, or losing control of themselves. These **feelings may provoke a strong urge to escape** or flee the place where the attack began (a consequence of the sympathetic "fight or flight" response).

This search made me wonder if the strong urge to escape could mean through suicide? If these attacks happened as often as described by the witnesses and were never treated professionally how devastating could these episodes have been on his overall mental health?

Well, the question I raised also had an answer on the internet which I found at the following URL

http://sg.paniccenter.net/support/viewmessages.aspx?forum=35&topic=55200&ForumName=@NewForumName&TopicTitle=Topic:%20Did%20you%20know

Prolonged and untreated panic disorders can sometimes cause side effects like social anxiety, **depression**, and agoraphobia. Since panic attacks can occur during social situations, it can sometimes cause someone to develop performance anxiety or social anxiety. This is particularly true if the attacks frequently occur during times of great stress for the patient. Another possible reaction to these triggers can be depression and lack of confidence, as the person continues to fail in his endeavors. The onset of these side effects not only have an effect on mental health, but can also make recovery even more difficult. As such, it is critical that the problem be diagnosed and treated as early as possible. That way, the damage it can do is kept to a minimum.

I continued my search and found my questions were certainly not new and had been answered in a study published in The New England Journal of Medicine in November 1989, The link between Suicide and Panic Attacks or Panic Disorder had long been recognized.
http://www.thefreelibrary.com/Panic+attacks+increase+suicide+attempts.-a08124445

New England Journal of Medicine November 2
Excerpt from Article:

Some psychiatric conditions, such as severe depression and schizophrenia, are known to increase a person's risk of suicide. But panic attacks and <u>panic disorder</u> defined as frequently recurring panic attacks, are also linked to a strong and largely unappreciated risk of contemplating and attempting suicide according to a new study. Surprisingly, people with panic disorder have a higher rate of suicide attempts than do severely depressed individuals, report psychologist Myrna M. Weissman of <u>Columbia University</u>

This finding is "quite remarkable" **and marks panic disorder as a major new risk factor for suicide,** *writes psychiatrist Peter Reich of the <u>Massachusetts Institute of Technology</u> Cambridge in an editorial in the same journal. Reich also notes that general practice physicians, who most commonly encounter panic disorder patients, <u>can help prevent suicides by recognizing and treating symptoms of the disorder.</u>*

This case continued as I followed up on other leads and details provided. The end result however indicated that his suicide was more likely associated to his drug use and mental health problems than a car accident.

Insurance Cases

SIU investigations refer to general investigations about most any type of claim that needs to be investigated and usually does not require any type of surveillance. These types of cases require good interviewing skills and analysis of the evidence to determine the cause or origin of an accident/incident. If someone slipped and fell in a supermarket, you would investigate what caused the fall, could it have been prevented? What can be done to prevent the fall from occurring again and was it a realistic accident. By realistic, I mean how often does this type of accident occur? Could it be that the person simply just tripped or slipped? Could it just have been their worn leather soles or a loose flip flop? In investigating an accident you need to look for any ambiguity with the accident. Proving or disproving the likeliness of the accident will take documentation. Is there any store video that shows the incident as it took place? Gather facts and statistics that may also cast some doubt on the incident actually being a liable accident. Accidents occur all the time but those that occur due to a problematic situation are those were liability may occur and thus damages may be brought against the property owner. With statistics, you may find that the store has over 200 register receipts daily and at a minimum, this would mean 200 people may walk through the same door or over the same threshold one customer tripped over. You may photograph the threshold and find it flush and without any obstruction which could have contributed to the fall. Secondly, I might speak or take statements from several patrons of the store in the parking lot after they have departed the store. I may look for an elderly woman or one using a cane and attempt to obtain a quick statement from her asking how many times a week she visits the store and for how many years she has been coming. I would then specifically ask her if she ever tripped in the area of the accident location. Obviously I am hoping to hear, "I have been coming to this store for 25 years and have had a hip replacement and use a cane. I usually come to the store twice a week and exit through those doors each time and have never tripped or ever felt the exit was dangerous or presented a hazard." I then ask if I can just take a quick picture, hold up my phone and snap her picture. During the statement I would have also asked the woman her name. The good thing about a parking lot is that I can see her walk tot her car and also get the tag to her car which will further give me her address.

Thinking on your feet on how to approach an investigation will vary from case to case. I was assigned a case where a hotel guest stated that the shower head shot off and hit him in the head while he was showering. I started by meeting the maintenance man and getting a full description of the type of shower heads he uses and any maintenance records for that specific hotel room. I then asked for access to the specific room with the original head that allegedly shot off and hit the subject. I took my video camera and set it up to record an attempt to duplicate the incident. I screwed on the shower head and turned the water on full force. With my video recording, I turned the shower head a half rotation off until final the shower head was being held on by just one thread. Water was spraying everywhere and finally as the last thread was loosened the head just dropped straight down into the tub. There was no pressure or force that could have turned the shower head in a dangerous projectile as described by the guest. I also secured a statement from the maintenance man about any similar accident of course finding that there had been none. I also photographed the threads of the shower water spout as well as the threads on the shower head itself to show they were not worn or damaged. I then confiscated the shower head itself as an evidence item. My final report determined that the accident could not have occurred as alleged.

Staged fraudulent claims and exaggerated claims of injuries purporting a libelous situation are the types of jobs we see most frequently from the insurance industry.

We can also investigate thefts, homeowner burglaries, auto thefts and even fires.

Sometimes we conduct parallel investigations acting as the middle man to gather information. In the case of a suspected arson, the fire marshal's office may be investigating the incident with a full staff of professional cause and origin experts. They may clearly feel it was an arson but are under no specific time frame to complete their investigation and produce a report. On the other hand though the property owner may want to be paid for his loss so that he can rebuild or re-locate. They may even want a per diem so that they can stay in a hotel while the insurance company processes the claim. The adjuster with the insurance company is on a tight time-line, but she cannot control the fire departments investigation. But the Professional PI should be able to introduce himself as an agent of the insurance company to get a feel for the direction of the investigation. If the Fire Department states this was and arson set fire then the case may quickly turn to who set the fire and why. A motive to set a car, house or business fire usually first falls on the owner. This is an investigation well within the scope and capabilities of any PI. Was the owner behind in his payments, was he/she having financial problems? Was there a problem with the business, was it failing. Was the car having mechanical difficulties or the home involved in a contested nasty divorce or the owners underwater in the evaluation of the property. If the fire was NOT an arson but a fire that started due to some faulty electrical work in a back addition, then the investigation may shift from a parallel gathering informational investigation to an active self directed investigation. The PI will want to know who did the electrical work in the addition as this party may be at fault for the loss. The PI will search for the building permits identifying the electrician. If there were no permits pulled and no plans or building inspections made then the work may have been done illegally and improper. Insurance companies do not cover illegal acts and the fire damage may not be covered.

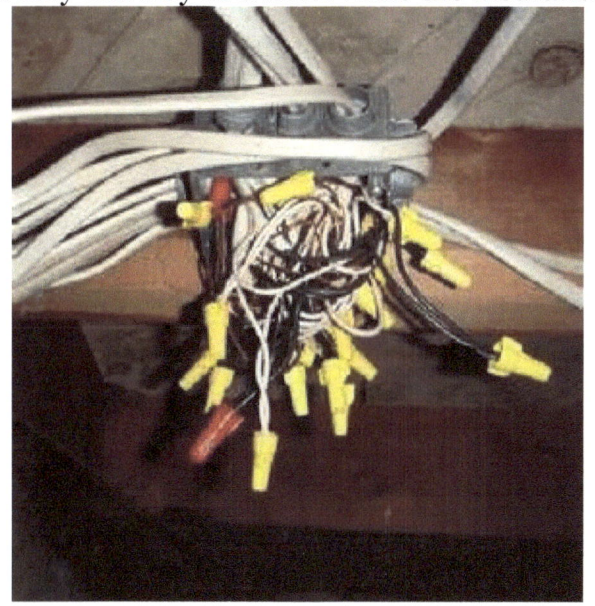

When investigating a homeowner burglary, we usually meet with the home owner, pick up a copy of the police report and look for the forced entry point. We cover each item stolen, where it was located, what brand it was and ask for any of the accessories that may go with the item such as a manual, remote control or to see pictures with the items in the background or being worn by the subject if it was jewelry. We are always trying to verify the validity of a claim. Ironically, I have investigated many homeowner burglaries and each time a TV set is reported as stolen, it is always described as a "Sony". If a fur coat is taken from the closet, it is always a "Blue Fox". I always ask to see where the coat was hanging in the closet and take a picture of the closet. Many times the closets are so full there isn't even room for a thick bulky fur. This is when I ask for pictures of the subject wearing the coat. If a video camera is stolen, I ask to see the box, the manual, the remote. Same holds true for a TV. I ask to see pictures of the same room with the TV present. Once again, there may be a financial motive for the owners of the property to have made the claim or loss. Some of the items may have been financed and the owners currently unable to make payments. There may have been a split in the household, two roommates leave and one takes property the other wanted or the property was taken by a family member or friends and the owner feels reporting it stolen is an easier way to handle the situation.

Whatever type of investigation you may be called to conduct chances are someone has worked a similar case before. Outlines of what to do and what to look for are prevalent within our industry.

Domestic / Infidelity Investigations

Our industry has a wide range of avenues to specialize in; perhaps the most prolific for small start-up agencies are Domestic Investigations, specifically Infidelity. The most successful agencies will learn to Flat Rate their pricing which is still lagging in the industry. As indicated I would suggest packaging surveillance 5 hours at a time ($250.00) and elicit the assistance of the client spouse. Next, creating a "window of opportunity" is the best approach to saving time. Have the spouse you are working for tell the significant other that they need to be out of town for work leaving at 6:00 p.m. and most likely being back the following morning. The significant other can also state they are going to help a friend move or assist a sick family member. What ever the case,  the destination needs to be at least three hours away and the spouse needs to call the other spouse right when they leave and again when they get to their destination. I suggest leaving at 2:00 p.m. - 3:00 p.m. so by 5:00 p.m. you are three hours away. Meanwhile, the PI is on the suspected cheater and having this window of opportunity is just too tempting to resist. If the spouse does not use the time period to see the other party then the relationship has probably been discontinued. If the client believes otherwise suggest doing the same thing on another weekend.

Forensic Computer Investigations

Another increasing specialized area of practice and also another "Flat Rate" opportunity to secure business. The client spouse can authorize the PI to forensically examine the computer or even install a key tracking software that will capture all correspondence, usually for a home visit of around $199.00. Statistics shows that 22 percent of men and 14 percent of women admitted to having sexual relations outside their marriage sometime in their past. And 17 percent of divorces in the United States are caused by infidelity. Results show that internet users devote three hours each week to online sexual exploits. Twenty-five percent have felt that they lost control of their Internet sexual exploits at least once or that the activity caused problems in their lives. Researchers think the vast majority of the millions of people who visit chat rooms, have multiple "special friends" and only 46% of men believe that online affairs are adultery. According to Divorce Magazine 80% think it's Ok to talk with a stranger identified as the opposite sex.

It is currently estimated that <u>one-third of divorce litigation is caused by online affairs.</u>

Because of the anonymity, affordability, and accessibility of Internet sexual resources, the computer can accelerate relationships. 57% of people have used the Internet to flirt. 38% of people have engaged in explicit online sexual conversation and 50% of people have made phone contact with someone they chatted with online.

The professional PI can utilize special industry strength software and hardware to retrieve the truth from any computer. This software can be easily loaded on a thumb drive for an at home visit by a field investigator.

A product called PC PANDORA http://www.pcpandora.com is a PC and Internet detective that hides on a hard drive and monitors all computer and Internet activity. This program will record and take snapshots of the websites visited, emails sent and received, Instant Messages sent and received, Chat room conversions and other computer and Internet activity that is done on a clients PC. This software can also be used as a key logger that will record secret passwords that someone may want to keep hidden. Once known they can be used to access other accounts on Hotmail, YAHOO, AOL or other web based email accounts. This is just one internet detective program that comes to mind and more sophisticated programs are developed all the time. You should consultant an expert in the field before deciding which to buy.

Other Domestic Investigations involve background checks on couples, renters, business partners and disputes between neighbors. Others may choose to support the corporate Human Resource industry and handle work related incidents such as conducting pre-hiring background checks, sexual harassment allegations, internal security and theft just to name a few.

Another large market that requires a very professional approach and preparation is to specialize in insurance related issues sometime overlapping with the aforementioned corporate investigators with the addition of some of the biggest accounts in our industry; Workers Compensation and General Liability Claims. Another avenue is to work directly for the Insurance Companies as a staff investigator in the Special Investigative Unit SIU, investigating auto, property and liability claims both personal and commercial Lines.

Then there are jobs with Criminal and Civil Defense Attorneys, seeking to provide a defense for their clients. It is very common for the PI to secure statements, locate witnesses and take pictures of an accident location to assist in the defense of the client.

Chapter Sixteen
Being a Witness

      I.   Deposition Testimony
      II.   Courtroom Testimony
      III.   Being a Witness is Serious Business
      IV.   Do's and Don'ts of Testifying in Court or Deposition

16. You've Been Served A Subpoena: Don't Panic

You've been served a subpoena to appear and testify in a lawsuit which you investigated or are a part of but not a party. The subpoena may direct you to appear at a law office to give deposition testimony or may direct you to appear in court to give trial testimony, and may request that you bring certain documents with you such as you report, notes surveillance tapes, photographs etc. In either event, you are upset that someone (sometimes a sheriff) has appeared at your home or workplace with a subpoena and apprehensive about what will be expected of you when testifying. You recall very little about the case and need to pull the file and refresh your memory, never just trust your recollection.

You should understand that the party calling you as a witness was required by law to serve you with a subpoena to assure your appearance and testimony. Service of the subpoena was not designed to embarrass you, but protect the parties to the lawsuit.

If you have questions about the subpoena, the scheduling of your testimony or the underlying litigation, you should speak to your office manager or sponsor. Always immediately notify the office and your manager. Your manager will next instruct to contact the client and determine who the attorney is on your client file. This attorney will be present during your deposition and will most likely want to meet with you before the deposition to go over your testimony.

Deposition Testimony

Witnesses are frequently asked to testify twice in connection with a single matter. The first time you testify may be on deposition. Deposition testimony is typically given in a conference room setting rather than in a courtroom. The purpose of a deposition is to find out what you know about the case. The lawyers for the parties, possibly the parties themselves, and a court reporter will be present.

You will take an oath to tell the truth. The court reporter will record all the questions asked by the lawyers and all responses given by you. The deposition may be taken many months or even years before the case is actually tried. The purpose of the deposition testimony is to record your recollections of the events at a time when they are relatively fresh in your mind. Afterward, testimony will be typed in a deposition transcript after it is given, and you will be given the opportunity to read and sign it. If you are at all concerned that the court reporter may have improperly recorded your testimony, you should exercise your right to read and sign the transcript and correct those areas in the transcript where your testimony is incorrectly recorded.

Courtroom Testimony

The second time you testify may be in a courtroom before a judge and possibly, a jury. You may wonder why you have to testify a second time when you have already given your deposition testimony. You should understand that the judge and jurors were not present when you gave your deposition testimony. In most instances the rules of court forbid the use of your deposition without the use of your live testimony. Remember that the lawyers investigate the case thoroughly and know what testimony they must present. If they judge your testimony to be essential, they will call you. Otherwise, you will not receive a subpoena. Also the cross examination in a trial will be harsher than it was during the deposition. The plaintiff's attorney now knows you a little better and also knows what you have to say. They have had time to analyze you from the first meeting and review all of your answers. They want you to believe you will see the same person, but most likely you will not. They will call you a spy and insinuate that you pry into people's personal lives. They will make any evidence you secured seem like it is unimportant or limited in nature based on the larger picture they want to promote.

An attorney once told me when they call you a spy, simple state "I take every precaution to be discreet and to protect the person's privacy". Because what the jury hears when they hear spy is that you are snooping and violating a person's privacy. Therefore no matter how many different ways they ask the same question my response should be the same. Just understand that we aren't spies, we are not government agents, nor are we trained spies or use spy gadgets to ease drop or bug someone's house. Furthermore, we should not see our investigative targets as enemies therefore we have no enemy combatants. We are no different than a police officer sitting off the side of the road to see if a speeder comes by. But again our simple answer to whether we spy on people is, **"I take every precaution to be discreet and to protect the person's privacy"**. We are not spying we are conducting ourselves in a discreet respectful manner. Because what we want to address is the undertone that we are not violating a person's privacy.

Being a Witness is Serious Business

Remember that your role as a witness in the judicial system is an extremely important one. Without witnesses, judges, and jurors could not fairly decide cases.

Never be argumentative or combative, with the plaintiff's attorney. He/She will do their best to get under you skin but listen carefully and answer to the best of your ability. Use your best efforts to present a clear and accurate answer.

DO's and DON'Ts for Testifying in Court or Deposition

1. Do go over the facts of the case in your mind prior to testifying. Separate what you remember from what you think you remember. You should always review with the lawyer who intends to call you as a witness.
2. Do answer as truthfully, accurately and completely as possible. Don't answer a question with half-truths or let your judgment about how the case should come out affect your testimony. Remember that you took an oath before testifying to tell the truth. A failure to tell the truth amounts to perjury.
3. Do correct any mistakes made in answering a question immediately.
4. Do speak slowly and loudly so that all concerned can hear your testimony.
5. Do dress neatly and dress professionally.
6. Do make estimations if a question requires you to do so, but be clear in your answer that your testimony is only an estimate.
7. If you were asked whether you have discussed your testimony with others before testifying if in fact you have. There is absolutely nothing wrong with discussing your testimony with lawyers or parties beforehand.
8. Do take a <u>subpoena</u> seriously. It has the force of a court order. That doesn't mean, by the way, that a judge has actually taken an interest in you (they are usually prepared by an attorney for a party) but a judge will be annoyed if you ignore a subpoena.
9. Do be honest and forthcoming with your testimony. That doesn't mean spill your guts out, but answer questions fairly and with intellectual honesty. You saw how badly a recent President looked when he tried to get cute with his testimony. Of course, also remember that perjury is a felony.
10. Do be honest and forthcoming with your attorney. Even if it is embarrassing, even if it makes you look like an idiot or a crook, it is better if your attorney knows. Giving your attorney insufficient information is like hiring a chauffeur and not telling him or her that your brakes don't work.
11. Do make yourself available to your attorney for discussions regarding the case, including working on discovery and preparation for depositions and trial. It is not a waste of your time if it helps you to win the lawsuit.
12. Do follow your attorney's advice about how to behave in the deposition or the courtroom. Don't be afraid to ask him or her if something is appropriate. It's one of the things that you are paying your lawyer for. Your attorney will tell you what he or she wants from you if you are deposed or have to take the stand in a trial.
13. Do dress as well as you comfortably can. A suit is best, for a man or a woman, but if your head spins and you gag at the thought of a tie or a skirt, dress as nicely as you can. If you are a police officer, military personnel, or cleric, your uniform is always appropriate. Your credibility as a witness is in some small degree judged by your clothing.

14. Do give your attorney everything in your relevant files, even if it is embarrassing or incriminating. If you have the document, the odds are that someone else does too.

THE DON'Ts

15. Don't attempt to answer a question unless you fully understand it. Ask the lawyer to rephrase the question. Don't guess at what you think the lawyer is after, make the lawyer explain the question to you.
16. Don't try to respond to a question if you don't know the answer. If you don't remember or know the answer to a question, say so.
17. Don't attempt to answer a question to which an objection has been made. When a lawyer makes an objection or the judge makes a comment, stop talking. Wait for a ruling by the judge. If he overrules the objection, you should answer the question. Listen to each objection made, so that you understand the basis for the objection.
18. Don't argue with the lawyers or the judge. Don't allow them to make you angry. Be cool, calm and attentive.
19. Don't guess. It is okay to provide a reasoned or thoughtful estimate, but do not simply guess or speculate as to an answer.
20. Don't be offended if you are told not to listen to testimony given by other witnesses in the case. There is an important reason for this rule. No one wants your testimony to be colored by the testimony of other witnesses. You will be expected to give your version of what happened rather than to parrot someone else's version.
21. Don't ever guess. You are in a deposition or on the stand to give facts, not to try to figure out what might have happened. Even if it makes you feel stupid to say it, sometimes "I don't know" is the right answer.
22. Don't help. It is human nature to want to explain things so that your listener understands. Resist the impulse. It is your opponent's job to get the answers. It is your job to answer only the question asked, and not help.
23. Don't try to be funny, unless you are actually Jerry Seinfeld. There are several reasons for not even trying. First, and most obviously, not everyone has the same sense of humor; some people, and there are judges in this category, have no humor at all. Second, your words are taken down by a court reporter to be read later. The court reporter does not take down facial expressions, gestures, or tones of voice. You can be saying "yes" in a sarcastic whiny voice while making quote marks with your fingers, and what will appear on the page is "Yes."
24. Don't get distracted. Pay strict and guarded attention to the questions being asked. If your attention wanders, you could make mistakes or misunderstand.
25. Don't answer a question you don't understand. If a question is vague or compound ("Did you go to the store and who did you see and what did you say to them?") or assumes something that isn't true, you have the right to have the question restated or rephrased.

26. Don't be afraid to ask for a break during a deposition. They can take hours, and it is inhumane to expect you to sit and squirm if you need a restroom break. BUT-
27. Don't' even think of asking for a break while you are at trial. Breaks are entirely in the control of the judge, and asking for a break (unless something dreadful happens, like you start crying) looks very bad.
28. Don't take any drugs or alcohol before you testify. This may seem obvious, but you'd be surprised. Remember that "drugs" also includes things like cold medicine, or even more caffeine than you are used to. You should also be careful what you eat before you testify. That isn't the morning to skip breakfast if you usually have it.

Chapter Seventeen
Terrorism Today

    I.   Introduction
    II.   Private Investigators and Terrorism
    III.   Different Types of Terrorism
    IV.   How to Report Terrorism Activity

17. Introduction

Terrorism may be something we will need to live with for many decades to come. The reasons behind terrorism associated with attacks on America and American Ideology is a vast topic for discussion. There are varying types of terrorism such as those home-grown related to idealistic thoughts, those related to religious radicals and finally those associated to purely pathological disorders.

I consider the Columbine and Sandy Hook shootings acts of terror from people with pathological disorders. I would argue that anyone involved in a terrorist act has some type of pathological disorder. After all, acts of terror are crimes, and we associate most criminal behavior with deviant or pathological disorders.

What causes a religious person to become radicalized to the point that they want to hurt innocent people has less to do with religion than it does to their own personal situation.

Many areas of the middle-east lack the social and religious freedoms more advanced societies enjoy. In a suppressed environment personal growth and educational opportunities can be stifled. Ignorance and feelings of hopelessness associated with no opportunity to advance their personal or family's financial well-being can be the formula for feelings of resentment or even hatred. People tend to look towards religion when things are bad. If you can not control your environment or circumstances often people tend to look towards their faith for guidance. When I lost my job in 1997, I made sure I didn't miss church on Sundays. Unfortunately faith can be used negatively when a misguided and demented leader attracts other similar misguided followers. Some of these deviants operate under the cloke of a religious organization trying to justify their promise or message by high-jacking a religious theme. There will always be groups and leaders that feel their circumstances are more tragic than others. We don't need to go far from home to find examples of this. The Reverend Jim Jones started the Peoples Temple to help homeless, jobless and sick people of all races. When former members claimed widespread abuse within the group, Jones started a colony in the jungles of Guyana where he hoped to build a tropical utopia. When a congressman visited the commune with three journalists to investigate the abuse claims, they were shot and killed when trying to leave. After the shootings, 913 commune members, including hundreds of children drank poisoned cool aid. Or, David Koresh (born Vernon Wayne Howell), the convicted leader of the Branch Davidians who raped girls as young as 12 years old. Finally more recently, Warren Jeff's of the Fundamentalist Church of Jesus Christ of Latter-Day Saints who was found guilty of sexual assault and aggravated sexual assault of children. Jeff's was sentenced to life in prison plus 20 years, to be served consecutively for sexual assault of both 12- and 15-year-old girls.

Radicalization can be defined as an opinion that differs from that of the moderate and most generally accepted. But sometimes these views and the way they are delivered can affect a person more differently depending on his or her situation. Mental Health is such a complex area of study that even the most advanced countries in the world including the US struggle to implement ways to identify it, treat it, manage it and un-stignafy it.

So pathologic leaders can convince mis directed people to do outrageous things including killing.

In the Boston Bombings the Tsarnev brothers became radicalized perhaps through different methods, but if we consider where they came from and perhaps what happened to them later we may find failures and feelings of frustration in their lives. Specifically the older Tsarnev who may have felt the frustration of not having the same opportunities as others, he faced problems with education, he wanted to be an Olympic Boxer and failed. He sought US citizenship and was denied. These failures and frustration combined with perhaps his own feelings of inadequacy and underlying psychological problems created a person ready to be used by another misguided deviant.

In most cases the people caught up in these types of horrendous circumstances lack their own defined purpose or ideas. People join groups for many reasons, some join for task concerns, jobs, social acceptance and interpersonal needs or attractions. Many people that join the military join to serve their country, but others join because it is an option in perhaps an otherwise option-less path. The reality is that people also join militias, and hate groups because they have no other groups to join or associate with. They have no personal path, no ideas or objectives of their own. They band together with other hooligans and are accepted into a group that feeds them, houses them, creates a sense of brotherhood set out to fight for a cause that in most cases is nothing more than a misconceived ideology by some radical unstable thinker.

A Professor who teaches at UC-Santa Barbara, called the Boston victims "canaries" and suggested that the U.S. had it coming because of our geopolitical fantasy of global domination. I would be concerned about even stepping foot in one of this professors classes as he seems to underestimate the complexity of America. While we may use drones and intervene in tumultuous situations around the world, <u>we don't plant out flag and seize foreign land;</u> we try to organize a stable government with people of that country. The US then works on an exit strategy to leave that country a more democratic and humanistic society. This is hardly what I would call word domination. Perhaps what the Professor was eluding to was our (Americans) competitiveness around the world and the fact that the planet is getting smaller as business becomes global. Any business or business person wants to dominate their market and capture market share, however this is rarely the initial driving force when the US enters a conflicted region. There are also those people that will promote conspiracy theories about everything and anything. Given most any circumstance a "spin" can be put on representing something entirely different than what it really may be.

The United States has always been a melting pot of cultures. It wasn't too long ago that the Irish and Italians came here and wanted help in their countries civil un-rest. Today's Iranian Americans and Iraqi Americans still have family members and relatives "back home" living under harsh conditions and suppressed human rights. Having the privilege of being an American, they feel it is their duty to do what they can to help those left behind. With a wife who is from Colombia, I know she would support any US policy that helps rid her homeland of drug trafficking. I see our presence in Colombia fighting narco-trafficking and corruption no different than helping free the Iraqi people from radical Islamists.

I recently took a trip to Morocco which of its approximate 33 million people, 99.9 percent are Muslims. My Muslim driver who spent his off-time as a nomad herding sheep stated that the younger population are being educated through satellite TV. Satellite dishes could be seen on the roof tops of almost every single house in each village we passed. With the average wage of a Moroccan only $9 US dollars a day, higher education is expensive and not affordable to most. It may just be though that those satellite dishes enable the younger generation to connect to the rest of the world and see it for what it really is and the future it may represent for them. Without such a connection, they have no idea what is happening around the world. In a place so large with so many uneducated people, I was amazed at the effect daily call for pray had on the people. With the call for pray ringing out over loud speakers strategically located throughout the town, people suddenly appeared in the streets. They would make their way to the town's Mosque for prayer. While I think religion is important, this type of daily repetitive religious beating seemed almost like brain washing to me. The event however was cultural, people know of no other way and this activity not just offers a religious reminder but it also adds structure and activity their lives. For many expectations of anything else more promising or life changing are very low, but those youths watching Satellite TV see things very differently and the affect it has on their lives will hopefully be educational and enlightening.

So, I say thank god for satellite dishes that bring the world to those who may be stranded elsewhere. Sane, socially adjusted, educated people don't become radicals. Any way we can promote tolerance and education will be ultimately good for the world.

Investigators and Terrorism

The purpose of this chapter might not initially be obvious however in early 2000, the State Department and now the Department of Homeland Security recognized that there was an invaluable civilian army of eyes around the country. With approximately 60,000 private investigators nationwide working the streets daily, making sure they realize the importance of their trained eyes can only add to the protection of our country and its' citizens. Unfortunately in this day and age, forces are at work around us to undermine the safety of our nation. The most notorious of these groups today is Al-Qaeda and their related organizations. With such an open society the ways in which a terrorist group might strike is abundant.

Al-Qaeda

The radical Islamist movement developed during the Islamic revival and Islamist movement of the last three decades of the 20th century, along with less extreme movements.

Some have argued that "without the writings" of Islamic author and thinker Sayyid Qutb, "al-Qaeda would not have existed. "Qutb preached that because of the lack of *sharia* law, the Muslim world was no longer Muslim, having reverted to pre-Islamic ignorance known as *jahiliyyah*.

To restore Islam, he said a movement of righteous Muslims was needed to establish "true Islamic states", implement *sharia*, and rid the Muslim world of any non-Muslim influences, such as concepts like socialism and nationalism.

Hamas (Islamic Resistance Movement)

Hamas was formed in late 1987 as an outgrowth of the Palestinian branch of the Muslim Brotherhood. Various Hamas elements have used both violent and political means, including terrorism, to pursue the goal of establishing an Islamic Palestinian state in Israel. It is loosely structured, with some elements working clandestinely and others operating openly through mosques and social service institutions to recruit members, raise money, organize activities, and distribute propaganda. Hamas' strength is concentrated in the Gaza Strip and the West Bank.

Hamas currently limits its terrorist operations to Israeli military and civilian targets in the West Bank, Gaza Strip, and Israel. The terrorist group receives some funding from Iran but primarily relies on donations from Palestinian expatriates around the world and private benefactors in Saudi Arabia and other Arab states. Some fundraising and propaganda activity take place in Western Europe and North America.

ISIS, after the U.S. invasion of Iraq in 2003, Abu Mussab al-Zarqawi came to Iraq to unite Sunni Muslims in the Middle East. Abu Mussab al-Zarqawi launched bloody suicide bombings and horrible executions targeting Americans, Shia

Muslims and others he saw as obstacles to creating a Sunni caliphate across areas of Iraq, Syria and Persian Gulf. While Abu Mussab al-Zarqawi was killed in a U.S. airstrike in 2006, thousands of foreign volunteers have since joined the movement to create an Islamic state and wage what they call "jihad".

What formerly known as "al-Qaeda in Iraq" was rebranded in 2006 as the Islamic State in Iraq and Syria (ISIS).

ISIS is thought to include between 3,000 to 5,000 fighters. The ISIS leadership has been targeted to reduce their organizational ability to occupy territory or continue to build strength. The biggest fear for Americans and our allies is the so called lone wolf who attacks soft targets with assault weapons or foreign volunteers who act as suicide bombers moving either on foot wearing suicide vests, or driving vehicles packed with explosives.

These types of attacks are difficult to anticipate and Americans have grown more conscious of our surroundings. Across the nation, we're all part of communities. In cities, on farms, and in the suburbs, we share everyday moments with our neighbors, colleagues, family, and friends. It's easy to take for granted the routine moments in our every day—going to work or school, the grocery store or the gas station. But your every day is different than your neighbor's—filled with the moments that make it uniquely yours. So if you **see something** you know shouldn't be there—or someone's behavior that doesn't seem quite right—**say something**. Because only you know what's supposed to be in your everyday.

Informed, alert communities play a critical role in keeping our nation safe. "If You See Something, Say Something" engages the public in protecting our homeland.

Different Types of Terrorism

Researchers in the United States began to distinguish different types of terrorism in the 1970s, following a decade in which both domestic and international groups flourished. By that point, modern groups had began to use techniques such as hijacking, bombing, diplomatic kidnapping and assassination to assert their demands and, for the first time, they appeared as real threats to Western democracies, in the view of politicians, law makers, law enforcement and researchers. They began to distinguish different types of terrorism as part of the larger effort to understand how to counter and deter it.

State Terrorism

Many definitions of terrorism restrict it to acts by non-state actors. But it can also be argued that states can, and have, been terrorists. States can use force or the threat of force, without declaring war, to terrorize citizens and achieve a political goal..

It has also been argued that states participate in international terrorism, often by proxy. The United States considers Syria the most prolific sponsor of terrorism.

Bioterrorism

Bioterrorism refers to the intentional release of toxic biological agents to harm and terrorize civilians, in the name of a political or other cause. The U.S. Center for Disease Control has classified the viruses, bacteria and toxins that could be used in an attack. Category A Biological Diseases are those most likely to do the most damage. They include Anthrax, Botulism, The Plague, Smallpox, Tularemia and Hemorrhagic fever, due to Ebola Virus or Marburg Virus.

Cyberterrorism

Cyber terrorists use information technology to attack civilians and draw attention to their cause. This may mean that they use information technology, such as computer systems or telecommunications, as a tool to orchestrate a traditional attack. More often, cyberterrorism refers to an attack on information technology itself in a way that would radically disrupt networked services. For example, cyberterrorists could disable networked emergency systems or hack into networks housing critical financial information.

There is wide disagreement over the extent of the existing threat by cyberterrorists.

Eco terrorism

Eco terrorism is a recently coined term describing violence in the interests of environmentalism. In general, environmental extremists sabotage property to inflict economic damage on industries or actors they see as harming animals or the natural environment. These have included fur companies, logging companies and animal research laboratories, for example.

Nuclear terrorism

"Nuclear terrorism" refers to a number of different ways nuclear materials might be exploited as a

terrorist tactic. These include attacking nuclear facilities, purchasing nuclear weapons, or building nuclear weapons or otherwise finding ways to disperse radioactive materials.

Narcoterrorism

Narcoterrorism has had several meanings since its coining in 1983. It once denoted violence used by drug traffickers to influence governments or prevent government efforts to stop the drug trade. In the last several years, Narcoterrorism has been used to indicate situations in which terrorist groups use drug trafficking to fund their other operations.

How to Report Suspected Terrorist Activity

Terrorist are constantly plotting and while we never know when they might strike, the safety of our people is our government's highest priority. As a group of Professional Investigators and Security Specialists keep an eye out for suspicious behavior or things out of place. Use your trained investigative eye and make note. Or act immediately by calling the local police department.

Take the following steps:

- Note as many physical characteristics of the person or persons involved in the suspicious event as possible. Report the suspicious party's sex, race, approximate age, height and weight, clothing, hair color and distinguishing characteristics (tattoos, accent, scars, facial hair and other identifying marks).
- Describe in detail exactly what you saw during the suspicious event. Know the time, location, what happened, who was involved and in what direction the suspects left. Your eyewitness account can aid law enforcement officials' efforts to apprehend the suspects. Take detailed notes of what you saw.
- Note characteristics of any vehicle the suspects used to make a getaway. The make, model, year, color, license plate number and any distinctive characteristics (dents, bumper stickers, tinted glass or paint chips) are all important details that can help law enforcement officials hunt the car down.
- Report peculiar incidents to your local police using their non-emergency number. Have your description of the suspects and notes regarding the incident ready. You may be asked to give your name and address. Remember that you are under no obligation to provide your personal information, although this may help law enforcement if they have further questions.
- Inform the Federal Bureau of Investigation of the suspicious incident. You can submit a tip by telephone, or anonymously, on their Web site (see Resources below). This contact information can also be found on the front cover of your local telephone directory.

- Call 911 only in an emergency situation. 911 is not the most effective source of help in cases of suspected terrorist activity which are not immediately life-threatening. However, suspicious unattended <u>vehicles</u> or packages left in public places may represent extreme public danger. Consider such a situation to be an emergency requiring the immediate attention of law enforcement officials.

Chapter Eighteen
Statement Taking

        I.   Elements of a Statement
        II.   Recorded Statement Format
        III.   Written Statement Format
        IV.   Principles of Interviewing
        V.   Interview Dos
        VI.   Interview Don'ts

18 CHAPTER 1 INTRODUCTION

I. ELEMENTS OF A STATEMENT

It's very common to conduct interviews and secure written or recorded statements when conducting an investigation. These statements may be crucial in providing corroborative supporting evidence or dismissive deceptive evidence showing the subject was untruthful. Statements are taken to document a subject's knowledge or facts about a matter and to memorialize this information while it's still fresh in their mind. Within the statement we will want to get as much personal information about the subject as possible keeping in mind that this case may go on for a year, two or several for that matter and being able to locate the witness at a later time will depend on the amount of information you secure about them now. So getting what we call identifying information about the witness as well as other family members will make locating them a lot easier when the time comes to produce them as a witness.

We know that statistically, about twenty-five percent of the nation's population moves every year for various reasons so the more information you can get about a subject without being too over bearing will prove well worth it if your witness is one of those that moved.

Interviewing is an art that you will get better at overtime. Confidence in your ability to understand what the witness is telling you is critical. If they are describing a complicated matter have them draw it out, show you pictures or even take you there. Don't move on in the statement until you understand every detail of what has already been said. Listen carefully as follow-up questions will clarify any uncertainty and are critical to getting those details that can be investigated afterwards to corroborate or pierce the falsehood of the witness' statement. You can never get too many details and through these details we obtain additional leads to pursue and verify.

Too often you hear investigators report, that the subject appeared untruthful because they neglected eye contact, fidgeted in their seat or sat with their arms or legs crossed. There are also verbal indicators where the subject asks you to repeat the question, there is a delayed response or the answer is overly specific or overly vague. While these are often indicators of lying, only facts that come from the subject's statement, proven and disproven will provide the documentation to verify the legitimacy of the statement.

If I hook you up to a lie detection machine, will the information it provides be accurate? The answer is simply YES. A lie detection machine does exactly what it is designed to do, read a person's heartbeat, record movement and perspiration. The art in the "Lie Detection", used ONLY as a TOOL, is in the operator's ability to establish reliable data. And regardless of the information, it can still only be used as a tool and the results are not admissible in court. Many Claims Investigators, especially those using this book will be new to the business and must understand that we don't rely on lie detection techniques to draw conclusions; we use them to keep probing and ask more questions.

I always act as if I believe their story to encourage more details, but if they are not coming, I ask questions that would seem to support their story if it were true to get those details that may be missing. As you get deeper in questioning and it is obvious to both parties that the statement is no longer making any sense, offer the person the opportunity to go off the record. Say to them, I think we both know that this is not going very well. I think it's time before you get in too deep to set the record straight. Nobody wants to commit insurance fraud over a simple accident. Let them know you will turn the recorder back on and get the real story and if they have to, have them withdrawal the claim.

Some of the most believable liars are criminals and drug addicts. Both are so used to covering up their tracks that lies come natural and they can be incredibly convincing. I just keep them talking so that I have as many details as possible. You may have heard the saying "Loose Lips Sink Ships" well that's exactly the principle behind getting as much information as possible. .

Recently I investigated an auto theft and the owner advised that her home had also been broken into. Apparently the thief broke into the house and stole the car keys. The owner of the car was hospitalized at the time and was relying on details reported to her by her son. The car had subsequently been involved in an accident near an office park and after the crash the car thief fled the area on foot. Footage of the thief was caught on an area businesses security camera. The person in the video looked very similar to the car owner's son. The image was grainy and distant, but the tall slender short dark haired twenty-year-old subject seemed to fit him perfect. He also had a somewhat unique gait which seemed to be noted in the footage.

Prior to interviewing the subject, I learned he had a history of drug abuse with his drug of preference the very addictive prescription pain killer known as Oxytocin. When I met the tall slender male he was wearing penny loafers, designer jeans and a sports coat. He began the introduction with a long story about his history and how my difficulty in contacting him was due to working with his father in Daytona Beach and going to school at night. During the interview he reported that he had been at the hospital with his mother for three days over the time period the house was burglarized. He had gone back and forth with a friend twice to get things for his mother but at the time the car theft and accident he was at the hospital. As I let him speak for almost two hours, he provided such incredible details. He advised that on the date of the accident at 3:00 a.m. which was actually five hours before the accident, he was returning to the hospital from one of those trips home to get some clothes and personal items for his hospitalized mother. He reported that he was driven to downtown Orlando by his friend Josh. At around 3:00 a.m. they stopped at a 7/11 on Orange Avenue near ORMC to purchase some items before actually arriving at the hospital. Later that same morning, he stated that he walked to that same 7/11 around 8:00 a.m. He stated that the same clerk who waited on him at 3:00 a.m. waited on him again at 8:00 a.m. He described the worker as a dark skinned "Indian" female in her 20's. He stated that he was certain she would remember him because, he was dressed in "Stewie" pajamas (from Family Guy), wearing a black jacket and high leather boots. He also stated that during his first visit there the young woman stopped him from leaving when he forgot to pick up the cigarettes he purchased. During the second visit she asked if he was still having a rough day. He also stated that when he returned, they had just served his mom pancakes and the hospital serves breakfast at 8:00 a.m. His mother who was listening in agreed with everything he was saying. Based on the subject's statement he could not have crashed the car in Sanford at 8:00 a.m. and also be in south Orlando at 8:00 a.m.

I determined that there are two 7/11 stores within walking distance of ORMC. One located at 1823 South Orange Avenue (referred to as the Kaley Store) and one located at 902 Gore Street. I determined that neither store had a female in her 20's working a third shift. Furthermore, the third shift girl would not have still been at the store by 8:00 a.m. The witness also stated that the clerk was a darker skinned Indian or Latin and neither store had any personnel that fit that description working the overnight shift. The managers in both stores agreed to review the video footage for that day and a follow-up call advised me that the subject was not observed in their store over the time period stated.

Later that evening I tried to call the subject to clarify if I had the right area or the right stores. I persisted with several more calls to the witnesses advising that what he had told me did not check out. He never responded.

Always go out and check the information provided in any statement. Talk to all of the people mentioned in the statement or visit any place they said they visited to see if it can be verified. You will find that through thoroughness you will become a successful investigator. There will be those that stop short of verifying all information or feel the drive to visit a location is not worthwhile. It's through these little acts of disregard or apathy that separates a good investigator from a bad one. As investigators, a large part of our work is investigating incidents or accidents. Incidents that occur at work to employees are investigated by the employers' agents, and companies that insure employers and their employees. Employers are expected to maintain safe environments for their workers. When a worker is required to clean the windows from the outside of a high-rise building, there are security procedures the workers follow to protect them from any workplace dangers. For instance they are required to wear tethers or body harnesses in case of a fall. Most of us can relate to having auto insurance to cover any injury in an automobile accident. Our auto coverage provides protection in case we are injured in the accident or whether we injury someone else. The coverage also reimburses us for the damage to our cars or the cars we struck in the accident. It also covers any other property we may have damaged if perhaps for example we ran into a fence or building that needs to be repaired. In my earlier statements, I mentioned that law enforcement agencies handle criminal matters however, when these incidents occur many times, a private party is brought into the matter. For instance, if a person is shot by an assailant during a robbery the Police will investigate the matter but so will the insurance company that insures the business and their employees. Since this shooting or incident occurred at work and the employee's injuries would be covered by their workplace insurance, the insurance company's representative would look into the matter for clarification of what happened. The worker at the same time may have been seriously injured and may seek his own legal representation to assure his best interests are protected. He may not be able to go back to work and may have a permanent personal injury or permanent disability. An investigator may be hired by the injured person's attorney to secure all of the facts of the incident.

So in any incident or accident, there may be law enforcement investigators working a case and private investigators representing different parties or sides of the matter. The investigators have different responsibilities and objectives. The Law Enforcement Officer is looking to apprehend the assailant. The Private Investigator hired by the employer or their insurance company is going to look into the workplace environment and the security provided to protect the worker from harm. The PI will start to show that the workplace did have the security required to protect the worker based on information they were able to collect during the investigation. Issues concerning crime in the immediate area as well as specific incidents of a similar nature occurring at the employer's specific location will all be collected.

OBJECTIVE

The topic of investigating Incidents and accidents covers a very broad spectrum. Many incidents and accidents occur while we are at work. Businesses need to know and understand the risks faced by their employees and the best way to understand them is to investigate the critical components of who, what, where, when, why, and how.

A good statement taker will need to pull details from the witness's memory. There will be details that they don't realize are important. Before going out, make sure you have a clear understanding of your objective. You can't conduct a thorough interview if all you ask is what happened.

Knowing and understanding the reason for the statement is key to even knowing what questions to ask. A client may ask for a statement simply to document their file. However, their purpose may be to determine liability, subrogation possibilities or to inquire about a possible pre-existing medical condition. There can be a million reasons why you are securing the statement and in order to do well in each instance you need to prepare. Always have a guide to follow as well as additional specific questions that may be relative to the issue and need to be answered. Always have a notepad to jot down questions that come to you while the witness is talking. So, before going out, make sure you have a clear understanding of your objective. You can't conduct a thorough interview if all you ask is what happened, who was injured, and who or what was responsible.

The following are a few examples of why one would be taking a statement in a particular type of claim.

Auto
Liability--Subrogation--Uninsured Motorist--Wrongful Death--PIP
Workers' Compensation
Compensability--Subrogation--Pre-exiting Condition
Slip and Fall
Liability and Subrogation
Medical Malpractice
Liability
Food Poisoning
Liability
Fire and Arson
Auto Theft
Property Theft
Property Loss

PREPARATION

Review your assignment and locate a good "base" outline appropriate to the type of claim. Have a note pad and diagram sheet available. Make your own list of questions as well.

All Statements will follow the basic format with an INTRODUCTION; BODY OF STATEMENT (questions); and a CLOSING (refer to following page for example).

PLAN AND CONTROL

Carefully plan the conversation, briefly outline your approach. Take notes, during the conversation. Listen to the interviewee's responses. Their responses should prompt additional clarification questions or follow-up questions referred to second and third tier questions. Remember, anyone listening to or reading the transcription from a recorded statement should have enough information to understand the incident or accident being explored.

INFORMALITY

Remember to use an informal positive approach. If you want a person to be your friend, treat him as if he is your friend; if you want a recorded statement, treat him as if he will give you one.

REVIEW

Review the claim and have all known facts well fixed in your mind.

COURTESY

Remember -- courtesy is essential.

II. RECORDED STATEMENT FORMAT

(Turn Recorder On)

Today's date is (date). My name is (your name). I am employed with (Agency Name), and I am representing (name of Client Company). I am at (the location where you are taking statement).

I am interviewing (name of subject) who was (involved in the accident/incident, witnessed, etc.). (Name of person) Are you aware that I am recording our conversation? (Response) Do I have your permission to do so? (Response)

    BODY OF STATEMENT

Depending on type of statement, refer to statement outlines and your own prepared notes and questions. Address the specific concerns of the client, such as any special questions indicated on the assignment sheet that must be covered. Be certain that you fully cover and understand how the incident or accident occurred. This should be a relaxed conversation so put your interviewee and yourself at ease. Don't be afraid to ask questions out of order. If a question comes to mind ask it. You can rarely ask too many questions.

    CLOSING

Ask:

Is there anything else you would like to add or clarify in this statement before I conclude the recording? (Response). (If response is no) . . . If there is nothing else, I will conclude this statement.

(Subject's name) were you aware that I was recording our conversation? (If the response is no, proceed with closing; If the response is yes, let the subject explain and ask follow up questions if necessary. Once you are through, repeat this statement again before proceeding.) (Subject's Name) Were you aware I was recording our conversation? (Response)) Did I have your permission to do so? (Response) (Subject's Name) Was everything you told me true and correct to the best of your knowledge and belief? (Response) Would you please statement your name for the final time. My name is (Your Name). Thank you for voluntarily giving this statement. (Turn Recorder Off).

NOTE

When taking a statement, avoid turning the recorder off once statement is started. If you do, you must say why the recorder is being turned off. When you turn it back on, you need to state that you are continuing with the recording and identify person and self again.

III. WRITTEN STATEMENT FORMAT

The most obvious difference between the two will be the means in which the statement is taken. Be ready to write for an extended length of time so find a comfortable writing position at a desk or table.

Make certain you are using carbonless, three part lined statement paper. This paper is available through a specialty office supply retailer. The top original white copy will be sent to the client with your report. The next yellow copy will be stapled to your notes and become part of the office file and the third part should be handed to the person whom the statement was taken from. If you do not have this specialty paper, using a piece of carbon paper inserted between the pages of an ordinary writing pad will create the same copies.

Fill in date, place of taking, and page number of statement in upper right hand corner.

The written statement should be taken as if the person wrote it themselves. You should however write the statement so that all vital questions are answered. Also, by the investigator writing the statement, the handwriting should be legible. The written statement should a continuous narrative without any paragraphs or blank spaces. If you make a mistake both parties should initial the correction. Below is an example of how the statement should be written.

Example:

My name is Veronica M. Brown and I am here today this 10th day of June with James Corn of Claims Resource Incorporated. We are here today in regards to the automobile accident, slip and fall, stolen property, etc., which occurred on (date) and (location). I am a 25 years old white female, born on July 7, 1965. I currently reside at 1276 Deer Lake Circle, Apopka, Florida 32712. My telephone number is

904-896-4629. I am married to Tim Brown who presently works for All American Gym as the manager (additional witness identification information). On the afternoon at approximately 2:30 p.m., I was driving home from having just picked my husband up from work. I was driving our 1993 blue Plymouth Voyager while my husband was seated on the passenger's side when he yelled look out! Just then I slammed on my breaks and skidded approximately 20 feet. We were both wearing our seat belts and I was only driving at approximately 45 mph so we stopped in time. The road was dry and it was a clear day. Since my husband was on the passenger side and staring out the passenger side window, he noticed a stampeding bull headed right for the road in from of us. We were driving on Old Winter Garden road heading south and my husband was starring east. The guy behind us had been tail gating me for about 5 miles ever since I left the gym. At about five miles on Old Winter Garden Road, the area gets real rural and I guess he felt it was a good place to pass. The guy who was passing me must have been looking for any oncoming cars because he sure didn't see that bull coming etc...

Remember, as this hypothetical example exhibits, each line should be continuous without any large spaces. This will prevent any room to alter or add information to the final statement that was not intended to be part of the statement. Whenever any corrections or error is made, be sure to have the interviewee initial the corrections. Number each page by using "Page 1 of 3; Page 2 of 3; Page 3 of 3", etc.

CLOSING

Have the interviewee initial each page.

Ask the subject whether there is anything else they would like to say with regards to this incident. Write exactly what they say. If they have nothing else to say, close with the following final statement and the interviewee's signature.

"I have read the above statement of _____ pages and it is true and correct to the best of my knowledge and belief." X   (Signature of Interviewee)

Detach the last (pink) copy of the three part statement paper and provide the interviewee with a complete copy of his written statement.

IV. PRINCIPLES OF INTERVIEWING

INTERVIEWING-is a specialized way of asking questions.

INTERVIEWING -is the art of extracting the maximum amount of truthful information from an individual.

INTERVIEW -is the questioning of a person who is believed to possess knowledge that is of official interest to the investigator.

An INTERVIEW is conducted for the purpose of gaining information that may establish the facts of an accident or incident and that may provide the investigator with leads which will further substantiate the validity of the claim.

In an INTERVIEW (claimants, witnesses, employers, supervisors, co-workers, etc.) the interviewee usually gives his account of the accident/incident in his own words and in his own way.

In an INTERVIEW, a specialized way and/or technique is used in asking questions.

WITNESS- one who has seen or knows something concerning the incident under investigation and is competent of discussing it.

(6- basic questions which must be exploited to the maximum in every interview).

WHO   WHAT
WHEN   WHERE
WHY?   HOW?

V. INTERVIEWING DO'S

1. DO provide a suitable place for the interview.
2. DO fix the time for the interview, if possible.
3. DO have the witness conform to your arrangements, if possible.
4. DO show some consideration for the witness, once he indicates that he is cooperating.
5. DO seat the witness and place him at ease.
6. DO seat the witness so that the light, if any, falls on him is possible.
7. DO show courtesy and politeness toward the ordinary witness.
8. DO create a motive for the witness to provide you with information.
9. DO assure the witness of protection of unnecessary disclosure.
10. DO distinguish between a witness and a bias witness.
11. DO seek to identify the witness's interest with yours, in the mind of the witness.
12. DO seek to win the confidence of the witness.
13. DO obtain basic personal details from the witness.
14. DO make an investigation of the witness before interviewing, if possible.
15. DO find out where the witness may be reached, before he leaves.
16. DO impress the witness with the importance of what he has to tell you.
17. DO ascertain the sources of the witness's testimony.
18. DO attempt to determine the truthfulness of the witness's testimony.
19. DO let the witness tell his story in his own words.
20. DO make an estimate of the consistency of the witness's story.

21. DO get the witness's story before he can consult others.
22. DO attempt to ascertain the basis of the witness's recollection of important details.
23. DO question continuously--most people talk.
24. DO interview witnesses when they are "hot."
25. DO observe the behavior of the witness, his reaction to questions, his hesitancy and other qualities which characterize his responses.
26. DO note all contradictions.
27. DO obtain documentary evidence; when possible, the originals.
28. DO change interviewers, if you find that you are "stymied" with a particular witness.
29. DO remember that there are no hard and fast rules.
30. DO keep all promises made to a witness.
31. DO look the witness straight in the eye.

VI. INTERVIEWING DON'TS

1. DON'T be rude, officious or impolite. There is matter in manner.
2. DON'T antagonize the witness.
3. DON'T deny or dismiss reasonable requests of the witness once he has indicated that he is cooperating.
4. DON'T interview more than one witness at a time.
5. DON'T lose control over the conduct of the interview.
6. DON'T "wisecrack" during an interview.
7. DON'T cross-examine or "grill" the witness.
8. DON'T let the witness know the purpose of the interview.
9. DON'T let suspicion fall on a witness whom you think is suspect, during an interview.
10. DON'T allow the interview to be interrupted, if you can possibly avoid it.
11. DON'T use only the question and answer type of interview.
12. DON'T lose track of, or dismiss, the witness until you have obtained from him all the information that he has.
13. DON'T ask more than one question at a time.
14. DON'T persist in following an unsuccessful approach.
15. DON'T place much credence in hearsay.
16. DON'T tell the witness what the "story" is; let him do the talking.
17. DON'T necessarily disbelieve an entire statement just because part of it is untrue or inaccurate.
18. DON'T ignore valid documentary evidence in favor of oral testimony.
19. DON'T assume that the witness is familiar with maps or military terminology.
20. DON'T fail to evaluate information accurately.
21. DON'T fail to obtain corroboration of testimony, if possible.
22. DON'T let the witness know how much you know.
23. DON'T lose your temper.

24. DON'T use profane language.
25. DON'T ignore your senses or common sense.
26. DON'T overlook any leads given by the witness.
27. DON'T overlook any slips made by the witness.
28. DON'T argue with the witness.
29. DON'T indulge in personalities.
30. DON'T allow the information that you get to go stale.
31. DON'T allow your prejudices against the witness, or otherwise influence your evaluation of the witness's testimony.
32. DON'T forget to note the witness's behavior and movements, i.e. any hesitation in answering questions; uneasiness; inability to maintain eye contact.
33. DON'T forget that there are no hard and fast rules to interviewing.
34. DON'T lie to the witness or make threats.
35. DON'T forget to indicate the witness's ability in your opinion to recount the incident if necessary in front of a judge and jury.

VII. GETTING STARTED

1. Call the interviewee and introduce yourself, and explain the purpose for your call.
2. Be prepared to fully identify yourself and have a business card available.
3. Dress appropriately.
4. Make certain your batteries are charged and keep spares handy.
5. The first thing to do upon meeting the interviewee is to put him or her at ease. Don't make a big thing of your recording equipment; treat it as a natural part of the procedure. Answer any questions asked but don't volunteer unnecessary detail about what will or might be done with the recording. If pressed, you can truthfully minimize the likelihood of its use in court but make no guarantees. You should know that the statement will be considered Hearsay and by itself would not be sufficient to enter into evidence. A statement cannot be cross examined so the party giving the statement would be required to testify if his statement or information was material to the case. Typically, we look at statements as a way to memorialize the information that person has while it is still fresh in their mind.
6. Explain what you are going to do is to ask a few questions beforehand and then you will turn the machine on and go over the same facts.
7. Pre-interview the witness. Ask the questions you intend to ask for the record. This tends to relax the witness and also prepares you for areas of the story that you may want to go into more deeply. Before recording the statement ask the interviewee to have a pencil handy. Invite him/her to make a diagram of the accident as a guide of his/her description. This will help prevent the interviewee from contradiction.
8. It will be a good idea to tell the interviewee that some repetition will be necessary for purpose of identification and clarification.
9. Place the recording device close to the interviewee. He/she most likely will

10. Should an interruption occur by the other party or yourself, you should keep the recorder playing and comment to explain the interruption and that the recording will be continued in a few minutes.
12. If the recorder is turned off, you must ask your subject if he/she would like to discuss anything that was mentioned while the tape recorder was off. A few reasons for turning the machine off would be for the interviewee to answer the phone, door, clear up a complicated matter.

WHILE RECORDING

1. Begin the recording by following the opening statement in the statement guide. Be sure to include the question -- "Do I have your permission to record this interview?" You must also establish that the witness understands the conversation is being recorded and that you have his permission to do so.

2. At the beginning of the statement, you should identify people, places, time and what is being done.

3. You should also establish the fact that they are giving you the statement voluntarily, without the promise of any reward and under no circumstances which would constitute a threat or duress of any kind. You need to establish the subject's educational level and their ability to read, write and understand the English language. You also need to understand and establish your subject's control of their facilities by asking if they are under the influence of any drug, alcohol or medication of any kind at the time of the taping. If they are under a doctor's care and taking some type of drug, you may want to establish what that drug is and at what time it was last taken by your subject. If, at any point and time during this statement, while your subject is providing you with specific information about circumstances which are important to your case, and you have any suspicion that the subject is taking some sort of medication, uses drugs or is a drinker, you might want to again ask him or her if at the time they observed, heard or were involved in these circumstances were they under the influence of any drugs, alcohol or medication.

4. If you are taking statements from more than one person at the same location, separate them. Do not allow one to hear the other person's statement.

5. Use good statement taking techniques during the body of the recording. Control the conversation with the aid of your statement outline. Keep the information factual and use open-end questions beginning with who, what, when, where, how, etc.

6. It is also important that you take notes during this recorded statement. You should have also already taken notes during any statement made prior to the actual recorded statement. Both sets of notes should be available to you in order to

formulate questions which will allow you to bring certain points out during the subject's statement.

7.   End the recording, as suggested in the statement guide, by asking if there is anything you haven't covered, any pertinent facts, which are felt to be important. If so, let them come out freely. Then ask if he has understood all your questions and if his answers are true and correct to the best of his knowledge. Make sure the interviewee repeats his approval of having his statement recorded. A final "thank you" ends the recording.

AFTER RECORDING

1.   After the recording and before you leave, run a spot-check on the record to make sure the machine was working.

2.   As soon as possible, while the interview is still fresh, summarize the important facts and your impression of the witness. Indicate how the information developed in the statement may affect the client's decision to "contest" or "settle" the claim and the reasons for your conclusions. This information should be reported on in your report and comprise a vital part of the report conclusion.

3.   In most cases your report will substitute for transcriptions of the recording so don't be afraid to elaborate in detail. Keep in mind that only at the request of the client will the record be transcribed.

4.   Your report and the electronic file (.wav or mp3) will then become a "material" part of the file. The statement file will be copied onto a CD and marked into evidence. Make certain that between the time you take the recording until you can download the file, the recorder is kept in a safe place.

5.   Remember you are not a licensed adjustor and should not be attempting to negotiate the settlement of a claim during your statement.

Please keep in mind that none of the following statement outlines in the manual are considered to be complete and comprehensive. Each case will warrant unique questions that apply to that case alone. They are merely outlines to reference and stimulate your own question-making process.

VIII. RECORDING TOOLS

It is always advised to take a statement in person so you can see the subject, study their body language and generally be more effective. However there will be cases where a statement may have to be taken over the phone. There are countless devices for taking statements over the phone from a landline. Most of these devices plug into the hand receiver and then have a separate mini jack that plugs into the recorder. When it comes to taking statement on your mobile phone, you will require an APP that allows you to download a program that will record both sides of the conversation. Your phone however may not be the best device and may have limitations of long statements so it's best to use a device that is specifically designed for this type of function. But some phones may not be compatible with such voice recording applications. In these cases, you will again need to rely on some hardware. Sony makes a microphone that plugs into your digital recorder on one end and an ear piece on the other. The ear piece's primary purpose is to capture the phone conversation you hear as you place your cellular phone over the ear with the microphone ear piece. The device was release in 2012 and is called the Sony ECM-TL3 Earphone-Style Mini Electret Condenser Microphone. I purchase my microphone ear piece on line through the Sony store for $19.99. Of course, in Florida you still need to notify the participants before recording any phone conversations. Even if the interview is not a formal statement, you can still tell the other party that the call is being recorded eliminating the challenges of having to write down all the information. It also prevents you from forgetting relevant information.

When choosing a digital recorder, make sure it allows you to download the file directly into your computer to transfer and save the file. Many recorders come with a separate USB wire and I have also found them with very nifty slide out USB connectors. These recorders can be found at large discount stores like WAL-MART or K-MART from around $25.00-$35.00. I am not a big believer in buying expensive equipment when there are so many devices that are reasonably priced and dependable. For many years now I have used the RCA VR5220-A Digital Recorder which takes two AAA batteries and has never let me down. Newer Digital Recorders will record files in MP3 which are smaller and easier to email. The newer recorders have climbed in pricing to over $50.00, but are well worth the extra money. The main key is that it has the capability to upload the statement to your computer. Some of the cheaper bands don't have USB upload which are of no value to the investigator so be careful.

After the recorded statement is over, you'll find yourself listening to the recording on your drive home or back to the office. This is the perfect time to recognize that you may have forgotten to ask a particular question. It's also the perfect time to call the subject back up and advise that you just realized you forgot to task them something. So get out your recorder and Sony earpiece and call them back to supplement the statement. Just start another recording and mention that this follow-up statement will supplement the previous statement taken.

IV. MAKING A CD COPY FOR CLIENT AND EVIDENCE

Once you're in the office, the statement will need to be downloaded to your computer. This is best done by following the instructions on your recorder. In most cases just by connecting your recorded to the computer, the software on the device will facilitate a download.

Set up a separate file on your computer marked "Statements" and make sure you drag and drop all recorded statements into this folder. The file names of the recorders will need to be changed during the transfer process so they are saved by witness/subject name.

Once the files as stored on your computer, you'll want to make two copies one for the client and one for the evidence room. DO NOT leave all your statement files on your computer without backing them up individually and numbering them individually (all evidence should be logged and numbered).

NERO

Is one of the more popular and mainstream software for copying data. Many of the basic versions are free to download. Once the software is downloaded onto your computer simply chose make a data disc and follow the prompts to browse for the file, in this case a statement or several statements and burn to disc. If you took multiple statements for one case, then there is no reason not to burn all of them on one disk (as long as they fit). Once a client's disk is made, simply duplicate the process and copy another disk to mark as evidence and store in an area away from your computer, typically a secure evidence room.

Chapter Nineteen
Statement Case Studies

I. Premium Fraud
II. Auto Repair Scheme
III. Brake Checking
IV. Slip and Fall
V. Staged Pedestrian Accident
VI. Apartment Fire
VII. Security Shooting

CASE STUDIES

The following is a compilation of various cases where statements were taken as part of the investigation. These statements were used to document the facts of a case as reported by the parties involved or witnesses. They were taken to clarify a matter and to document the incident while the information is still fresh in the mind of the person being interviewed. The report samples are based on my own reporting format and yours or your company may prefer the reporting in a different format. I routinely take photographs of each person interviewed and accident or incident locations. In accident cases, I take picture from each driver's perspective as well as any other pertinent matter. Most pictures are taken with my smart phone. Some cases involving fine details should be photographed with a high resolution digital camera.

CASE I – PREMIUM FRAUD – FALSE GARAGING

Mrs. Santiago was in the back seat of a vehicle driven by her daughter. Her son Christian was seated in the front passenger's seat. The daughter was driving a car insured by her father. The car was reportedly left at his ex-wife's house while he traveled to Washington on a business trip. He claimed he drive to Kissimmee and had his family take him to the airport and they brought the car back to Kissimmee while he was away. He indicated that anyone at the house had permission to use the car while he was away. The adjuster handling the claim saw that Mr. Ramero had two cars and was the only listed driver on both cars. He insured both cars stating that they were garaged at his Tampa residence. Since Mr. Ramero could not drive two cars at the same time and had no other listed drivers, his insurance on the second car was greatly discounted. Many times insurance can be purchase online, making acts like this go undetected until something major goes wrong. For an adjuster, the two cars are a "red flag" and the newly licensed driver operating the car also fits similar acts of fraud.

As you read the case, I approached this investigation thinking that the car was most likely always in Kissimmee and never in Tampa. I was prepared to get the truth from the teenage driver, however when Mr. Ramero arrived, I spoke to him briefly and stated that I would need proof of his airline ticket and out of town travel. He clearly knew the cat was out of the bag and I offered him an opportunity to come clean. Lying to me and furthering the deceit, meant the Insurance Company would take this very serious as the more time we have to spend determining the truth, the greater the severity of the incident. If he lies to me during our recorded interview, it only provides the ultimate evidence I need to show he intentionally misrepresented material facts of the case in order to gain coverage. This was a classic act of fraud that was disrupted by the investigation. Had this case not been investigated, it's possible the deceit could have played itself out.

As you review the case, make note of the manner in which I report my findings and the report format I follow. These reporting formats are my own style and are only included as an example.

Details of Investigation

Investigator: John Bilyk / Claims Resource Incorporated / (877) 274-2000 / www.claimsresource.cc

Dates of Investigation: Wednesday, August 15, 2013 (12:15 p.m. – 5:47 p.m.); Thursday, August 16, 2013 (5:25 p.m. -6:15 p.m.)& Friday, August 17, 2013 (6:05 p.m. – 7:18 p.m.)

Pertinent Information: On Wednesday, August 15, 2013, I was contacted by SIU Ross to immediately proceed to contact the claimant's attorney and request permission to talk to the unrepresented, minor driver. Since the minor driver was reportedly living with her mother the claimant Vicki Santiago, I needed to secure Ms. Santiago's approval prior to speaking with her daughter. Reportedly, the daughter was not represented although her mother was.

Attorney Contact
Farrow & Rogers- 407.836.2560   Wednesday, August 15, 2012

I learned that the attorney on the file Neal Ricardo had this case in his Kissimmee office and it was being handled by the Attorney's assistant "Lucy". I reached Lucy's extension and advised I was heading out to the claimant's residence to speak with the unrepresented minor child, Victoria Ramero who was driving our insured's vehicle. I advised that if there was a issue with this contact to p[lease call me immediately on my cell phone number. I also advised I would like to also secure the recorded statement of their two clients, Vicki Santiago and Christian "Santiago" Ramero, who were both passengers and reportedly injured in the accident.

SIU Contact

I contacted the SIU and asked if it was okay if I also did a neighborhood canvass while I was in the area. It was discussed that while in the neighborhood, I should have a picture of a silver 2000 Mazda Protégé to show to the neighbors in determining if perhaps the car was left (garaged) at this residence as opposed to Tampa with insured as it was insured and registered.

Internet Picture - 2000 Mazda Protégé

A generic looking color picture of a silver 2000 Mazda Protégé was downloaded and printed prior to leaving for the neighborhood inquiry.

Personal Visit – Ms. Victoria Ramero
2528 Dome Ridge Court   Kissimmee, FL 34744
3:15 p.m. – 5:22 p.m.

Initially the address was provided as 2526 Dome Ridge and once finding this address was not correct, I returned to my office to run a database address search. The address search showed that the correct address was 2528 Dome Ridge Court. The address search however also showed that two other addresses, seemingly more recent, had also been used since the claimant reported the Dome Ridge Court address. These other two addresses were PO BOX 41162, Kissimmee, FL 34742 and 1043 Metro Resorts Place, Kissimmee, FL 34744.

5:47 p.m.

Nonetheless I returned to the same neighborhood and conducted my inquiries of the resident at 2528 Dome Court as well as the surrounding neighbors. I found the current occupant in 2528 has been there less than one month. A vehicle in the driveway had Texas plates #DB2BI81. The resident in 2526 stated that before the current resident in 2528, there was an American couple at the house and before that a Spanish family occupied the residence. He described the Spanish family comprised of the claimant Vicki Santiago who he identified only as a woman in her late 50's early 60's, a male believed to be Christian and a young female, possibly Victoria. I then showed him the picture of the silver 2000 Mazda Protégé and he stated that he had never seen that vehicle at the residence. He did state that he recalled seeing a green Dodge Caravan and possible a white Honda Civic. He believed the young male person worked at "Lockers" as he wore a shirt with the company's logo.

1047 Metro Resorts Place
Kissimmee, FL 34744   Thursday, August 16, 2012
5:25 p.m.

I proceeded to the claimant's newer address located in a vacation resort now being converted to long term apartment rentals. The community is gated however I was eventually permitted access inside. Upon proceeding to the claimant's residence, no one was home. I waited in the area a short while but after finding they had still not returned home, I exited the area.

1047 Metro Resorts Place
Kissimmee, FL 34744   Friday, August 17, 2012
6:05 p.m. -7:18 p.m.

Once again I returned to the claimant's neighborhood, this time finding both the claimant Vicki and Christian present at the apartment. I introduced myself as a representative of AUTO NORTH, her ex-husband's insurance company. I advised both of them I needed to speak to Victoria Ramero who was reportedly in the pool at the time. Christian left to go get her and while remaining waiting, Ms. Santiago pointed out a large scare on her forehead. I didn't want to give her the impression I didn't care so I took a picture of the scar. I did remind them that they were both represented and that I called their attorney to advise him of this contact. Neither subject had been contacted by their attorney on how to proceed, but I advised that we should not discuss the matter. I reconfirmed though that young Ms. Victoria Ramero was not represented although they stated she was seeking some treatment. I did not discuss the case with either of them but did take the opportunity to obtain a photograph of Mr. Christian Santiago Ramero as well.

As I waited for Christian to walk to the community pool and retrieve Victoria Ramero, I was advised by Ms. Vicki Santiago that the insured, Mr. Hector F. Ramero was on his way to the house. I didn't know if he lived there or was just visiting. I remained tight lipped until he arrived just moments before Ms. Victoria Ramero.

When Ms. Ramero arrived she was clearly wet and had her bathing suit on. She went to the back of the house changed then returned to the front room. I asked her to wait momentarily while I speak to her father, the insured Mr. Hector Ramero in private.

Interview – Recorded Statement of Insured Hector F. Ramero

We walked outside and I asked Mr. Ramero where he lived. I wanted to get it straight whether the insured was estranged or not from his family. He told me that he did live in Tampa at the address I had on records of 12261 Mill Street #305, Tampa, FL 33626. I next asked him how many cars he currently has insured under his own name and he responded two. I next identified myself as a licensed investigator and showed him my state license. I told him I had come to this location to question the driver of the car (his teenage daughter) specifically about her possession and use of the car. I told him I had some questions about the story that the car was left while he went to Washington. I could see the anguish in his face and asked if perhaps he just wanted to clear the whole matter up as from this point further it could only get worse if the truth didn't come out. He stated that he bought his daughter the car around June 11, 2013, in Orlando and that the car was given to her. It was meant for her and for her only as his son Christian Ramero already had his own car. Furthermore the car was kept at 1047 Metro Resorts Place, Kissimmee FL 34744-5131 and was never in Tampa or used by him (the insured).

At this point, I advised I would notify the adjuster of this new information and suggested he also call or follow-up after the weekend. He stated that he would like to be able to retrieve his vehicle since he is under the assumption he is not insured. I also walked with him back into the house when he told his ex-wife that she needs to forget trying to get money from his insurance company because he is not insured. I did not render any opinion on what may happen next or how his wife's' attorney may proceed. I think he was just relieved that the truth came out and that no one was seriously hurt.

With the new information coming directly from the insured, I did not proceed with Ms. Victoria Ramero's statement.

<u>Electronic Update</u>   <u>Sunday, August 19, 2013</u>
<u>5:00 p.m.</u>

During this investigation, I maintained contact with the SIU, Shane Ross. Following my completed efforts, I was instructed to submit my full written report for review. The secured recorded statement of Mr. Hector Ramero will be sent directly to the adjuster via US mail.

Status: Closed

Thank you for the continued opportunity to be of service. Should you have any questions regarding this investigation, please contact my office at (877) 000-0000 or direct them to my e-mail.

Enclosure: CD/Recorded statement of Hector F. Ramero sent to Claims Handler via US Mail.

END OF REPORT

CASE II – AUTO REPAIR SCHEME

The Insured, Mr. Randall obtained a quote to have his car repaired then worked with a friendly repair shop that agreed to do the repairs at a significant reduction. When Mr. Randall went to pick up his car and wasn't happy with work, he took it to another shop. The new shop found unrepaired items as well as an inferior paint job. Mr. Randall tried to indicate that damage had been missed by the appraiser and needed more money. The insured had also told the adjuster that the first repair company was paid the entire amount and the Insurance Company's check was signed over to the repair shop. When a copy of the check was ordered by the adjuster it clearly showed it was cashed by the Insured not Performance Detail. When stories don't match, many times an investigator is assigned to look into the matter, thus the reason for the referral. By ordering an investigation, we were able to intervene in this matter before any additional work had been done. The new repair shop saw us in person so knew this claim was being watched.

Details of Investigation

Investigator: John Bilyk / Claims Resource Incorporated / (877) 000-0000 / www.claimsresource.cc

Dates of Investigation: Tuesday, January 9, 2013 (3:19 p.m.- 5:25 p.m. & 5:15 p.m.) & Wednesday, January 10, 2013 (10:55 a.m. – 12:33 p.m.)

Pertinent Information: This investigation was received on a rush basis and requested to be initiated immediately. I was advised that the claimant's vehicle was appraised at having $7,860.98 in damages. A check was sent to the claimant for the total of the repair. According to the repair shop, the claimant spent the repair proceeds and couldn't pay the repair shop and wanted to make payments. The claimant agreed to have only certain repairs performed to lower the repair costs. The claimant kept the balance of $7860.98 and the shop actually received a total of $4300.00.

The claimant now alleges that the shop didn't complete work or do all the work needed for repairs. The claimant wants damages that the shop didn't address, which he knew weren't addressed. He has now taken his car to another facility and is requesting more money.

I was requested to visit the Body Shop identified as Performance Detail in Miami and then meet with the claimant to sort out what exactly happened.

Performance Detail 786.944.5582   Tuesday, January 9, 2013

I called the shop and spoke to the owner Mr. Luis Rodriguez. He provided the body shops physical address of 200 SW 46th Avenue Miami, FL 33223. I introduced myself and he agreed to meet with me and attempt to resolve this matter.

Performance Detail -200 SW 46th Avenue Miami, FL 33223

I arrived on site to an unmarked warehouse and small single bay unit and met Mr. Rodriguez. He seemed very straight, but just starting out in business and didn't have much in the way of an office or filing cabinet. Mr. Rodriguez agreed to provide me with a recorded statement.

Recorded Statement of Luis E. Rodriguez DOB 06/27/1986

Mr. Rodriguez while a bit disorganized and newly in business appear to be straight forward and truthful. He advised that the claimant did not sign over any Insurance Company check to him. In fact, the claimant told him he had not coverage and needed to pay for the damage out of his own pocket. Apparently the claimant knows a mutual friend who recommended Luis to him because this body shop is about an hour from the claimant's residence in Boynton Beach. The claimant however reportedly is a welder and works in Miami off Okeechobee Road at Jims Grinding. Mr. Rodriguez stated that the claimant dropped his car off at his shop so he could inspect it and come up with a price to repair the vehicle. Mr. Rodriguez stated he never saw any appraiser's estimate.

After the inspection, Mr. Rodriguez stated that the car needed $1700 for parts and he would charge $2600 in labor. The claimant paid the $1700 in parts which Mr. Rodriguez had no receipt. He then went to Mr. Randall's place of work and picked up an additional $900 in cash. When the car was done, Mr. Randall paid another $1700 final payment for a total repair cost paid to Performance Detail by Mr. Randall of $4300.00. Mr. Randall always paid cash and the only document Luis Rodriguez had of the work is the enclosed work order that doesn't identify the source of the parts, the costs of the parts or even what parts were put on the vehicle. (See attached work order exhibit #1).

Mr. Rodriguez is a young guy and has only been in business for about six months. Mr. Rodriguez feels he was doing a friend of a friend a favor by doing the repairs as inexpensively as possible since he was told there was no insurance money.

When the car was completed, the appraiser came to his shop and inspected the finished vehicle and notice the front left steering arm needed to be replaced. This is when the shop was sent a payment directly to replace the arm. Mr. Rodriguez states he replaced this item and had the receipt for the part (enclosure #2).

While by no means does Mr. Rodriguez appear to have a top rated body shop, the facts about the money between him and the claimant appeared truthful. (Mr. Rodriguez' full recorded statement is enclosed).

Telephone Call Eric Randall – 565.222.3664
5:33 p.m.

I contacted the Randall household in the evening since he was working and thought that perhaps we could meet in the evening. I reached his wife who stated that the claimant works the second shift and doesn't get off until 2:00 a.m. She provided me with his cellular number of 544.955.7668 so I could contact him and discuss meeting. I called him on his cellular phone and left a message. He called me back and we discussed meeting the following day at 11:00 a.m. at his residence.

Electronic Update –SIU Mr. Ross Smith
5:56 p.m.

Immediately following my conversation with Mr. Rodriguez an update was provided to the SIU. We also discussed a request to have a copy of the front and back of the Insurance Company Check paid to the claimant which Mr. Ross forwarded to our office. The claimant had stated that the entire proceeds where paid to Performance Detail.

Personal Visit- Claimant's Residence- 12204 Redlake Drive
Boynton Beach, FL 33426   Wednesday, January 10, 2013
10:55 a.m.

The claimant resides in a secured gated apartment complex where he rents. Mr. Randall met me outside in the parking lot area. His wife later joined us to listen in on the conversation. Mr. Randall agreed to provide me with a recorded statement.

Recorded Statement Eric Randall DOB 5/12/1974 SSN 266-33-XXXX

Mr. Randall confirmed that the Insurance Company sent him $7860.98 paid directly to him and he used $4300.00 of the funds to pay Performance Detail. He used another thousand to buy tires and rims. He used the remainder to pay his rent as he had lost his job and was facing eviction. He stated that he understands that the rest of the costs are on him and not the responsibly of the carrier. He acted as if he didn't know why I was present and stated that he doesn't want to get involved in any "fraud". Contrary to what I had been told in the initial assignment, Mr. Randall made no attempt to hide the fact that he cashed the check. In fact the check shows the casher's Florida DL #R333-345-74-042-0. This is the same number that I observed on his driver's license when I asked him for identification. His signature is also on the back of the check. Mr. Randall confirmed he chose Performance Detail because they had a mutual friend. He also paid much less than he was given so he understands that now if he expects to get any further work out of Pro-Detail he will have to resolve this on his own. At the same time the claimant told me his car was located at X-Quisite Auto, located at 1230 W. Lantana Road, Boynton Beach, FL. This is about 15 minutes from the claimant's house and he wanted me to come visit the location. He stated that putting everything aside that there appeared to be one item that the car still needed that the appraiser never saw. This was a right knuckle. I agreed to accompany him to X-Quisite Auto. The claimant's full statement is enclosed).

X-Quisite Auto - 1230 W. Lantana Road, Boynton Beach
12:01 p.m.

Here I met the owner and learned that he and the claimant had been talking to Mr. Shiner of North AUTO INSURANCE to cover the cost of just the right knuckle paid directly to the business. I also was shown about $1,000 worth of work that needed to be performed and was on the original appraisal but not performed by Performance Detail. The shop also stated that the paint job was done in a contaminated booth and had specs of air and particles in the paint. This however again was a matter that needed to be handled between the claimant and Luis Rodriguez. It seemed very clear when I left that the claimant agreed to take care of all other matters and that the payment for the right knuckle would end any further claims.

Electronic Update   Wednesday, January 16, 2013
10:15 p.m.

During this investigation, I maintained contact with the SIU, Mr. Ross. Upon completion of this investigation, I forwarded my full written report for his review.

Status: Closed

Thank you for the continued opportunity to be of service. Should you have any questions regarding this investigation, please contact my office at (877) 274-2000 or direct them to my e-mail.

Enclosure: #1 Performance Detail "Work Order"
             #2 Steering Arm Part Replacement Receipt
             #3 CD / Statements of Rodriguez and Mr. Randall

END OF REPORT

CASE III – BRAKE CHECKING

In this case we represented the tailgater. The woman driver indicated that she had to brake for a child on a bike but the witness stated this was untrue. The concept of Assault by Brake Checking is a new phenomenon but her actions contributed to this accident and we panned on playing the "criminal charge card" if this matter got out of hand with her personal injury attorney. The attorney got wind of our plans and ended up dropping his client feeling the fight and time wasn't worth the effort. It was our field investigation that led to the discovery of the witnesses which turned this case around dramatically.

Details of Investigation

Investigator: John Bilyk / Claims Resource Incorporated / (877) 000-0000 / www.claimsresource.cc

Dates of Investigation: Thursday, April 18, 2013 (12:34 p.m.); Monday, April 22, 2013 (1:13 p.m.); Friday April 26, 2013 (12:54 p.m.- 1:33 p.m.); Monday, May 13, 2013 (1:56 p.m.); May 14, 2013 (3:33 p.m.); Wednesday, May 22, 2013 (11:03 a.m.- 3:31 p.m. & 6:33 p.m.)& Thursday, May 23, 2013 (9:33 a.m.- 2:11 p.m. & 5:30 p.m. – 7:00 p.m.)

Pertinent Information: On Thursday, April 18, 2013, I was advised by SIU, Ross Smith to conduct an accident scene investigation by securing statements from the claimant and any witnesses I could identify. Mr. Smith forwarded me the Police Report purchased from Buycrash.com as well as the claims file notes, insured's information and recorded statement. I reviewed all documentation before proceeding with this investigation.

Telephone Contact -Claimant Trina Ann McCormichale
Telephone Number 352.989.0959   Monday, April 22, 2013
1:13 p.m.

I called the claimant and found she answered the phone during the middle of the day. I advised that the purpose of my call was to inquire as to who represented her. She stated that she did not know the specific attorney however they were with Rogers & Rogers.
I did not discuss the case or make any further inquiries and thanked her for her assistance.

Law Offices of Rogers & Rogers 352.552.4459   Friday, April 26, 2013
12:54 p.m.-1:33 p.m.

I contacted the Law Offices and was advised that Attorney Rogers' assistant Michelle Antia was handling this matter. I was advised to send a letter to her attention at mantia@rogersandrogers.com. I compiled the letter and sent it via email to her attention.

Law Offices of Rogers & Rogers 351.542.4459   Monday, May 13, 2013
1:56 p.m.

I called the law offices and again was put through to Ms. Antia's voicemail. I left a detained message asking to take her clients statement and asked if she received my letter.

Law Offices of Rogers & Rogers 351.542.4459   Tuesday, May 14, 2013
3:33 p.m.

I spoke to Attorney's assistant yesterday and she stated that she never received my letter? I resent the same letter to her attention but emphasized that I wanted to secure her clients statement.

Ms. Antia 351.542.4459   Wednesday, May 22, 2013
11:03 a.m.

I sent an email to Attorney Rogers attention reporting that I wasn't sure if they still represented Ms. McCormichale. I advised that I had made numerous attempts to speak with Ms. Antia whom I was directed to no avail. Ms. Antia returned my call, but I was apparently on the other line. She left the most bizarre message stating that she never received any letter from me and has no idea what I am calling about. I immediately called her back and left her a message stating exactly what my intentions were. I also immediately sent her an email making the same request to secure her clients statement. To date I have received no response.

SIU Contact
12:40 p.m.

After this last message, I got the impression they were just stalling because it just didn't make any sense. I also advised the SIU, Mr. Shane Ross that I was still proceeding with the investigation.

Leesburg Police Department 352.787.2121
1:11 p.m.

I reviewed the Police report obtained through BUYCRASH.COM and saw that the investigating officer had put the insured name in the witness box. I had an address but I wanted a name to go along with this information. I spoke to Sonia in records who stated that she would get with Patrolman Secrest and have this information corrected and get back to me.

Telephone Contact Insured- Mr. John Murray
1:31 p.m.

I contacted the Insured and obtained a description the motorcycle as well as the motorcycle operator. The insured advised that the motorcycle was a Harley Davidson black and silver in color and it was driven by a male subject in his 30's tall and thin build with no facial hair. As I was talking to the Insured, he mentioned that the claimant had tried to back her off by hitting her brakes earlier at the intersection of Lone Oak and Main Street. He then stated that she did it again on S. Lone Oak in front of several witnesses who were outside their house at the time. He stated that the claimant stopped for no reason as there were no kids crossing or near the street. Stating "no reason" seemed an incomplete answer so I pushed him more until he stated what he meant was that she stopped to get him off her tail because she felt he was following her too closely. At that point, I realized her actions where what seemed to have caused the accident not the Insured's. I asked if he would allow me to visit him and he reported he was off work on Thursday, so we agreed to meet Thursday at noon-time at his house in Leesburg.

Witnesses Address -20260 Hwy 27 Clermont, FL 34715
2:44 p.m.- 3:12 p.m.

I proceeded to this location and found it was a trailer park called Bee's RV Resort. I spoke to the manager who based on the description didn't know anyone at the park that currently fit that description. I advised that I was working on a name so if she didn't mind I would call her back to see if the name sounds familiar. She state that I could reach her at 352.429.2116.

Leesburg Police Department 352.787.2121
3:31 p.m.

I called Sonia back at Leesburg PD and learned that Officer Secrest would not be on shift until 6:00 p.m. She however stated that she spoke to him and he also had the witness's telephone number. Sonia became skeptical that I even had a copy of the Police Report because she stated that the witness's telephone number was on the report. With the recent law requiring affidavits to secure police report information, Police Departments are very reluctant to help anyone over the phone. I told her we purchased the report through BUYCRASH.COM and that the witness's telephone number was not on the report. She ran her own check and was surprised to see that the witness's telephone numbers are in fact redacted from the HSWV Crash reports from BuyCrash.com. I tried obtain the witnesses telephone number but she just wouldn't do it stating that there may be a legal reason it is withheld. She stated that I would have to talk to the Patrolman or his supervisor at 6:00 p.m. tonight. I left a message for Patrolman Secrest to call me as soon as he could.

Leesburg Police Department 352.787.2121
6:33 p.m.

I called and spoke to patrolman Secrest's supervisor Sergeant MacDill. He stated that he was going to meet with Patrolman Secrest and have the Police report corrected with the proper name. He however stated that I would have to come to the Police department in the morning to obtain a copy of the full report and submit a sworn statement affidavit per 316.066(3)c). I advised the Sergeant that I would be driving from Kissimmee so please have the report available for pick-up tomorrow.

Leesburg Police Department Leesburg FL   Thursday, May 23, 2013
9:33 a.m.- 10:45 a.m.

I made a personal Visit to the Leesburg Police department and found the report ready for me to pick-up. I secured the Actual Leesburg Police Report which had the witnesses name corrected as well as his telephone number. The witness was identified as John Jacobs with a corresponding telephone number of 561.319.1992.

Bee's RV Resort -352.429.2116
10:55 a.m.

I spoke to the manager again and asked if she knew Mr. John Jacobs. She stated that she did but that he no longer lived in the park. She stated that he lived with his mom and dad and that they left no forwarding address.

Telephone Contact Witness John Jacobs 561.319.1992
11:11 a.m.

I called the witness and received his voicemail. I left a detailed message asking him to call me.

Telephone Contact Insured 352.552.4444
11:20 a.m.

I called the insured and left a message stating that I was in route to his house as arranged.

Insured's Residence 30 Larry Street, Leesburg, FL 34748
11:42 a.m.- 12:44 p.m.

I arrived at the Insured's and observed his crashed Buick parked off to the left of the house in the grass. The Insured stated that the Police have advised that the inoperable car needs to be removed from the front of the property. I proceeded to introduce myself and the Insured agreed to provide a supplemental statement.

Recorded Statement of John Murray DOB 3/27/1984

The claimant reported that the accident occurred around the area of 120 S. Lone Oak drive. He reported that there was a black family outside that saw the whole accident. He also reported that there was another incident where the claimant stopped abruptly. He stated that the claimant was "angry" and while he had backed off from the prior incident she stopped the second time more abruptly. The claimant has a hard time communicating what actually happened but he did state that "she stopped and caused the accident." He stated that she was playing a game and agreed that she stopped on purpose. He didn't think there was anything wrong with her and stated that she walked fast while talking on the phone and spoke to the motorcycle witness and the black family. He stated that her stating there were kids in the street was no true.

After the statement the claimant agreed to show me where the black family lived. We both entered my vehicle and drove about .5 mile from his residence to 120 Lone Oak Drive. I then returned him to his house and thanked him for his assistance.

120 S. Lone Oak Drive, Leesburg, FL 34748
1:10 p.m.-1:27 p.m.

I proceeded to this location and spoke to three people an elderly man, a female in her young late 20's and a male subject in his teens identified as Trevon Been. Mr. Been agreed to provide a statement of what he witnessed.

Statement of Trevon Been DOB 1/12/1994

Mr. Been stated that on the day of the accident he was outside with his two other brothers. Her stated that one of his brothers was on a bike but that they were no were near the road in fact they were on the porch 30 feet away. He stated that he saw the accident happen he saw the claimant hit her brakes a couple of times then slam on the brakes causing the front of her car to dip and the back to raise up high. He stated she even skid her tires stopping so abruptly causing the insured's car to go under her car. He also stated that there were no kids in the street. He stated that "she stopped to see if he would hit her". He stated that the Police came five minutes later and he told them the same story. (Mr. Been's full statement is attached).

Accident Location Surrounding Area
1:33 p.m.

The accident occurred in front of 120 S. Lone Oak Drive. Across the street there is a chain link fence bordering the roadway and a vacant home.

The witness lives to the left and there house is out of view. To the right there is a chain link fence that runs along the street the next house on the right is vacant.

These pictures show the image of the street from the insured drivers perspective traveling south on S. Lone Oak Drive.

Telephone Contact Mr. John Jacobs – 561.319.1994
1:42 p.m.

I called Mr. Jacobs again and left a second message.

2:11 p.m.

Mr. Jacobs returned my call and stated that he was at work in Leesburg and not supposed to be on the phone. He advised that he told police everything he had to say and while he was reluctant to get involved he stated that I could call him back at 5:30 p.m. after he got off work.

5:30 p.m.- 6:13 p.m.

I called Mr. Jacobs back and introduced myself. He agreed to provide me with a recorded statement over the phone.

Recorded Statement of John M. Jacobs DOB 1/17/1993

Mr. Jacobs supported the other two statements stating that there were no kids in the road or even near the road. He further confirmed that the nearest people were the black family outside with one teenager on a BMX type bike. He also corroborated the other two statements saying that the claimant stopped for no reason other than to cause an incident. He said she gave no warning and he had to lock up the rear tire of his bike which caused him to go into a slide and almost hit insured. He said he told police and they said oh "she brake checked him". But she didn't just brake check, she slammed on brakes and stopped suddenly. He stated that the claimant was about 18 feet from her and he was about twenty feet from the insured. He stated that he purposely stayed back because she did a similar brake check at the intersection of Main and S. Lone Drive. After the accident he stated that the claimant got out of car and said to motorcycle guy "did you see how close he was following me" and nothing about any kids or children. He also stated that there absolutely were no children in the area and this was not a true statement. He stated he knows this for certain because after almost hitting the insured he rode his motorcycle around both vehicles and there were no kids anywhere. The witness's full statement is attached and he is well spoken and would make an excellent witness.

Internet Law Article
6:15 p.m. – 7:00 p.m.

I did some internet searching and found similar cases across the country and in Florida have been seen as acts of assault where slamming on the brakes was considered "Intent to Frighten".

I have enclosed the following article to better explain this point.

What you may not know is that this tailgate stopping action can lead to both civil and criminal assault charges and can block the front driver from any injury recovery if it actually leads to an accident.

First, let's think about the idea of assault charges. Ask yourself what slamming on the brakes is supposed to accomplish?

The easy answer is to say "to get the other car to back off." But there is an underlying answer that is more important, it is "to scare the other driver into thinking they might rear-end the front car so that they decide to back off." This is the important distinction.

Slamming the brakes is intended to cause fear, fear of a potential accident and possible injury.

The Crime of Assault, in many states, includes any action that is intended to cause fear of immediate harm in the mind of another person.

In Maryland, there is even a specific Criminal Jury Instruction under the category of Assault called "Intent to Frighten." To be found guilty of 2nd Degree Assault in this context, the state must prove 4 things:

That the front car driver committed an act with the intent to place the driver of the second car in fear of immediate physical harm;

That the front car driver had the apparent ability at the time of the action to actually cause physical harm;
That the driver of the second car (or any other person in the area) was reasonably put in fear of physical harm; and
That the front car driver was not legally justified, or acting in self-defense.

Let's analyze these elements in this context. (1) You intentionally slammed on your brakes, with the intent to scare the second car into thinking if they don't slow down there might be an accident – Check; (2) you are driving a hunk of steel weighing upwards of a ton and if an accident occurs, it is likely to cause at least a minor injury – Check; (3) someone was actually put in reasonable fear that they might immediately be hurt as a result of your action — Maybe; (4) there is no legal justification for slamming on your brakes to scare someone – "he was tail gaiting me" is not a valid justification here.

So, with 3 of the 4 elements being fairly obvious, as long as there is some proof or good faith belief that someone was actually scared as a result of your actions, you just committed an assault.

Florida Police Officer's "Blog" on Slamming on Brakes Topic

I've had this happen to me once. I made the arrest for aggravated assault, the state attorney actually upgraded it to aggravated battery because the person was "jolted" as a result of the accident..........it stuck and the guy pled out......I've heard of other cases, but didn't follow them.

It definitely fits the assault/battery statute here in Florida.....but only an idiot would admit to "slamming on the brakes just so he would hit me".......stupidity he/she deserves to go to jail.....too much road rage and too many idiots causing injuries/death on the roadways.

Electronic Update   Tuesday, May 28, 2013
3:12 p.m.

At this point, it appears there is a case that the claimant slammed on her brakes to scare the claimant and lied about there being children in or near the roadway. Statements from two witnesses, Mr. Bell and Mr. Jacobs confirm what the Insured had a difficult time communicating.

The Law Offices of Rogers and Rogers, specifically Michelle Antia has not assisted or responded to many of our attempts to set an amicable time to interview her client. At this point it seems this case should be submitted to DIF as a Fraud Referral and may also meet the guidelines of criminal assault.

Pending any further developments, I am closing my file in this matter. If future responses are received from the Law Office of Rogers and Rogers I will notify your office to see if we are to proceed.

Case Status: Closed

Should you have any questions regarding this investigation, please contact my office at cases@claimsresource.cc

Enclosures: #1 CD with statements of:
        a. Insured John Murray
        b. Witness Trevon Been
        c. John Jacobs

       #2 Official Leesburg Police Report (5 pages)

END OF REPORT

CASE IV – SLIP ANF FALL

Ms. Harkow stated that she got up in the middle of the night and went to go use the bathroom only to slip and fall on what she stated was water on the floor. Upon investigating the incident, I learned from the maintenance supervisor that there had been no reported water leaks in the room and no maintenance records of any water related repair. I inspected the room to try and see what she may have tripped on. I looked for a broken or uneven tile, loose carpeting or perhaps an uneven threshold at the bathroom door, but none existed. I learned a security officer was the first responded and I tracked him down at another job he held. Upon taking his statement, he indicated that the woman seemed to have just showered and had a wet head. He believed she had just gotten home and showered. At the same time though he stated that she was had slurred speech and moved slowly and recalled seeing prescription bottles on the night stand. He also recalled the subject stating that she just passed out. From the investigation, this was clearly not a slip and fall where the hotel neglected some hazard that caused the accident. Ruling out the hotel being at fault and documenting all the facts while they were still fresh in everyone's mind was a precautionary measure against any future law suit. I later learned that the woman's father called and wanted a full reimbursement of the woman's two week stay until he was presented with the facts from our investigation at which time he dropped all demands.

Details of Investigation

Investigator: John Bilyk / Claims Resource Incorporated / (877) 274-2000 / www.claimsresource.cc

Dates of Investigation: Monday, December 10, 2012 (3:13 p.m.); Monday, December 17, 2012 (12:07 p.m. - 6:15 p.m.) & Tuesday, December 18, 2012 (9:01 a.m.- 4:30 p.m.)

Pertinent Information: Prior to initiating this investigation, I reviewed all information provided by the SIU, Mr. Coates. This information included a detailed description of the accident, the claimant's name and insured contact information.

Doralto Beach Resort – Insured Contact, Ms. Tina Gonzalez
<u>305.797.0065 Extension 3300   Monday, December 10, 2012</u>
<u>3:13 p.m.</u>

The insured's property is called the Doralto Beach Resort. It is a famous Miami Beach Hotel dating back to the 70's when reportedly bands such as the Beatles performed there. I called the hotel and the insured contact Ms. Gonzalez was very pleasant and helpful. I learned the claimant was staying in room #944 at the time of the incident. I also learned that the room is booked through December with some periodic changes in guests specifically on Monday December 17, 2012, after 2:00 p.m. I could gain access to the room and we agreed to meet on that date.

Doralto Hotel 6777 Collins Avenue
Miami Beach, FL   Monday, December 17, 2012
12:07 p.m. - 3:44 p.m.

As agreed, I visited the hotel arriving in the later afternoon after check out and prior to the next guest's check-in time. I was accompanied to the room by Ms. Gonzalez. I examined and photographed the room. The entrance, hall closet and bathroom are all tiled. There were no broken tiles or any uneven surface. There was also no threshold under the bathroom door. As we discussed the way the hotel operated I was advised that the Customer Service Manager manages, maintenance and guest issues. I was advised this person was Mr. Steve Ruiz.

Mr. Steve Ruiz Customer Service Manager

In this hotel, any room repairs, guest complaints or closures of rooms for maintenance are tracked by Mr. Ruiz and the hotels software he uses. He agreed to provide me with a recorded statement.

Recorded Statement of Mr. Steve E. Ruiz

Mr. Ruiz has been working at the hotel for 3.5 years. He stated that room #944 did not have any reported leaks, or problems that could have been associated with the guest's fall. Nor have there been any repairs or changes made to that room since her incident. This subject stated that the day after the fall, he visited with the claimant to see how she was doing and he stated that she seemed to be speaking very slowly. It was a characteristic that stood out to him for such a young and beautiful girl. He described her as a blonde haired 5'5 inch female in her early 20's. He stated that he visited with her the day after the incident. He stated that it is very common for young adults to come to their resort for the club experience. He went onto review her billing portfolio and found she paid for the hotel using an online travel company (Travelocity), but that she paid the add-on Resort Service fee of $15.00 a day for amenities like the gym and beach chairs. He said it is not uncommon for a guest that feels the hotel was responsible for something to ask for a credit of some sort but she paid her full bill when she checked out on May 16, 2012. From the resort Information Invoice (attached) it appears she checked in on May 9, 2012 and checked out on May 16, 2012.

Mr. Ruiz also stated that he reviewed the report prepared by the first responder and since it was 5:50 a.m., that person would have been a security guard. He stated that according to the guard's report, it stated that the guest reported that she "passed out". (Mr. Ruiz' full statement is enclosed)

Security Department

I next visited the Security Office and inquired about the security guard on duty the night of the incident and the report compiled. I obtained a copy of the report (enclosed) which clearly indicated that the claimant stated to the security guard that she "passed out". The security guard on duty that night was a Mr. Mark Paty, badge # 405.

Human Resources

I went back to Human Resource Office where I had first met the insured Contact Ms. Gonzalez. I enquired about the Security Personnel Mr. Mark Paty and learned he was no longer with the Resort. She pulled his personnel file and I reviewed same. I determined Mr. Paty's personal information to include his SSN 589-50-2308, address 5640 NE Miami Court, Miami, FL phone number 7886.985.8419

Attempted Contact Security Officer/ Witness Mark Paty 786.985.8419
4:45 p.m.

I called and left a message for Mr. Paty. He called me back a few minutes later and stated that he was running errands and that he would not be able to meet today. He stated that possibly tomorrow he would have more time before he went to work at 3:00 pm. I stated I would call him in the morning.

Telephone Contact Mr. Paty
9:11 a.m.

I started to call Mr. Paty early and left several messages. At around 12:00 p.m. I elected to proceed directly to his house.

640 NE Miami Place, Miami, FL
12:53 p.m.- 1:43 p.m.

I arrived at Mr. Paty's house and found no one present. I spoke to several people outside and after several minutes his brother arrived in the area. His brother stated that he had also been trying to reach Mark. He stated that Mark works at the Blue Diamond hotel. I searched the internet and found The Blue Diamond Condominium Resort located at 7115 Collins Avenue, Miami Beach.

Blue Diamond Condominiums
2:22 p.m. - 2:41 p.m.

I proceeded to this location and found these were condominiums and while Mr. Paty was reported to work here he was not scheduled to work this day.

2:55 p.m.

As I was just leaving the area, Mr. Paty called me and stated that his phone's battery had gone dead and he had just arrived at work and was charging his phone when he heard my messages. He stated that he was at another place he works identified as 8801 Brickell Key Boulevard in downtown Miami. He advised that the building was a private high-rise condominium structure and he was working the front security desk. I advised that I needed to come to his location and meet him and he obliged.

Statement of Mark Paty
8801 Brickell Key Boulevard, Miami, FL
3:27 p.m.

I proceeded into downtown area of Miami off Brickell Avenue and the inter-coastal waterway. Mr. Paty was working in an upscale high-rise condominium complex as the front desk attendant. Mr. Paty confirmed that he recalled hearing Ms. Harkow state that she does not remember what happened as she passed out. He also stated that she appeared as if she had just got home and he believed her hair was wet as if she had also just showered. He also remembered her talking slow and saw what appeared to be prescription medicine bottles on her night stand. She did not smell of alcohol, but appeared as if she had been up and had just come home and showered. She may have been under the influence of something but he didn't think alcohol. He stated he was certain that she did just wake up to use the bathroom.

SIU Electronic Update   Friday, December 28, 2012

Following the completion of these efforts, I forwarded my final report to the SIU, Mike Mathews.

Case Status: Closed

Should you have any questions regarding this investigation, please contact my office at cases@claimsresource.cc

Enclosures: #1 – CD statements of Mr. Ruiz and Mr. Paty
              #2 – Copy of Security Incident Report
              #3 – Copy of Information Invoice (check-out)

END OF REPORT

CASE V – STAGED PEDESTRICAN ACCIDENT

Mr. Brooke thought he would hang out at a local Feed store until he found an unsuspecting victim. When 75 years old Mr. Rogers exited, Mr. Brooke knew he had found the perfect target. Right as Mr. Rogers started to back out, Mr. Brooke made a bee line directly to the rear of Mr. Rogers's car and acted as if he had been struck by the backing vehicle. The only factor Mr. Brooke over looked was an outdoor security camera that captured everything. It would have been an easier case had we been able to get that video or at least a copy from the local police department. Once learning the video was not an option, securing a statement from the manager that had seen the video was the next best piece of evidence to use to fight the demand. Upon contacting Mr. Brooke's attorney and advising him what we had he dropped Mr. Brooke as a client. As the case continued we attempted to reach Mr. Brooke but he refused to meet.

Details of Investigation

Investigator: John Bilyk / Claims Resource Incorporated / (877) 274-2000 / www.claimsresource.cc

Dates of Investigation: Monday, January 6, 2014 (10:19 a.m.); Wednesday, January 8, 2014 (11:50 a.m.- 12:55 p.m.); Friday, January 10, 2014 (9:55 a.m., 2:23 p.m. & 3:35 p.m.); Monday, January, 13, 2014 (1:11 p.m.-1:44 p.m.)& Tuesday, January 14, 2014 (12:05 p.m.- 4:36 p.m.)

Pertinent Information: On Monday, January 6, 2014, I was requested to follow-up and attempt to secure or view security video footage currently in the custody of the Miami Police Department or attempt to locate another copy from the originating business Sheila's Feed & Garden Supply. This security video from Sheila's Feed & Supply reportedly captured the actual incident in which the claimant claims he was struck by the Insured.

Investigation   Wednesday, January 8, 2014
11:50 a.m.

I reviewed the assignment, the police report and a report prepared by an Independent Adjuster. The Police report # 13-737611 indicated that the responding Officer was J. A. Trecker, Badge # 44841. Officer Trecker states in the narrative that "PED 1 failed to make any attempt to move out of harm's way and continued to walk into the back of VEH 1". The officer clearly seems to indicate that this matter was avoidable by the pedestrian. As such, the SIU wanted to also evaluate the video having more extensive experience with staged accidents or deliberately planned accidents. I spoke to the IA as requested and found they could not corroborate the Officers narrative statement and had not secured a copy of the security video.

Police Department – 305.931.6500
12:12 p.m. – 12:20 p.m.

I learned that Officer Julie Trecker had advised that her copy of the video had been turned into evidence and she no longer had access to the video. Her immediate division supervisor was identified as Sergeant Figuerero. Both he and Officer Trecker work the 6:30 a.m. - 5:25 p.m. shift. I left a detailed message for Sergeant Figuerero asking him to contact me.

Wonders & Flankers Attorney at Law – 305.226.9700
12:55 p.m.

I called the Law Offices of Wonders & Flankers and asked to speak with Attorney Marc E. Wonders, the Attorney on the letter of representation sent to INSURANCE COMPANY. I was advised that Michelle was the case manager on the file but them was put with Ms. Susie Mathews who stated that she was handling the file. She indicated that arranging a recorded statement was fine with the Attorney but that they have had some difficulty contacting their client. She indicated that his phone is a "Magic-Jack" internet phone that makes reaching him a challenge. She stated that he usually treats once a week and would leave a message with the doctor for him to call the office so that an amicable time could be arranged for the statement. I provided Ms. Mattos with my direct contact number.

Miami Police Department - 305.931.6500
Follow-up   Friday, January 10, 2014
9:55 a.m. & 2:23 p.m.

I again called the Miami Police Department and spoke to the Captain, who stated that he would speak with Sergeant Figuerero. I called back again and was told that Sergeant Figuerero advised that the video would not be release but he did not comment about whether I could come in and personally view it myself. I left another message asking for a response to this request.

Telephone Contact DIF – Field Office
Investigator Captain Michaels 305.972.8622
3:35 p.m.

I spoke to the Investigator Michaels and asked if he had any suggestions on having the opportunity to get a copy of the security video at least have the opportunity to watch it at the Miami PD. He stated that he could lend no assistance but that upon completion of our investigation to forward the matter as quickly as possible and they would review the file and video.

Sheila's Feed & Garden Supply
Telephone Contact 305.932.9775   Monday, January 13, 2014
1:11 p.m. – 1:44 p.m.

I contacted the feed store and spoke to Mr. Gonzalez, the store Manager. He stated that the assistant Manager Fred Jacob handled the entire incident with the patron/insured, the police and the claimant. He stated that after the incident, he met with the police and made them a copy of the incident. As per their store policy, a second copy of the video was made and sent to the owner who has still not be able to locate the second copy. Having heard that Mr. Jacob watched the video and made the copies, Mr. Gonzalez agreed to allow me to secure a recorded statement from Mr. Jacob. We agreed to Tuesday, January 14, 2014, at 2:00 p.m.

Sheila's Feed & Garden Supply , Inc. 513 South Avenue
Miami, FL 33612   Tuesday, January 14, 2014
12:05 p.m. – 4:36 p.m.

As I arrived I observed the stores exterior camera located to the left of the front door covering anyone coming in and out of the front door. The business is located directly on Nebraska Avenue which has a high flow of traffic. Directly across the street to the north perpendicular to South Avenue is a low income apparent complex. It does not appear to be unusual for people from this complex or the side street to walk through the Feed Stores parking lot which is located on the corner. The positioning of the camera not only covers the front door but also the 4-5 spaces in front of the door and those headed towards Nebraska. I again met with Mr. Gonzalez who stated that the owner was on vacation until Saturday, January 18, 2014, so that he could not follow-up with him concerning the video copy he might have or was looking for. We agreed to touch base on this matter the week of January 20th after the Owner returns home. Meanwhile he introduced me to his assistant manager who took me in the office where the security camera monitor is located. From the office I observed the actual angle of the cameras and the area of coverage depicted in this position.

The top image is from the actual security camera and the Insured, Mr. Brooke was believed to be parked in the space where you currently see the silver compact. The next car over almost out of screen is a dark SUV and that direction is west towards Nebraska Avenue.

After speaking briefly, I learned there were no other potential witnesses and that Mr. Jacob handled the entire incident from responding to the initial incident, speaking with the claimant, reviewing the video and copying the footage for the Police. He agreed to provide a recorded statement.

Recorded Statement Fred Jacob DOB 1/2/1979

Mr. Jacob has been working at the feed store for 3 years. On the date of the incident, he stated that he had recalled seeing the claimant and two other individuals hanging around outside the exterior of the business. This activity in itself is not unusual because people in this area sometimes come up close to the business to get out of the sun or to learn against the building and just hang out or wait for someone. He stated that the Insured, Mr. Brooke is a regular customer but that the claimant was not known nor was he a customer on this day. He described the claimant as a darker skinned male wearing a do-rag.

He stated that the car was already in motion when the claimant came into the security camera picture and walked into the back of the car. He stated that it looked faked in his opinion. The other two people he was with, a woman and a child, they were not with him but stayed behind and after the incident occurred those to other people didn't react surprised about the incident. They just walked over and didn't seem overly concerned or worried like you would expect after someone you know is hit by a car. The witness stated that having seen the video and during his interaction with the claimant he just didn't believe he was injured. After the incident, the Insured left because he felt threatened by the claimant. While the insured left and called the police, he later returned. The claimant remained at that location the entire time and stood outside yelling and causing a major disturbance. He was swinging his arms and walking around. Just by his movements, he didn't seem to be injured at all. When the police returned so did the fire department and an ambulance. The claimant left via the ambulance (the entire recorded statement in two parts is attached).

SIU Contact

Following this interview, I contacted the SIU and discussed the matter. I advised that I was still waiting on the opportunity to secure the claimant's statement, however based on the witness and the police officer's comments; both felt the incident was staged. Therefore, I was instructed to prepare this interim report for the SIU to facilitate a quicker referral to DIF.

Electronic Update   Thursday, January 16, 2014

During the course of this investigation I maintained contact with the SIU, Ms. Jenny Davis.

At this time, I am forwarding this interim report and will continue to pursue the claimant's statement through his attorney.

Case Status: Open, pending claimant's statement.

Enclosure: #1 -CD Recorded statements from witness Fred Jacob

Should you have any questions regarding this investigation, please contact my office at cases@claimsresource.cc

END OF REPORT

CASE VI – APARTMENT FIRE

The Harbor Apartments had just been bought by a new company when an electrical fire broke out. The new company was in the process of doing everything they could to repair the reputation of the complex as well as make repairs to a complex that prior management had somewhat neglected. Then another fire broke out and the tenant who was a maintenance man immediately stated it must have been another electrical fire. The new owners of the apartment complex needed the fire investigated immediately. The press had already showed video of the fire on the local news and continued the concern that another electrical fire had broken out at the Harbor apartments. To management the publicity, the corporate owners wanted to know everything they could about the fire. Typically in these cases we conduct what is referred to as a parallel investigation speaking to whomever we can and at the same time trying to stay in touch with the fire department to determine what they know. During a conversation with a fire department officer, I learned the fire was not electrical and started on the porch of the second floor property. I spoke to the manager of the complex who reported that the tenant was a smoker. I interviewed the tenant who reported that he doesn't smoke on the porch he smokes inside the apartment. He however stated that his girlfriend's son, smoke small cigars and since they smell so strongly, he is not allowed to smoke them in the house and usually smokes on the porch. IT was also determined that the son had been smoking a "cigarillo" on the porch balcony 30 minutes before the fire. In the fire departments estimation, this coincided with the start time of the fire.

Details of Investigation

Investigator: John Bilyk / Claims Resource Incorporated / (877) 274-2000 / www.claimsresource.cc

Dates of Investigation: Wednesday, May 8, 2013 (9:02 a.m.); Thursday, May 9, 2013 (3:39 p.m. -6:00 p.m.) & Monday, May 13, 2013 (9:59 a.m.- 2:12 p.m. & 4:17 p.m. -5:01 p.m.)

Pertinent Information: On Wednesday, May 8, 2013, I was contacted by the SIU, Mr. Sam Gates and requested to secure the statements of the Property Manager and any person identifiable as responsible for the fire. I was also requested to secure a copy of the Fire Marshals and tenants lease where the fire occurred.

The SIU provided me with contact information for my insured contact on the property, Ms. Christine West.

Telephone Contact – Harbor Walk Apartments Property Manager
Ms. Christine West 813.884.1821   Thursday, May 9, 2013
3:39 p.m.-4:44 p.m.

I spoke to Ms. West over the phone and she requested that I put together what I needed in writing and send it to her attention. I prepared an email and sent it to her email address at Christine_West@venetian.net. We then agreed to meet on Monday at 11:00 a.m.

Early New Articles Review
6:00 p.m.

Early news articles clearly raised the concern that this may have been an electrical fire. There was an electrical fire in February 2013, which was referred to as an electrical short but I would later hear from the Property manager that this was attributed to too many items plugged into a power strip. The news fueled this concern that the new fire may also be electrical in nature. This was an early report by the Tampa ABC Action News. http://www.abcactionnews.com/dpp/news/harbour-walk-fire-ignites-resident-fears.

The local channel 10 did the same story raising concerns that the fires may be linked to electrical problems at the complex but according to Hillsborough County Code Enforcement there had been no violations and it was too early to speculate if this was also electrical in nature.

http://www.wsls.com/story/22065586/3-alarm-apartment-fire-in-west-tampa

Personal Visit- Harbor Walk Apartments – 8302 Crystal Harbor Drive
Tampa, FL 33615   Monday, May 13, 2013
9:59 a.m.- 2:12 p.m.

I made a personal visit to the Harbor Walk Apartments and met with Ms. Christine West. After speaking momentarily, she agreed to provide a recorded statement.

Recorded Statement Ms. Christine J. West DOB 11/6/1969

Ms. West advised that she was present on the day of the fire. She has worked regular shifts since the fire and has not been advised or contacted by anyone concerning any injuries or vehicle damage. She stated that the fire was initially spotted at the unit of their landscape worker, Ricardo Gonzalez. It was around 11:30 a.m. when the fire started and the worker, his girlfriend and her son where all in the apartment at the time. They had plenty of time to get out of the building and also make certain everyone else was evacuated. Most tenants were at work at the time. Ms. West provided me the most recent rental agreement for Mr. Gonzalez, which has a work4rent agreement (attached 5 pages). Mr. Gonzalez is provided an apartment valued at $595.00 a month in return for 20 hours a week. Ms. West had also just received the Fire Marshall's Cause and Origin report which stated the fire occurred on the balcony and the cause of the fire was a pipe or cigar. Ms. West had asked if this included cigarettes since the employee Ricardo Gonzalez smoked. The fire investigator said yes, and added that the young man in the apartment admitted to the investigators that he was smoking on the porch about a half hour earlier which seemed to coincide with the time the fire started. I obtained a copy of the fire marshals report. (Ms. West' full statement has been enclosed)

I next met and introduced myself to the landscaper and tenant who receives his rent for free under the apartments Work4Renk agreement. He agreed to sit down and provide me with a recorded statement.

Ricardo Perez DOB 3/24/1975 SSN 582-27-XXX

I asked Mr. Gonzalez if he had any form of renters insurance but he did not. He started out telling me he didn't smoke or at least not out in public where anyone could see that he smoked, but I told him Ms. West has seen him many times smoking on property. He then stated that he smokes inside his house and has no reason to smoke on the porch. He tried to state that the fire was most likely from the light switch outlet but I advised that the fire and arson investigators determined that it was from a smoking device. He stated that no one was smoking on the porch, but I told him his girlfriend's son stated to fire investigators that he had just smoked on the porch. He then said that he was in the room with his girlfriend who was still sleeping, so maybe the boy went out on the balcony unbeknownst to him. I told him the cause of the fire appears to be a pipe or cigar and asked if the boy smoked a pipe. He thought I meant crack or pot so I asked does he smoke either and he said no. He said he smokes those "cigarillos" (which the kids call blunts). They are flavored thin cigars and he stated that he purchases them at the local convenience store. He stated that he doesn't let the boy smoke them in the house because he doesn't like the smell. He stated that his girlfriend is not on the lease as she wasn't staying with him full time but was there a lot. Then her son also moved in with them but he didn't want to inherit the whole family so he told her the boy could not stay and she has since moved out. The employee stated that they had a lot of time to make sure everyone got out of the apartments and most were empty with the exception of the "old man" downstairs, whom they alerted and got out. He stated that no one was hurt and no cars were damaged in the fire.

The employee told Ms. West that he was working at the time as he should have been doing. But he stated in this statement and the statement to the fire investigators that he was inside when the fire started. It appears that while he was supposed to be working he was still in the apartment. The claimant stated that his girlfriend's name was "Angelique Vasquez" and her son's whom he knew as "Danny Dominguez". He stated he didn't know their birth dates.

The employee holds no other full or part time job. He does do some graphic design work from home but has not formal employer. His girlfriend reportedly works for a telemarketing company, her son's employment is not known. (The employee's full statement is enclosed)

National Database – Address Cross Reference and Name Searches
4:17 p.m. – 5:01 p.m.

I referred to a national database to do an address search and cross reference possible names matches for the girlfriend and her son. I identified the claimant's girlfriend as Angelique Katherine Vasquez DOB 11/14/1974 (38) SSN 073-53-9343 and her son Benito "Danny" Dominguez DOB 2/4/1994 (21) no verifiable SSN.

SIU Electronic Update   Wednesday, May 15, 2013

During the course of this investigation, I maintained contact with the SIU. As it turns out the Fire Marshals report just released May 9, 2013 states that the "area of origin" for the fire was the exterior balcony and that the "heat source" was a pipe or cigar. This puts to rest any speculation the fire was electrical or in any way related to the fire in February 2013. Furthermore the employee/tenant stated that his girlfriend's son smoked cigars and according to the fire investigators he had been smoking a half hour earlier on the balcony around the estimated time the fire started. Fortunately, there were no injuries or vehicles damaged.

Pending, review of this matter and any further follow-up request, I will close my file.

Case Status: Closed

Should you have any questions regarding this investigation, please contact my office at cases@claimsresource.cc

Enclosures: #1 Tenant Lease -Ricardo Gonzalez (5 pages)
              #2 Fire Report (6 pages)
              #3 CD with statements of:
                  a.   Property Manager Christine West
                  b.   Tenant/Employee Ricardo Perez

END OF REPORT

CASE VII – SECURITY SHOOTING

The apartment complex had just opened and within two weeks' time there was already a shooting on the property. The apartment complex' corporate owners didn't know what to expect next. Would they be sued by the victim? Could their entire investment suddenly be at risk? How did the perpetrator penetrate the gated complex? All of these questions would be answered as the person shot was the security guard who had just arrived for his shift. As soon as he got there he was approached by a subject whom he thought had a question but it turns out he wanted more than just information. The subject grabbed the security guards gun and shot him in the leg then demanded his car to make his getaway. Since the purpose for a security guard is to thwart off criminals, the guard knew when taking the job that there may be some danger involved in the position. After all he was carrying a gun while doing his job. So, once we determined it was the security guard who was shot and not a tenant, the apartment complex' corporate owners breathed a sigh of relief.

Details of Investigation

Investigator: John Bilyk, CFE / Claims Resource Incorporated / (877) 274-2000 / www.claimsresource.cc

Dates of Investigation: Monday, October 22, 2012 (10:10 a.m.); Thursday, October 25, 2010 (1:17 p.m.- 5:30 p.m.) & Thursday, November 1, 2012 (3:55 p.m. – 7:57 p.m.)

Pertinent Information: Prior to initiating this investigation, I reviewed all information provided by the SIU, Mr. Coates. This information included a detailed description of the accident and a copy of the incident report from the on-site property manager.

Telephone Call Insured Contact
Wendy Riles 854 .249.6714   Monday, October 22, 2012
10:10 a.m.

On the above date I left a message for my Insured Contact Ms. Riles. Her voice mail message stated that she would be back on Thursday October 25, 2012

Return Call Ms. Riles   Thursday, October 25, 2012
12:10 p.m.

I call Ms. Riles who advised that I should call the Regional Manager, Isabelle Mattingly at 954.7797950. I then called Ms.

Mattingly that advised she would call the on-site property manager, Ms. Falls and advise that I was on my way.

Insured Apartment Complex- Sorrento at Sarasota
8991 SW 41st Street, Sarasota, FL 33025
1:17 p.m.

Here I met with Ms. Falls who was actually quite knowledgeable about the incident and therefore I proceeded to take her recorded statement

Recorded Statement Property Manager Ms. Falls

Ms. Falls reported that she received a call from resident Porchia Cinder who lives in Building 4 unit #102. Ms. Cinder's phone number is 727.724,9256. According to Ms. Cinder's file she works at Northwest Farms with a phone number of 727.493.1600. The phone call came in around midnight but Ms. Falls did not hear the message until 5:30 a.m., as she was getting ready for work. Reportedly, the victim was not an unknown party but instead a Security Guard coming to duty. He had just arrived and was on the phone to check in with his office. He was employed by Best Security. At the time of the shooting, several building were still unfinished and the General Contractor/ First Construction hired the guard service to protect the unfinished buildings. At that time the electronic gates were also not working yet or in use, so anyone could come and go unlike today where a security access is required to enter the community. The guard/victim was identified as a black Haitian male. The attacker was reportedly also a black Haitian man and was being spoken to in Creole. The guard thought it was a joke until he was shot and pulled from his car. It's uncertain if there was a struggle or if the guard was shot with his own gun or the assailants.

According to Ms. Falls, she observed a trail of blood starting on the main entrance road just west of the mailboxes and leading to the sidewalk near the office. There was reportedly another guard on the property, but he was in the back near the unfinished buildings and apparently not around to help. Ms. Falls explained that she tried to identify the Security Officer and called Best Security, but never received a response. She never had anything to do with the guard service since they were hired by the GC.
After the statement we walked the property and she pointed out where the incident occurred. The picture to the left depicts the entrance to the community. He stopped just past the open gates near the side walk in his car. After being pulled from his car and shot in the leg, he then walked back towards the gates and stopped in the picture to the right in front of the mailboxes building where the blood stops and he was apparently assisted.

Best Security 305.919.9400

After several calls I reached the reported owner Neal Blackshear. He was very reluctant to provide any information. I asked for the guards name and address so I could check up and see how he was doing. He stated that he really don't know much as he was not involved in the incident. It sounded odd that the owner didn't know much about one of his guards getting shot. He deferred me to his HR

Manager, Ms. Brown and stated that she would call me back. I asked if he could at least me the name of the guard/victim. He paused and then advised his name was Elliot Winters.

To date the Human Resource Manager has not called me.

<u>Sarasota Police Department, Sarasota Florida</u>
<u>3:55 p.m.-4:20 p.m.</u>

I visited the Sarasota PD and found case #120903902 still an open investigation being conducted by Detective Sam Tort and therefore the report was not available. I called Detective Tort at 727.602.4162 and asked if he could return my call.

<u>Florida Department of Agriculture-Division of Licensing</u>
<u>5:01 p.m.</u>

I checked the States Website for Security Guards and found only one Elliot Winters, with an address in Palm Bay, a Central Florida city.

WINTERS, ELLIOT
License Number   Expires   Status
D 16666670 11/17/2013   LICENSE ISSUED

Physical Address
1332 HOLBROOK RD NW
PALM BAY FL 32907

<u>National Comprehensive Database</u>
<u>5:30 p.m.</u>

I ran a national database and found an Elliot Winters DOB 1/20/1983 SSN 0866-76-4617 at 3464 Cluster Road, Sarasota, Florida 33025-4179. I also found another address with an overlapping October date. This address was 1644 NW 24th Place, Madeira Beach, FL 33054.

Continued Investigation Locate Elliot Winters- 3463 Cluster Road
<u>Sarasota, Florida 33025-4179</u>   <u>Thursday, November 1, 2012</u>
<u>3:55 p.m.</u>

I arrived at the above address and found this townhouse apartment occupied by Mr. Jean who also works at Best Security. He and Elliot use to be roommates but since the accident he stated that Elliot's WC check was not enough to maintain his share of the rent so Elliot moved in with some family. He did not know the address, but knew it was on 24th Place. He did however have Elliot's cellular phone number of 954.391.0332.

Elliot Winters – Telephone Contact 727.391.0332
6:12 p.m.

I called the number provided and reached Ms. Winters. He confirmed that his address was 1644 NW 24th Place, Madeira Beach, FL 33054.
He reported he moved back in with some cousin's but was going to look for his own place. I asked if I could come and meet with him and he complied.

Claimant Current Address
1644 NW 24th Place, Madeira Beach, FL 33054
6:36 p.m.- 7:57 p.m.

I arrived at the above address and was greeted at the door by Mr. Winter's younger cousin. He invited me inside and walked me to a bedroom in the back of the house off the back porch. I met Mr. Winters who was lying in bed watching television. He agreed to provide a recorded statement.

Recorded Statement-Elliot Winters DOB 1/27/1983 SSN 084-74-4447

I identified the subject by his state issued Security Guard License. He advised that he used to live in Palm Bay when he first applied for a security guard license. Mr. Winters advised that he had just reported to work and was checking in with the office, when the attack occurred. He stated that Best Security has a special number the guards use to call in to when they arrive onsite for their shift. He was going to relieve another subject that was already present but working in the back. He stated he didn't remember the other guards name but knew he was an African American Male. The subject identified himself as a Haitian male and reported that the male that car jacked him and shot him in the leg also appeared to be Haitian. The subject reported no ties between him and his attacker. The subject stated that the post is an unarmed post and he is an unarmed guard. When the attacker approached him he said in Creole, "do you speak Creole". He then said put your hands up and the subject put his hands up even though he never saw a gun. He then said give me all your stuff and pulled the subject from the car. The attacker then for no apparent reason shot him once in the lower leg, shin area and the bullet exited from his. The subject never saw the gun, but heard and felt it. He fell to the ground and starting yelling for help. He doesn't quite remember how far he ran but he remembers several people coming out of the buildings and he yelled that guy took my car pointing as the attacker left in the subject's car. The subject then stated that someone had called an ambulance which he left in. He stated that he is on Worker Compensation and initially only received a little over 200 hundred dollars but didn't know it was just a partial check. He just received a check for around $425.00 which seems to be his set biweekly amount. He had never reported his car stolen so I assisted him in calling Guardian Insurance and reporting the stolen vehicle. The subject told me that he had been contacted by Detective Saint Fort and advised that his car had been recovered and is currently being stored at Midtown Towing. The car however is stripped and the subject feels it is totaled.

The bullet entered the lower front of the subject left leg and exiting through his calf. His doctor told him it may take a year for him to fully recover as the bullet tore up a lot of nerves leading to his foot and it hurts him to walk without crutches. He was appreciative that RS Management, LLC showed an interest in his condition. (For more information please listen to the recorded statement attached).

Electronic Update   Friday, November 1, 2012

During this investigation I maintained contact with the SIU, Mike Coates. During this time we discussed the fact that the victim was a Security Guard and was there to guard and provide security to the unfinished apartments. As a Security Guard, it appears unlikely any potential claim for lack of security seems to be moot. Secondly, this activity occurred during his scope of employment and as a Security Guard would have understood the dangers involved in his occupation and trained to expect the same. It's unfortunate that he underestimated his attacker as he thought it was a prank since there has never been any problems at the Insured's Property, Sorrento at Sarasota.

Having completed the assignment, the SIU advised me to submit my full written report and send the Claims Handler, Ms. Blank the statements on CD.

Case Status: Closed, pending further authorization to proceed as directed.

Thank you for the continued opportunity to be of service. Should you have any questions regarding this investigation, please contact my office at (877) 274-2000 or via e-mail at cases@claimsresource.cc.

Enclosures :   #1 – CD Statements of Ms. Falls and Mr. Winters

End of Report

Chapter Twenty
Preparing for A PI Position

    I.   Introduction
    II.   Your Resume
    III. What type of Job Am I Interviewing For

20. Introduction

Our goal is to provide you with useful information that will help you in your pursuit of a career in the professional Private Investigations industry. And, of course interviewing for a job will be essential and many companies have assessment tests to calculate how well you know the industry.

Part of the process will be how well you can compile your thoughts and whether these thoughts are *adapted to the reader based on the facts of the case.*

One of the entry level tests is for the applicant to watch video taken by a surveillance investigator. You watch the film and then report on what you saw. Sounds simple right!

Well let's say you should at least practice this on your own and look for any mistakes or ways to make your report more concise. Maybe your choice of words can be improved so take some video then write out what you saw (based on the objective for the assignment) and let someone else read what you wrote and critique your report.

So after you shoot some video, type up a brief paragraph describing your observations to see how well you can recall and describe what you saw. Don't keep going back to the video, look at it once, make notes then write. If you are doing surveillance on a person suspected of exaggerating their injuries, then your details should relate to the physical movements and noted physical capacity of the individual with a direct focus on the stated injury reported to you by your client and how it may or may not impact the activity observed.

Along with checking your detail and writing, an employer they will also want to gage your knowledge of the industry through questions regarding privacy issues, the use of pretexts, different types of investigations, procedures and industry specific terminology. A classroom education can only teach you so much and there is no replacement for actual field experience. There is no doubt the more you work in the field, the better acclimated you become to the over all work of an Investigator. Surveillance is one of the largest fields in our industry and is an art that you will perfect through repetition and practice. Getting use to using your camera will improve your surveillance results. The quicker you can pick-up, turn on and focus your camera the better your footage will become. It is not uncommon to take your camera to a supermarket or busy commercial location and attempt to video the subjects going into the store and then exiting. I would suggest you spend several hours each weekend shooting video and then review the video and critique it. Look for how shaky the video may be. Do you start and stop the video? Is the video clear, is the subject in the full screen with his head at the top of the screen and his feet at the bottom? Are parts of your car in the video? Did you have to move around the parking lot to get the best video possible? How did you prepare for when the subject exited the store?

The next step in your training is to then go to a neighborhood and start to follow a random person out of the neighborhood and see where they go. If they stop at a convenience store are you able to start your filming just before they exit their vehicle and enter the store? If not what can you do to increase your ready speed. Getting video of a person exiting their vehicle and going into a store is a crucial piece of documentation a seasoned investigator will obtain and something a client will look for to access your talent.

An experienced manager can tell how long you have been in the field just by reviewing your video. Perhaps even worst is that when we see less than acceptable video, we think one of two things, this person is new or the worst case scenario, this person doesn't care about their work product. Therefore your final product is very important. As you start out focus on quality NOT quantity, five minutes of great video is better than 10 minutes of blurry or out of focus or shaky video.

What Type of Job Am I Interviewing For

I have talked about some of the different types of cases the professional PI conducts. Some Agencies you may apply to will be general PI Agencies and cover all aspects of the business. These are usually smaller companies that rely on a broad spectrum of work options to keep their investigators busy and the cases coming in. Others will specialize in Claims work or Criminal and Civil Defense. Go on-line and review the Agencies web-site and spend time researching the meaning of any content you read.

The more professional agencies typically look to specialize in one aspect of the industry. Specialization enables the investigator to concentrate and improve in the overall quality of the product they deliver.

Your Resume

Having hired hundreds of investigators, I can tell you that hiring managers usually spend about ten seconds looking at your resume. Make sure the Resume is no longer than one page. Your goal is to get an interview not tell your whole life story on paper (which won't be read). In our business simple and to the point is better. Don't send a copy of your investigative certificates, diplomas, driver's license or any other documentation unless they ask for it specifically.

Make sure the resume is typed and an original copy is brought with you to the interview. Have your resume printed on nice neutral color paper. If you use a telephone number make sure you answer that number not a house phone that you never answer. Same goes with the email address, check it often. Most employers will call you to discuss your resume and then decide if they want to proceed further. Again keep the conversation professional, you still need to get in front of the hiring manager in person. The more versatile you are the more attractive you appear to the employer. You need to realize you may be needed in another town, state or that a lot of driving is required. There is also probably 50 people applying for the same job you are so understand that its not what the company can do for you its what can you do for the company. You need to get use to this concept because this is a performance oriented business. High pressure, results oriented with no complaining or excuses.

Being a PI is a lot like being an entrepreneur, you need to be resourceful, independent and results oriented. Anyone that requires a lot of hand holding or doesn't understand how to get results won't last in the industry. But don't be afraid by all of this tough talk, you'll get the hang of it, but you need to stay focused and work hard. You may find yourself spending more time to get something right than originally expected. There is nothing wrong with putting in extra time to learn.

We want people who appear aggressive, communicate well and are career focused. I want to hear that you see yourself managing a staff of investigators in whatever town, region or state the company may need you in five years. I don't want to hear that you have applied to five police departments and are waiting on a call back, or plan to go to law school. I want to hear how you are going to contribute to the growth and success of the company. This starts by understanding that your manager is the person who wants to train you and has the experience and knowledge that you need.

Resume

Joe Davis
1915 Eastview Drive, Sun City Center, FL 33573
Telephone 706.399.9753 / Email DavisJ@email.sc.edu

Objective: Secure a position with a Private Investigative Agency or Insurance SIU department specializing in Claims Investigations and Surveillance. Utilize my passion for investigative work and desire to outperform expectations and deliver results.

Education: The Best College 8/2014
　　　　　　　A.S. Private Investigations

Experience: Private Investigator's Class "CC" license 8/2012.

Courses Taken:

- Surveillance Procedures and Techniques
- Locate Procedures
- Statement Taking (Written and Recorded)
- Taking Clear, Steady Video and Video Capture
- Report Writing
- Statute 493 Rules and Regulations
- Legal Issues of the Professional Investigator
- Being a Witness and Testifying

Ranked Top 10 Student

References: Al's American Bail Bonds, Plant City
　　　　　　　　Allen McCoy 813.546.1376

Keep Improving

Once your hired or in business, keep working on improving your service. This should be an on-going priority of the professional investigator. Do you deliver a professional looking report? Do you enclose pictures in your report? Do you use an on-line system to track and deliver your product to the client? Does the client have access to your files/reports 24/7? Is your equipment up to date or is there a product that will improve the look or quality of your investigation.

A good quality camera IS IMPORTANT. So is a back-up camera and a reliable covert camera. These are basic pieces of equipment that keep getting better with new technology. Something as simple as having a digital tape recorder that can deliver .wav or mp3 files of your statements by email to your client or a printer that prints your logo labels on your DVDs all improve the look and quality of service you offer.

And finally, remember customer service is everything. Treat your clients like gold and deliver results. Clients are hard to come by and it costs more money to look for new clients than does to keep the ones you have satisfied.

About the Author

John Bilyk has been a career Private Investigator for over 33 years. Originally from Philadelphia, he graduated from West Chester University with a degree in Criminal Justice. He joined a Private Investigative Firm 1982, specializing in Insurance Claims Investigations. He has worked, directed or supervised more than 50,000 cases and is considered an expert in Business Risk Mitigation and Claims Investigations.

John Bilyk has always been a strong believer in continuing education. He attained his Certified Fraud Examiner designation, CFE status in 1995. He was licensed and practiced as a PI in 12 States throughout the U.S. and the Commonwealth of Puerto Rico. With offices throughout the country he understands the challenge of operating a multi-state operation dealing with varying states rules, regulations and compliance issues.

As a Director and Board Member, he organized the first Associates Degree program in Florida for Private Investigations through the Institute of Specialized Training and Management (ISTM), later purchased by City College.

As a lifelong Private Investigator he is devoted to the private investigations industry, teaching, writing and training. He has trained hundreds of investigators who have made Private Investigations their career.

This book was written as a guide and example of what a career professional Claims Investigator does, the types of cases they work and examples of the process, procedures and reports.

"The decision to become a Private Investigator was a life long dream and an overwhelmingly satisfying career. I hope you too can enjoy the same success and wish you the best in your endeavor".

John C. Bilyk Jr., CFE